The Psychoanalytic Theory of Greek Tragedy

The Psychoanalytic Theory of Greek Tragedy

C .   FRED   ALFORD

Yale University Press   New Haven and London

Designed by Sonia L. Scanlon.

Set in Berkeley type by Tseng Information Systems, Inc.

Printed in the United States of America by BookCrafters, Inc., Chelsea, Michigan.

Library of Congress Cataloging-in-Publication Data

Alford, C. Fred.

The psychoanalytic theory of Greek tragedy / C. Fred Alford.

    p.   cm.

Includes bibliographical references and index.

ISBN 0-300-05708-3 (alk. paper)

1. Greek drama (Tragedy)—History and criticism—Theory, etc.   2. Psychoanalysis and literature.

I. Title.

PA3131.A59   1992

882'.0109—dc20   92-13469

              CIP

A catalogue record for this book is available from the British Library.

10 9 8 7 6 5 4 3 2 1

For Jim Glass, fellow traveler

Contents

Preface

What if the insights into the human psyche contained in Greek tragedy were somehow more profound than the psychoanalytic theories often used to explain them? The answer, of course, is that we should never know this, as our theories would reduce these insights to the terms of psychoanalytic theory. I have tried to take this possibility seriously, which does not mean that I have somehow solved the problem, an instance of theoretical incommensurability. Taking the possibility seriously means reading the tragedies in such a way as to privilege their fundamental concerns, which I take to be the following: how to live in a world in which justice and power, right and might, often seem to have nothing to do with each other? how to deal with the fear that my own aggression and violence will overflow and violate all that I care about? how to confront my own death, and the deaths of those I love? how to act responsibly in the absence of freedom? how to make this inhumane world a more human place, and so comfort myself, and offer comfort to others?

These are the topics of the chapters that follow. It would be foolish to claim that these are the ur-themes of the tragic poets, the categories by which they truly apprehended the world. I cannot know this, and in any case these themes are ones to which my readings in psychoanalytic theory have attuned me. Nevertheless, I have tried to take the big themes of the tragic poets seriously, which has meant, in effect, modifying psychoanalytic theory in a very eclectic fashion when it has not seemed adequate to them. The title of this book thus has a double meaning. Insofar as it seeks to reconstruct in psychoanalytic terms the tragic poets' view of the psyche and its world, it is the psychoanalytic theory *of*, that is, belonging to, Greek tragedy. At the same time it is a psychoanalytic interpretation of the works of the tragic poets. It is in my attempt to move back and forth between these two projects (which in the end may be simply one, similar to what another intellectual generation called *verstehen*, or sympathetic understanding of another's world) that characterizes this book.

I believe that the worldview of the poets could be summed up by the phrase "humane antihumanism," for they generally hold that human beings neither "know [nor] control their basic nature and desires," which is how Alexander Nehamas defines the humanism to which Martin Heidegger is opposed. Nor does it ever occur to the poets that man's "*humanitas* or *Eigentlichkeit* lies in his capacity to wrench free of his determinations," which is how Luc Ferry and Alain Renaut define humanism. This does not lead the tragic poets to withdraw from the problem of how humans might create a decent and humane world in light of these circumstances, however. On the contrary, it only gives this human project added impetus. From time to time I compare the tragic poets' approach to this issue—how humans might create a humane *activa vita* in a world that was not made for the human being—with that of Heidegger, as well as with those of several postmodernists. Here too the poets represent a perspective that is in danger of being overlooked, in good measure because it does not fit neatly into contemporary categories.

I have found several video productions of the tragedies useful, not only for teaching but for imagining what it might have been like to have been in the audience at the Theater of Dionysus Eleuthereus. The production by the National Theatre of Great Britain of Aeschylus' *Oresteia* trilogy is most valuable in this regard. Sophocles' Theban Plays (*Oedipus the King, Oedipus at Colonus,* and *Antigone*), produced by the BBC and Films for the Humanities, are also useful, even if the costuming and staging are intrusive and offensive. The Kennedy Center's production of Robinson Jeffers' *Medea* is powerful. Michael Cacoyannis' Hollywood-style production of *Iphigenia at Aulis* is a fine film if judged on its own terms. Unfortunately, there exist no decent videos of Sophocles' *Philoctetes* or *Women of Trachis* or Euripides' *Heracles, Iphigenia in Tauris,* or *Alcestis*. Although these are less well known, it is by no means clear to me that they are in any way lesser works.

Discussions with Blake Kessel, whose dissertation on Greek tragedy I have had the pleasure of supervising, have been helpful, as have discussions with Vanessa Friedman, who with Kessel helped me teach an undergraduate course in Greek tragedy. Joanna Papandreau of the Classics Department at the University of Maryland helped me with the ancient Greek. My friend Martin Rosensky and my wife, Elly, both possess a tempered humanity that has helped me better understand the human world. Roger Lewin has helped me approach the sorrow and the pity of tragedy with the seriousness it deserves. My continuing debt to Jim Glass is expressed elsewhere. Gladys Topkis, senior editor at Yale University Press, has never interfered with my creativity. What more could one say of an editor?

Introduction: Psychoanalysis and Greek Tragedy Today

All sorrows can be borne if you put them into a story or tell a story about them.—Isak Dinesen

I shall not approach the psychology of Greek tragedy as one might approach the physics of Aristotle: as an enterprise of considerable historical interest but hardly capable of challenging contemporary theories. On the contrary, I shall argue that there is much to learn from the psychological assumptions of Aeschylus, Sophocles, and Euripides, not only because their views are similar to modern ones but because they are different. In particular, the characters of Greek tragedy (some more than others, of course) often lack a certain inwardness. It was, it seems, part of a theatrical convention not to focus upon the inner lives of the characters. Most of the formal elements of tragedy, such as the controlled staging (use of masks and special boots, or *kothornoi;* stylized gestures), difficult poetic language, action that takes place offstage, and so forth, served to distance the audience from the protagonists, including from their inner lives.[1]

If this was the case, how can we learn from the poets' psychology? Is not psychology, especially psychoanalysis, the study of inner states? Is not the psychoanalytic attitude one of reflection upon the inner sources of conduct? If the Greek poets did not reflect thus, can their psychology be of more than historical interest? I shall argue that psychoanalysis need not be seen as reflection upon inner states, one's own or others. The loosely structured Greek self, acted upon by its passions as though these passions were external forces such as gods, is actually phenomenologically quite accurate. To analyze the play of these passions as though they were uncontained and uncontrolled by the self may be quite fruitful, even if this is not the last word. In fact, if analysts such as Jacques Lacan and Melanie Klein are correct, it may be that moderns think they control their passions far more than they do. Much, but hardly all, of modern psychology may be a defense against truths intuited by the poets.

Mine is not the first psychoanalytic study of Greek tragedy, though it is surprising that there exist many more psychoanalytic studies of Plato, at least in English. My approach is best characterized by distinguishing it from two others, George Devereux's *Dreams in Greek Tragedy* and Philip Slater's *Glory of Hera*. Devereux argues that most accounts of dreams in Greek tragedy are psychoanalytically plausible—that is, compatible with Freud's explanation of how the unconscious works, using symbolism, condensation, and so forth. Furthermore, this psychoanalytic perspective provides a standard by which to judge the tragedies: the more psychoanalytically plausible the dream, the greater the play. A plausible dream will have a greater unconscious resonance with the audience and thus will be experienced as more powerful, even if the audience does not know why.

Devereux's thesis has validity. A psychoanalytic account may help us to explain the aesthetic appeal of a work of art in terms of its unconscious resonance. The problem, to put it simply, is that Devereux's approach guarantees that we shall learn nothing new from the Greeks themselves, but only how well they conform to Freud's categories. In the case of Aeschylus' *Persians,* for example, we learn from Devereux that Xerxes' yoking of the Hellespont must "certainly be viewed as the son's symbolic sexual defilement of his mother."[2] Aeschylus, however, seems to have intended something different, the yoking of the Hellespont (which is echoed in Atossa's dream) representing Xerxes' hubris in joining what the gods had held asunder. There is a connection between these interpretations, of course. Like bridging the Hellespont, incest is an impermissible crossing of boundaries. Nevertheless, Devereux's psychoanalytic interpretation seems not to add to our understanding but rather to reduce the Greek intellectual struggle regarding man's proper relationship to the gods to an instance of the Oedipus complex. What if the Greek interpretation of the dream were more profound than Freud's? My account is designed to leave open this possibility.

Slater's study is less problematic, in part because his goal is to explain not Greek tragedy but Greek family life. He regards the tragedies as evidence; they are not themselves the subject of his study. Slater argues that the system of weak, diluted marriage in classical Athens led mothers to relate to their sons in a profoundly ambivalent manner, alternating between seductive behavior and hostile ridicule. The result was men with a fragile sense of themselves, especially of their masculinity. This fostered a culture in which invidious displays of aggression and unrestrained competition in every aspect of life were common, as men sought to bolster their weak egos by overcoming other men. The title of Slater's book translates the name *Heracles*. It is intended to capture the bitter irony of the Greek mother-son relationship, for the goddess Hera was Heracles' chief tormenter. In a chapter entitled "The Multiple Defenses of Heracles," which draws heavily upon Euripides' *Heracles,* Slater argues that virtually every pathology associated with the Greek mother-son relationship is embodied by this hero.[3]

True enough, and more besides, as subsequent chapters will show. Nevertheless, Heracles also acts with great courage in Euripides' play, deciding to live in dignity and remorse rather than kill himself, after having killed his wife and children in an act of madness induced by Hera. Heracles makes this decision after Theseus reassures him that his pollution can be overcome by love. These themes too, such as how love might help overcome feelings of being polluted by one's own badness, or how one might live responsibly in an unfree world, are worthy of psychoanalytic attention. Yet the psychoanalytic perspective that Slater employs guarantees that none of these themes will be considered—not simply because it is based on Freud's view rather than on that of my favorite analyst, Melanie Klein, but rather because Slater's approach is too reductive, almost guaranteeing that the larger issues will be ignored.

Consider, for example, Slater's elaboration of the theme of the poisoned breast in the myth of Heracles. According to the myth, Heracles wounded Hera in the right breast with an arrow during the battle of Pylus, in which the gods participated. This is, says Slater, a permutation of another account, in which Hera suckled the monster Hydra so that it might eventually kill Heracles with its poison in the contest they were destined to have (see Hesiod, *Theogony,* 313ff). Furthermore, says Slater, it is significant that it was the right breast of Hera that Heracles wounded with his arrow, for in the Western world "right is good or primary, left is evil or secondary."[4] Anyone who is familiar with the work of Klein, founded as it is on the distinction between the good and bad breast, will see that there is much to work with here! Yet to pursue the story of Heracles in this fashion, finding in it Kleinian rather than Freudian primitive symbolism, would be little improvement. What is needed is an account that is true to the larger themes of the myth, such as how one may assert responsibility in the absence of freedom. The Kleinian theory is relevant here, but it must be applied with subtlety and abstraction and in conjunction with other accounts.

Rather than reduce Greek tragedy to the categories of psychoanalysis, my goal is to "enlarge" psychoanalysis itself. Operationally, this means that if there are important themes in Greek tragedy that do not seem explicable in terms of psychoanalytic theory, the theory will be revised to take them into account. The text will set the standard.

Though he does not follow this approach in a programmatic fashion, instead claiming to apply modern psychiatric categories to the tragedies, Bennett Simon in *Mind and Madness in Ancient Greece: The Classical Roots of Modern Psychiatry* actually comes closest to my own approach, insofar as he moves with a light hand between ancient and modern categories, not hesitating to reinterpret modern categories in light of ancient insights. I trust that my more studied, less Freudian, approach to enlarging psychoanalysis retains a similarly deft touch.

I do not reject other psychoanalytic works on Greek tragedy out of hand. It depends. Freud's interpretation of tragedy in *Totem and Taboo* as a dramatic reenactment of the primal crime, the tragic hero serving as scapegoat (*pharmakos*) for the guilt of the entire community, is profound, informing much of my chapter 3.[5] On the other hand, Heinz Kohut's distinction between tragic man and guilty man is one I have not found useful.[6] It may be that Kohut's definition of tragic man in terms of his inability to realize his nuclear self fits certain modern tragedies, but it does not fit ancient Greek tragedy, as chapter 5 will make abundantly clear. Erik Erikson's brief comments on *Oedipus Tyrannus* are fruitful, however, especially insofar as they emphasize the importance of intergenerational, not just oedipal, issues.[7] In general, however, Simon seems correct in his implication that most psychoanalytic interpreters lack a tragic heart, and so fail to capture fully "the pain, pessimism, and grimness of tragic drama." Where I disagree with Simon is in his attempt in *Tragic Drama and the Family* to psychoanalyze Euripides. Rather than ask what personal psychological conflicts Euripides was wrestling with in *Medea*, for example, I ask what conflicts Euripides might have been "holding" for the culture.[8]

Of course, it is not quite as simple as merely stating that I shall let the text set the standard. In "Oedipus without the Complex," Jean-Pierre Vernant argues that the Freudian account of Greek tragedy imposes a theory on the plays, reads the plays in light of this theory, and not surprisingly finds its account confirmed. Vernant's structural approach, on the other hand, "takes as its starting point the work itself as it comes to us, in its own particular form. This is then studied from every point of view possible in an analysis appropriate to the particular type of creation."[9] Only then does it draw its conclusions. Hogwash! Problematic as the Freudian account is, the alternative does not take the texts as they truly are. Who could know this? All interpretation is the imposition of concepts. The alternative to the imposition of Freudian concepts is the imposition of better concepts.

What this might mean is clarified by Peter Winch's "Understanding a Primitive Society." Winch treats the matter of understanding a different society as akin to translating a foreign language. Any translation of a term or concept from one language to another must involve a certain violence to the original. Nevertheless, some translations are less violent than others, as they come closer to capturing the original understanding. For example, Winch argues that Alasdair MacIntyre's interpretation of Azande witchcraft in terms of modern science ends up making the Azande look like stupid scientists. This is, says Winch, because MacIntyre is so alienated that he can only see the world in terms of production and consumption. In fact, Winch notes, Azande witchcraft has more in common with how moderns understand religion: as a way to come to terms with contingency, as in "Thy will be done."[10]

Seen in this fashion, the Azande may have something to teach us. We have at least the possibility of learning from them, which means enlarging our own categories in light of our understanding of theirs, because we are not reducing their understanding to the framework of our own—or at least not as much as if we treat witchcraft as stupid science. In the end, this is the goal, says Winch: to understand how other cultures come to terms with the fundamental "limiting notions" that all of us as humans face, such as birth, sex, death, and the struggle to find meaning in existence. If we let it, such understanding may broaden our own horizons, which means creating new possibilities for good and evil. "What we may learn by studying other cultures are not merely possibilities of different ways of doing things, other techniques. More importantly we may learn different possibilities of making sense of human life, different ideas about the possible importance that the carrying out of certain activities may take on for a man, trying to contemplate his life as a whole." [11]

This is what I want to learn from the psychology of Greek tragedy. The reductive character of the accounts of Devereux and Slater is not due, it is apparent, to their failure to read the texts with sufficient care. *Pace* Vernant, their studies are overly reductive not because they impose categories, for they must, but because they impose the wrong categories—categories insufficiently rich and profound to capture the great themes of the tragic poets. Their readings (Devereux's more than Slater's) reduce something important to something less important. To correct this it is neither necessary nor possible to go to the "texts themselves." Rather, we must find better psychoanalytic categories. These categories will not, in most cases, result in an understanding equivalent to that of the poets but may, as Winch suggests, allow us to learn something from those poets.

A psychoanalytically relevant example may help to explain this point better. Artemidorus' *Interpretation of Dreams* (second century AD) reveals that the ancient Greeks interpreted dreams quite the opposite of Freud. Manifest sexual content was regarded as symbolic of the latent, and more real, issues of security and status. To take an example, to dream of having intercourse with one's male or female slave is a good sign, for slaves are the dreamer's possessions and signify that he will take pleasure in his own possessions as they increase in number and value. Similarly, a man who dreams that he has two penises will gain more wealth than he requires, "for it is impossible to use two penises at the same time." [12] Or, as Michel Foucault puts it in his study of Artemidorus, sex is the signifier, not the signified. [13] This perspective is not unique to Artemidorus. In Herodotus' *Histories*, Hippias dreams that he is sexually united with his mother, and concludes with pleasure that he will reenter Athens, restore his power, and die there of old age. "There is no trace in this symbolism," says Vernant, "of the anxiety and guilt that are peculiar to the Oedipus complex." [14]

From the ancient Greek perspective, one looks not for incestuous desires and the like, but for themes of dominance, profit, invasion, and injury.

Not surprisingly, Devereux does not think much of Artemidorus. (Freud thought more; my criticism of the interpretation of Greek tragedy in terms of Freudian analysis generally does not apply to Freud, who was far more interested in using Greek terms to illustrate his concepts than he was in interpreting particular tragedies.[15]) In suggesting that we take the Greek perspective more seriously, I am not suggesting that we fall down dead before it either. There may be something to learn from Artemidorus and Herodotus about dreams, but they could be wrong, or only half right. A perspective that remains open to all these possibilities is needed. I find it by asking if there is any psychoanalytic view current that comes closer than Freud's to providing a sympathetic translation of the Greek concepts, one that seems to respect the Greek viewpoint while remaining comprehensible in contemporary psychoanalytic terms. In this case the psychology of Jacques Lacan works, because Lacan argues that it is not the desire of the self for the other but the desire of the self for itself, for its own wholeness and potency, that motivates. Sex serves the needs of the self, not vice versa. In this regard, Lacan can illuminate an aspect of Greek thought. In other respects he cannot, for he programmatically ignores the connectedness of the self to others that was so central to the Greek experience.

My approach is profoundly eclectic, downplaying issues of theoretical consistency among the psychoanalysts I draw upon. The theories of Klein and Lacan are incompatible—or rather, incommensurable. Nevertheless, each illuminates an important aspect of Greek thought. At different times each provides the best translation of a Greek concept. This is what I consider most important: to be as true to the intent of the Greek poets as a psychoanalytic approach can be, which means, in part, being willing to sacrifice theoretical consistency. In fact, by the end of this book it should be apparent that the Greeks had a fairly consistent perspective on issues which we today call psychoanalytic. It was simply inconsistent with any current psychoanalytic theory. But that is to be welcomed. Otherwise psychoanalysis would derive no benefit from taking the plays seriously. The tragedies tell a story about human life the wholeness and fullness of which has never been equalled in the West. It is my goal to show that psychoanalysis can measure up to this ideal, even if no particular psychoanalytic theory can. One must make a choice (and I do not think it a tragic one) between fidelity to a particular theory and fidelity to the truths of the poets. I have chosen the latter.

TRAGEDY, PSYCHOANALYSIS, AND STRUCTURALISM

Though psychoanalytically informed, my approach is similar to the structuralist perspective, insofar as it focuses not on what is given but on how the given is created and maintained. Like the structuralist perspective, mine focuses on "the subsurface tensions within the system, the dynamic pulls the culture has to allow, resist, and contain in order to exist. The 'achievement' of classical Athens, then, appears less as the crystallization of a marmoreal harmony than as an open equilibrium between competing values and unresolvable polarities," to quote Charles Segal.[16]

From this perspective tragedy will reflect the anxieties of the audience rather than its confident truths. Although tragedy is part of a civic ceremony, one would expect it to question whether the polis can contain its citizens' anxieties. In fact, this is precisely what tragedy does, as Vernant points out.[17] Thus, although I find Vernant's optimism regarding how well we can decode tragedy misleading, his general approach—to see in tragedy clues as to how the social order deals with its antimonies—seems correct.

Not only this. Charles Segal, drawing heavily upon such structuralist interpreters of tragedy as Vernant, argues that the code of Greek tragedy is an antimony, or "unresolvable polarity," between wild and tame, an opposition which is mirrored in almost every aspect of life in such oppositions as raw and cooked (food), *physus* and *nomos* (philosophy and law), civilized and savage (family and religion), and so forth. Like the structuralists, I too desire to "reveal the 'deep structure' of society's concern and its modes of organizing reality." Unlike them, I am not interested in demonstrating that "each code is homologous with every other code."[18] Rather, I try to show that a fundamental confusion runs through Greek life, so that what is good and what is bad are thrown into deepest doubt. If one wants to call this the code, so be it. My concern, in any case, is not to map its presence but to explain the psychodynamics behind it.

The term *structuralism* carries a lot of baggage and could for several reasons be misleading. A number of authors not known as structuralists, such as E. R. Dodds, A. W. H. Adkins, Vernant, Alvin Gouldner, and Slater, pursue what are in effect structural analyses, insofar as they focus on disruptive undercurrents of Greek life such as its love affair with irrationality as a retreat from the burden of identity, the theme of Dodds's famous book.[19] *Structuralism* as it is used in the present book includes the works of all these authors. It is a term of focus, not of method.

The term could also be misleading were it seen as an alternative to deconstructionism. The structural approach reveals the tragic poets to be deconstructionists, insofar as they used the traditional form of tragedy, as well as its status as a civic celebration, to take apart the values and assumptions that constituted this tradition and status. Although it might seem that such an account fits Euripides better than Aeschylus, I shall argue that it suits all three poets almost equally well. My approach is in no way exemplary of what is today called deconstruction but neither is it its opposite. I too produce another text than that of the poets, as every critic must. Indeed, the deconstruction-ist doctrine of intertextuality (texts refer only to other texts, "the world as wall-to-wall text," as Edward Said puts it), although absurd when pushed to extremes, makes a useful reminder that the tragedies are first of all texts. Even though they refer to tensions in the culture, they are not culture but text and must be analyzed as such. Thus, chapter 3, devoted to blood rituals, refers to the anthropological literature on the subject, mindful, however, that ritual in tragedy is not the same as actual ritual. Sometimes structuralism tends to forget this and needs the reminder found in the doctrine of intertextuality.[20] These texts are also dramas, another point that will not be overlooked.

FIVE QUESTIONS AND THREE PARTS

Following are the five questions addressed in this book:

• How may men and women live morally and well in a world in which good and bad are confused, and often reversed, so that it is hard to tell the difference?
• How may men and women come to terms with the experience of feeling polluted, contaminated by the badness in themselves and others?
• How may men and women establish connections between life and death, so that death is not a meaningless termination of everything?
• How may men and women live responsibly in the absence of freedom?
• How may men and women live decently together in a world full of evil, hurt, and pain?

Where do these questions come from? From my own readings of the Greek tragedies; readings that are, of course, informed by my familiarity with, and interest in, psychoanalytic theory. In this regard I fail Vernant's test. Like Freud, I find in the tragedies themes that I have already identified as important from my readings in psychoanalysis and philosophy. (But no one, I have argued, could pass Vernant's test anyway.) Are these the most important questions that humans face? I do not know. Certainly they are important, but others may be equally crucial.

Missing, it might be pointed out, is the question "How may men and women build a more socially just world?" Thus, it might be concluded, the poets have little to tell us about social theory. Against this conclusion, I shall argue in chapter 6 that this question is missing because the poets pose an even more fundamental one in its place. Before social justice comes pity, mercy, and de-cency. Not justice tempered with mercy, but mercy tempered with justice is the ideal of the poets. Aristotle's view of political friendship is similar (see *Nicomachean Ethics*, 1159b20–1161b10) but a pale shadow of the poets' ideal.

How the poets answer these five questions depends more on the question than the poet. The first part of this book, "Confusion," subsumes the first question and concerns the poets' critique of the propensity of their culture to confuse good and bad. As cultural critics, the poets do not so much answer the question as raise the issue, even though they outline what an answer would look like: to end the confusion, men and women would have to act more nobly than the gods. The second part, "Death," considers the second and third questions, exploring the poets' study of their culture's failed attempt to come to terms with violence and death. Against violence and death Greek culture set more violence and death, a solution that only made things worse. In a word, the second part deals with failed attempts to sort out the confusion analyzed in the first part. Part three, "Life," looks at the fourth and fifth questions and examines the more positive teachings of the poets: how to live responsibly in the absence of freedom and how the polis might be civilized through an overflow of the civilizing emotions. These teachings constitute the tragic poets' solutions to the problems raised in the first two parts. In chapter 6, particularly, I shall contrast the poets' solution to the more traditional solutions of political philosophy.

An appendix applies the analytic framework developed here to the portrayal of the self in Homer's *Iliad* and *Odyssey*. Although Homer falls outside the direct focus of a book on Greek tragedy, the appendix is nonetheless theoretically important. It is often argued, and more often simply assumed, that there is a line of ideal psychological development running from Homer through the tragic poets to Plato, in which the fragmented, relatively incoherent Homeric self first becomes conscious of itself in tragedy—the discovery of mind, as it has been called. Only in the philosophy of Plato, however, does the self become a free, self-conscious, and responsible agent. Here I imply a criticism of the last two steps of this ideal development from tragedy to Plato, arguing that Plato is better seen as constructing defenses against the tragic poets' insights into the truth of the human condition. Such an argument has implications for the first step of this development as well.

No Comedy?

In Aristophanes' *Frogs*, Aeschylus accuses Euripides of introducing women "who say that life is not life" (1082). Here is the difference between comedy and tragedy, as Segal suggests.[21] Greek comedy restores unity and affirms simplicity in the face of chaos and complexity. Because I am most concerned with chaos, complexity, and difference, I shall focus on tragedy. I shall, however, pay more attention than is usual to some of the lesser-known plays of Euripides, especially *Heracles, Alcestis, Suppliant Women, Ion, Helen,* and *Iphigenia in Tauris*. (The plots of all the tragedies discussed are summarized in the text, those of the lesser-known plays being summarized in greater detail.) In fact, the last three plays are often called comedies, both because of their happy endings and their convoluted, romantic plots. I argue that the absence of simplicity and grandeur in these plays—that is, the absence of beautiful form and the "tense and ordered calm" that goes with it—allows us to see the confusion at the heart of the poets' world more clearly. Beautiful form obscures as much as it reveals. I say *poets,* because I shall read all three poets from this Euripidean perspective.

PSYCHOANALYTIC THEORIES DRAWN UPON, MAKING REFERENCE TO THE TRAGEDIES

Throughout the tragedies, in Aeschylus almost as much as in Euripides, characters express doubt about the goodness of the gods. Are the gods jealous of human success and happiness? Or just jealous of the greed and hubris success so often engenders? Aeschylus' *Persians* gives both answers (see 97ff, 157ff, 740ff).[22] Conversely, are the gods worthy of esteem because they are good or merely because they are powerful? If only the latter, then what should be the standards of human goodness? Questions like these not only constitute the most fundamental human concerns, they also generate anxiety. How can I protect the good from the bad if I do not know which is which? For Melanie Klein, contemporary of Anna Freud and founder of object relations theory, there is no more fundamental anxiety than this, that we shall confuse good and bad, love and hate, and so destroy all that we really care about.

Klein

According to Klein, this anxiety originates virtually at birth, in the young child's fear that his or her frustration with mother will lead him or her to harm her. The child fears this because he or she depends on mother so much and also because the child soon comes genuinely to love mother. Can he protect mother from his own anger quickly comes to be his deepest concern. Klein talks about all this in terms of the good breast and bad breast, symbolism (though a strict Kleinian would not regard it as such) that need not concern us here. In another book I have dealt with Klein's theory at length, and the reader desirous of more details can find them there.[23] Here I care only about those aspects of Klein's theory that help to explain the poets' anxieties about the gods.

In order to protect those she or he loves, the child comes to hold good and bad rigidly apart, as though the bad mother and good mother were two separate people. Klein calls this organization of anxieties and defenses the paranoid-schizoid position, a dramatic term that should not make us think that it is sicker than it is. By *paranoid* Klein means that the child projects her or his hate and love into the world, originally into mother, and finds it there in the form of persecutors: fantastic fears of being attacked which reflect the child's own aggression. By *schizoid* Klein means that the child holds good and bad rigidly apart, so rigidly that an actual and original whole, mother, is seen as if she were two beings: good mother and bad mother. Schizoid, or splitting, thus refers to the ability to hold two (or more) contradictory ideas in the mind at the same time.[24] Often splitting is reinforced by idealization and devaluation, in which the good is grossly idealized in order that it may be more firmly separated from the bad, which is completely devalued. Indeed, the single best and most visible sign of splitting is excessive idealization, evidence that the intrusion of the bad appears so threatening that the good must be rendered sublime and perfect in order to protect it. Conversely, the best sign of emotional integration and maturity is the ability to tolerate the ambivalence of the good.

Klein goes on to argue that securely established paranoid-schizoid defenses are absolutely necessary to the child's emotional development. Long before emotional integration can take place the child must be able to hold good and bad apart, allowing her to be crystal clear about what is good and what is bad in the first place (actually, of course, too clear: the world is more complex). Rigid paranoid-schizoid defenses also increase her confidence that she can protect the good from the bad. Donald Meltzer comments upon Klein's *Narrative of a Child Analysis,* her record of treating a ten-year-old boy named Richard, by noting that Richard's core problem was *inadequate* splitting-and-idealization. He "could not keep the destructive and Hitleresque part of himself from crowding in on and taking over the good part." Because of his inadequate splitting-and-idealization (Meltzer runs them together with hyphens as though they were one process), Richard tended to confuse good and bad, leading to greatly heightened paranoia (for example, was the helpful maid a good object or a bad one?), hypocrisy, and confusion.[25] Though he is no Kleinian, Robert Jay Lifton reveals a similar phenomenon in his study *The Nazi Doctors.* Many of the Nazi doctors, particularly those who worked in the concentration camps, dealt with their guilt and anxiety by reversing good and bad, so that killing became healing, and healing killing.[26] Before they could commit ultimate evil, they had first to convince themselves that it was good.

The poets' account of Greek anxiety about the gods as well as Greek cultural confusion generally about what is admirable and shameful reflect these same processes. Confusion or the reversal of good and bad served to diminish anxiety over a world in which goodness and badness could no longer be distinguished or separated. In this respect, of course, I am not being true to the intent of the poets, for I assume that the gods are human projections: alienated anxieties and passions. But perhaps Greek belief is not so simple in this regard either. Many argue, for example, that Euripides was an atheist, seeing the gods in just this fashion. From this Kleinian perspective I shall begin the next chapter with an account of Aeschylus' *Oresteia* trilogy. The anxiety that Aeschylus confronts is the (accurate) perception that the Olympian, or sky, gods share much with the Furies, being almost equally vindictive and bloodthirsty. Rather than simply insisting upon their separateness, however, Aeschylus seeks a higher integration, one that puts the Furies in their place while not denying their power. They are still monstrous, but they are monstrosities contained in the service of justice.

Klein wrote an essay on the *Oresteia*, arguing that this resolution represents what she calls depressive integration, in which the rigidly separate categories of good and bad are integrated under the leadership of the good (it is called *depressive* because the child originally despairs of being able to bring good and bad together without destroying the good).[27] Often this leadership is expressed in terms of the desire to make reparation, a key Kleinian category, for the harm done, generally in fantasy, to the good. My interpretation of the *Oresteia* is not as optimistic. I see more than a touch of what Klein calls manic denial, in which integration comes a little too easily. And much confusion remains. Certainly the poets who came after Aeschylus were never as optimistic about the prospects of genuine depressive integration. Whereas this claim may seem obvious with regard to Euripides, I argue that it fits Sophocles as well.

This Kleinian-inspired account, used to address my first question (about how men and women can live in a morally confused world), and drawn upon to a lesser degree to answer the second and fifth (how to come to terms with badness and how to live responsibly in an unfree world), makes no assumptions about Greek family life and the like. Rather, it is strictly phenomenological, focusing upon how the passions are projected into the world, creating a universe that is then reintrojected and experienced as objective. Which, of course, it has become. The world that the passions create is, above all, the world of culture. This links my account to the structural one. I assume that anxieties reflected in the culture reflect the anxieties of its members. My guess is that these cultural anxieties were exacerbated by the mode of family life that has been analyzed by Slater, but this is not my primary concern. I wish instead to show how our understanding of these cultural anxieties can be enhanced by a Kleinian reading.

In the Kleinian view the passions live a virtual life of their own. The protagonist does not so much have these experiences as carry them, as in the cliché (so appropriate to Greek tragedy), "You don't choose love; love chooses you." This relatively structureless aspect of Klein's account, in which the passions are almost more real than the person who experiences them, makes her theory especially appropriate to Greek tragedy. Nor, I shall argue, is that account entirely false, a view that moderns have somehow superseded. As the psychoanalyst Jacques Lacan points out, the belief that we control our passions is generally a defense: a false self built on repression to defend against the infinitely needy subject.

Lifton

In *The Broken Connection,* Robert Jay Lifton argues that Freud is mistaken to hold that man does not fear death because nonbeing has no unconscious equivalents. Says Freud, "it is indeed impossible to imagine our own death. . . . In the unconscious every one of us is convinced of his own immortality."[28] On the contrary, says Lifton, many of the most profound anxieties, such as loss of object, desertion, castration, and ego disintegration, are symbolic death equivalents: the way in which we conceptualize death, and the only way we can. As Charles Ryder puts it in Evelyn Waugh's *Brideshead Revisited,* "Next to death, perhaps because they are like death, he feared darkness and loneliness."[29] For Lord Marchmain, and perhaps for us all, darkness and loneliness have become symbolic death equivalents. Through them death becomes our leading anxiety. In a word, death comes to encapsulate all the terrors of life. How are we to deal with our eventual nonbeing, an event that sometimes seems to mock and render meaningless all our activities, achievements, and plans? Freud said, "If you want to endure life, prepare yourself for death." To this Lifton adds, in effect, If you want to live well, prepare to die well. What does this mean?

Man is a symbolizing animal, says Lifton: his relation to virtually everything, including death, is mediated through symbols. To prepare to die well, and so to live well, means to establish symbolic connection with symbols of transcendence: with valuable persons, ideas, and activities that will continue after your death. A personal example may help to explain this. On the frieze of my campus library is Carlyle's saying "In books lies the soul of the whole past time." Sometimes, on my way over to the library, I feel that I am a participant in this literary culture. For a moment my soul partakes, as it were, of the soul of the whole past time. I trust that this symbolic connection allows me to become part of a larger order, an order that will, I hope, continue into the future, even as I someday will not. The psychological mechanism involved is *projective identification,* in which I symbolically identify a part of myself with other people and ideas. Obviously there are many ways to participate, via projective identification, in the imagery of transcendence, such as living through children and grandchildren, participating in a religious tradition, being part of nature and its great cycles, and joining in what Lifton calls experiential transcendence, a sense of oneness with the All, in which time and death disappear.

Because projective identification is such an important concept in Lifton's work as well as in my explanation of how Greek tragedy works its effect on the audience (chapter 6), it will be fruitful to explore the idea for a moment before continuing with Lifton's account. In projective identification, a term originating with Klein, a part of the self, as well as the emotions associated with it, is symbolically (that is, in the imagination of the projector) forced into another, who is then regarded as a container of that part of the self. Though strict Kleinians reject projective identification's conceptualization as an interpersonal phenomenon many non-Kleinians prefer to view it as a relational encounter. As Thomas Ogden puts it in *Projective Identification and Psychotherapeutic Technique,* in projective identification "feeling-states corresponding to the unconscious fantasies of one person (the projector) are engendered in and processed by another person (the recipient). . . . In association with this unconscious projective fantasy there is an interpersonal interaction by means of which the recipient is pressured to think, feel, and behave in a manner congruent with . . . a specific, disowned aspect of the projector."[30]

Projective identification is not necessarily bad or pathological, even though it always involves a certain alienation of self, in which part of the self is split off and experienced in others. Projective identification may, for example, represent an attempt to communicate with another by almost literally sharing emotions. Most of the protagonists of Greek tragedy are florid projectors. Not all are pathological. Not by its presence but by the degree to which projective identification is associated with fantasies of omnipotent control over the recipient of projection, is key in determining the degree of pathology involved.

Projective identification is a psychoanalytic concept, and Lifton refers to what he practices as psychoanalytic psychiatry. In the end, however, terms are unimportant.[31] Important, in this context, is only the content of his theory. Is it psychoanalytic? The answer can only be yes. *The Broken Connection* is a reinterpretation and criticism of Freud's account of the *Todestrieb,* based primarily on the work of Otto Rank and to a far lesser degree on that of Carl Jung. In fact, one might well argue that Lifton remains closer to the spirit of Freud's late metapsychology (beginning in 1920, with the postulation of the Todestrieb in *Beyond the Pleasure Principle*) than any analyst except for Klein. How many other analysts have made the Todestrieb their central analytic concept? To be sure, Lifton would abandon the dualism of Freud's drive theory for an account that makes the symbolic unity of life and death central. In support of this argument, he turns to Rank's unitary position regarding a "primal fear, . . .[which] manifests itself now as fear of life, another time as fear of death." Going on to associate this primal fear with a "loss of connection with the greater whole," Rank provides the intellectual underpinning for Lifton's claim regarding the fundamental continuity of life and death.[32]

All this does not argue for the correctness of Lifton's position. That is a difficult and complex issue. Rather, these considerations are intended only to demonstrate that Lifton is working strictly within the psychoanalytic tradition, for the counterargument is sometimes made about him. To be sure, Lifton abandons Freudian drive theory, emphasizing instead man's search for meaning via his creation of symbolic images. In so doing, however, Lifton follows what represents perhaps the dominant path in psychoanalytic theory today, moving from drives to object relations, especially as these are conceptualized intrapsychically as part of the self—what Lifton calls image-feelings of connection or separation. Unlike many object relations theorists, however, such as W. R. D. Fairbairn or Harry Guntrip, who conceptualize the self strictly in terms of its relationships, Lifton characterizes people's quest for vitality (a feeling of aliveness, of moving forward) in almost drive-like terms: as a search that emanates from needs deep within the self that generate a source of energy for life akin to what Aristotle called *energeia,* a font of activity in the world.[33] These aspects of Lifton's work, coupled with the fact that most of the chapters of *The Broken Connection* begin with a statement of Freud's position on an issue, then criticize and alter it, put Lifton squarely within the Freudian tradition. The key measure of that tradition is not whether an author agrees with Freud (or there would be no Freudians), but whether Freud remains the starting point. He does for Lifton.

About Lifton's position that we come to fear death via various symbolic death equivalents, such as loss of object, or ego disintegration, it might be asked whether we *really* fear death. Or do we fear the splitting, fragmentation, and loss of connection that these death equivalents evoke? In the end this is, I think, a distinction without a difference. Lifton's position seems to be that men and women are virtually programmed with a knowledge of death.[34] I would put it a little differently. When we die we really *do* cease to exist as personalities (at least in this world), so that all our connections really *are* lost to us and the self *really is* obliterated. Not only is death the paradigm of many other losses; it is in fact the final loss, in which all other losses must culminate, against which all other losses are measured. But despite the fact that death truly is obliteration, fragmentation, and loss of connection, it need not be merely and only this. Death may also have meaning. If, that is, men and women can substitute more abstract, symbolic connections, what Lifton calls images of transcendence, for the more immediate, less abstract images of self and other that generally predominate in our mundane lives. This, though, cannot be a merely individual act. It requires cultural resources—culturally elaborated images of transcendence—such as religion has traditionally offered.

Some cultures make it more difficult than others to invest in the images of transcendence. Classical Greece was one such culture. Another may be our own. The result is that death anxiety gets played out in various ways, often quite destructive. Jean Baudrillard argues that "from savage societies to modern societies, the evolution is irreversible: *little by little the dead cease to exist.* They are thrown outside of the symbolic circulation of the group."[35] Things were quite different, says Baudrillard, in other societies. So-called primitive societies saw no real division between life and death. As Douglas Kellner puts it: "One lived with the dead—their spirits, memories, achievements—and was early on initiated into the realm of the dead oneself, dying a symbolic death and being reborn into a symbolic world in which there was no difference between life and death. In these societies, symbolic exchange between life and death continuously took place."[36]

The tragic poets, however, suggest that life (and death) was not this simple in classical Greece. In reading the plays one is continually struck by how dead the dead really are. The body and psyche (a term whose Homeric meaning is simply "shade") seem so closely bound that they die together. Plato's *Phaedo* addresses precisely this anxiety. The ancient Greek thus had difficulty establishing symbolic connections between life and death or securely holding the memories of loved ones. The family, by far the most important symbol of continuity for the classical Greek, is, of course, constantly under threat in the Greek tragedies, most of which concern the murder of family members by others. Nor does this difficulty lead simply to quiet desperation and the like. It leads instead to the cultural disintegration that Euripides writes of, fire not ice. We seem to face a similar problem, a deficit of images of transcendence, today.

Lacan

Lacan's analysis of the self, his chief concern, begins with his study of what he calls the mirror stage ("le stade du miroir"), in which the child first comes to recognize its image (*moi*) in the mirror. The image, says Lacan (in an account that is as much metaphor as developmental psychology) comes to be regarded as more real, more coherent, and certainly more ideal, than the actual self. The image in the mirror is whole and complete; the actual self is lacking (*manque*). What we desire most of all is ourselves: the ideal of perfection that is alienated in the mirror and never recovered, because it never truly existed in the first place. Lacan's analysis suggests that many of the images and ideals of mature selfhood valorized by most modern Westerners, such as autonomy, free will, and the unity of experience, are defenses against the lack in being of the real self. Rather than being the achievements of integrated selfhood, such ideals serve, like the image in the mirror, to defend the real self against its emptiness and longing. For that is what the real self is: the entity that longs for what it never can be—itself, whole and free.[37] Even those who admire the Greeks, emphasizing how important it is to understand them on their own terms, often take a condescending attitude toward the Greek self. John Jones concludes his

On Aristotle and Greek Tragedy with the statement that "it turns out to be our bad luck that Greek tragedy is superficially intelligible in a modern way."[38] This means that we must take extra pains to avoid imposing our own categories onto it, as we will be readily ensnared by apparent similarities. Yet, in this same book Jones argues that Antigone's concept of self is so weak and undeveloped (and Jones by no means sees her as exceptional) that she cannot think hypothetically. Her "apprehension of self in absent circumstances is so shifting and feeble. . . . In short, she knows no adequate modern 'you' which would give an adequate modern sense to the question: 'What would you do if it were a husband or child lying unburied?' "[39]

Jones is, in fact, doing what he cautions against (to be sure, he is addressing a disputed passage, but that changes nothing here). He is imposing a modern category on an ancient one, finding the ancient one feeble and inadequate by comparison. Against such an approach, I want to suggest that the Greek self was less defended by ideals of autonomy and self-control than the modern self but not for that reason more "feeble." I do not make my argument in the name of cultural relativism and tolerance. On the contrary, if we regard many of the attributes of the modern self as defenses against a lack in being, then a self characterized by such defenses is not more mature or developed: it is just more heavily defended. We would not call someone with a neurotic, narcissistic belief in his or her absolute autonomy more mature than someone who lacked such a belief. That is just what the mature, modern self is for Lacan—a neurotic, narcissistic defense.

Because Lacan's account is particularly dense and difficult it will be elaborated further in chapter 5, where it is used to support the Greek view that man is responsible without being free. Much of this elaboration involves contrasting Lacanian psychoanalysis with existential psychoanalysis, founded by Jean-Paul Sartre, which touts man's absolute freedom. Aspects of the schemes of Klein and Lifton will also be developed further in the appropriate chapters. One additional psychoanalytic concept, that of *holding,* a term closely associated with the psychoanalytic theory of D. W. Winnicott, is developed in chapter 4. Relatively straightforward, the concept is explained in the text.

The Psychoanalytic Theory of Greek Tragedy Is
Object Relations Theory

At this point the thoughtful reader may be saying to him- or herself that I am being too eclectic: all these theorists and all these concepts simply do not fit together. About this I ask the reader to withhold judgment. My goal is not to combine a bunch of different theories but to show how this eclectic mix is held together in an account of Greek tragedy that gives each a place in a narrative of human existence. Eclecticism is not my ideal. But the reality dealt with by the Greek poets is so subtle and differentiated that no single psychoanalytic theory can come to terms with it.

The reader should not get the wrong impression about my eclecticism, however. The theorists chosen are not incommensurable. None, for example, is a drive theorist or an ego psychologist. Klein and Lifton are object relations theorists, at least under the broad definition of this term. Lacan is not, but it is on this point that my psychoanalytic theory of Greek tragedy parts company with him: on his willful ignorance of human relatedness. As is well known, psychoanalysts can be divided into two camps: those who stress the importance of drives, Freudians of every stripe, and those who stress the importance of relationships. For drive theorists, psychic conflict stems from the intensity of the drives, from the way drives often seem about to overpower the ego, the agency charged with their control. Indeed, Freud often wrote of the puny ego, squeezed between the demands of the drives on the one hand and the demands of society, as embedded in the superego, on the other. The press of the drives upon the psyche, the urgent demand that they make for fulfillment, makes emotional life turbulent and conflict-ridden.

Object relations theory takes a different perspective. By "object relations theory," however, I mean something more general than the British School with which it is often associated—analysts such as W. R. D. Fairbairn, Harry Guntrip, and D. W. Winnicott. I mean rather an approach that sees psychic growth and psychic conflict as stemming from the ambivalent emotions we feel toward others: we often love and hate the same person. Such emotions may split the self, alienating it from itself and others. Reconciled and integrated, these same emotions may also heal the self. For purposes of diagnosis and treatment, object relations theorists generally focus upon the quality of the self's connection to others. Not only are these connections visible in a way that mind is not but many object relations theorists hold that these connections and relationships *are* the self.

In evaluating the quality of these connections, the most important questions are whether the self participates in whole-object relationships and whether it can do so with constancy. "Whole-object relations" refer to the self's ability to avoid splitting its objects into all good and all bad part-objects. Such relations require the toleration of ambivalent feelings toward others, a characteristic of what Klein calls the depressive position. "Object constancy" refers to the ability to hold an image (internal object, as it is called) of the other in the mind during the other's absence, not indiscriminately connecting with whatever object happens to be present. Neither our inability to reflect on our own sources of conduct nor our ability to control our desires is central to the object relational view of the self, though both are desirable. Central is the self's ability to connect with whole others over time.[40] All sorts of interesting consequences flow from this insight, including the possibility that the self portrayed by Homer, as well as that of the tragic poets, is more "developed" than that idealized by Plato and even moderns.

Lifton is in effect an object relations theorist, as noted previously. Relations with objects, valued people and ideas, constitute the connections that help us overcome the terror of death. Klein is often seen as the founder of object relations theory, even though she never explicitly broke with drive theory. It is true, as Harry Guntrip puts it, that for Klein external objects (such as people) serve primarily as recipients of projective identification. But, as he points out:

> The result comes to much the same thing in the end, namely the development of an inner world of fantasy that is actually object-relational, and is a counterpart of the ego's relations with the world of real objects. . . . This is the real core of Melanie Klein's work. By a very devious and quite unnecessary theoretical route, based on hypotheses that hardly any other analysts but Kleinians accept, she arrived at the fundamental truth that human nature is object-relational in its very essence, at its innermost heart.[41]

I approach Klein from this perspective.

Lacan is not an object relations theorist. As E. Victor Wolfenstein puts it, Lacan's approach "involves a regress from deeds to words and from words to texts . . . from the self engaged with an object to the self engaged with the self as an object, and then to the self as the absence of the object and of itself."[42] In this regard Lacan parts company not only with object relations theory, but also with the poets. Alhtough there remains much of value in Lacan's work, it will have to be separated from his withdrawal of the self into the no-self.

ANTIHUMANISM WITH A PLACE FOR HUMANS

From a number of different directions, the civilizing power of reason—the contribution of reason to civilization—has come under increasing attack in recent years. Among its critics are postmodernists, as they are called, such as Michel Foucault, Jacques Derrida, Pierre Bourdieu, Jacques Lacan, and Jean-François Lyotard, who in various ways argue that reason gets men and women into trouble because it is an instance of humanism, understood as the principle that the world is susceptible to human reason because it is organized along rational lines. Central to this critique of humanism is the later work of Martin Heidegger, particularly his "Letter on Humanism," as well as his essay "What Is Metaphysics?" Yet intellectual life is nothing if not ironic, and recent revelations about the extent of Heidegger's involvement with National Socialism have raised the question of whether a critique of humanism must not eventuate in an antihumanism that is simply inhumane.

In fact, the question is terribly complicated, depending in good measure on how one defines humanism, as well as the nature of the alternatives. I have found it useful to turn to the Greek tragic poets for insight into this issue. They offer a valuable perspective in part because their nonmodernism is not a reaction to Modernism, at least in the current sense of the term. They are modern in subjecting myth to standards of the polis, as Jean-Pierre Vernant defines tragedy (see chapter 2, below). However, this aspect of the poets' modernism is not what is today called Modernism, as it does not assume that human beings either "know [or] control their basic nature and desires," which is how Alexander Nehamas defines the humanism to which Heidegger is opposed.[43] In this sense the poets' perspective accords with that of Heidegger, as Heidegger himself appreciates. But though the poets are not humanists, they are not antihumanist either. I shall not enter into the debate over whether Heidegger is an antihumanist (I do not believe that he is; to characterize the human essence in terms of its relationship to Being does not constitute a subjective humanism, but it is not antihumanism), but I shall argue that the tragic poets represent an alternative to humanism that neither Heidegger, nor the postmoderns, nor even most moderns have fully grasped.

"Wozu Dichter in dürftiger Zeit?" We need poets, says Heidegger in his later works, to name the Holy. The poet speaks Being, and so brings traces of the vanished gods into the cosmic night. The poet speaks Being because he uses language not as an instrument to control Being, but as the house of Being: an opening in which Being might appear. Through poetry, one may grasp the god who is "near yet hard to grasp," a god remote from traditional theology, who presides over long-lost Being. In a word, the poet is shepherd (*hüten*) of Being, to use Heidegger's famous phrase from his "Letter on Humanism." Though Hölderlin is Heidegger's favorite poet along with Rilke, Heidegger does not exclude the Greek tragic poets. On the contrary, the tragic poets wrote at a decisive cusp in history, he argues, in which man's openness to Being was being clouded by the rise of philosophy. Heraclitus' *agchibasin,* which Heidegger renders as "letting-oneself-into-nearness" of Being, was about to be overcome by "metaphysics."[44] With the tragic poets, however, Being had one final chance. Heidegger concludes his "What Is Metaphysics?" this way.

In Being all that comes to pass in what-is is perfected from everlasting. The last poem of the last poet of the dawn-period of Greece—Sophocles' "Oedipus in Colonos"—closes with words that hark back far beyond our ken to the hidden history of these people and marks their entry into the unknown truth of Being:

> But cease now, and nevermore
> Lift up the lament.
> For all this is determined.
> (ll. 1777–1778)

This is not the place to develop a critique of Heidegger's philosophy. I have turned to Heidegger to make a single point. Whatever the merits of his praise of the pre-Socratic philosophers, Heidegger gets *Oedipus at Colonus,* and the tragic poets in general, just wrong. The tragic poets sought not to build a house for Being to appear. On the contrary, they wished to build a house, or rather a polis, in which man might find some human comfort and companionship in the face of a capricious Being (to use Heidegger's terminology for a moment) that cares nothing for human happiness and fulfillment. Put baldly, the poets sought, unsuccessfully, to build a house to keep an inhuman Being out. This difference with Heidegger arises not because the tragic poets were humanists, for they agree with Heidegger that to ask about man's nature requires that one look beyond man himself. Not only this. Whereas Plato would have man "know himself" by understanding his relationship to Ideas, Heidegger and the tragic poets agree that this larger order has little to do with *nous,* "reason." This is their shared antihumanism. For the tragic poets, however, this larger order is either incommensurable with, irrelevant to, or incompatible with (it varies with the poet and the play) a meaningful human existence. Man should know the traces of this larger order, what I am calling Being, as best he can, particularly as these traces (Heidegger's *Spuren*) are communicated through the beings of gods. But primarily so that he might stay out of its way as best he can.

This difference between Heidegger and the tragic poets is reflected in the poets' embrace of everyday life, even though the poets never mistake everyday life for the sine qua non of existence. Heidegger, on the other hand, exhibits an "antipathy toward everydayness [that] has been noticed, in a general way, by numerous commentators." For Heidegger the thoughtless willing and wanting of everyday life leads Being to hide itself ever more thoroughly, which is why he turns from "face-to-face" (*Gegen-einander-über*) relationships to an encounter with a more distant Being.[45] The tragic poets, on the other hand, manage to embrace everyday life, while still being concerned with the thoughtless willing and wanting—what they call hubris—that gets men into trouble, precisely because it violates a larger order. Never failing to appreciate the claims of the larger order, the poets never sacrifice this world to it, recognizing that although this order makes a claim on men, it is not human. One sees this, for example, in Sophocles' *Antigone,* in which Creon's refusal to recognize the claims of the larger order leads to his destruction at the hands of Antigone, whose motives seem entirely her own: private, personal, and strictly human (more on this theme in chapter 4). In the poets' account men must respect Being, but it is not their home. Their home is with other humans.

With the term *Being,* I am designating what might be called the fundamental principles or characteristics of reality. While I do not think this violates

Heidegger's intent, my definition hardly captures the depth of Heidegger's understanding of the term. Not only this: to define Being is perhaps itself the problem, as though we might understand Being by categorizing it in human terms. Nevertheless, I have found it useful to do so, not so much in order to understand Heidegger as to understand the tragic poets. For the key point is that the tragic poets write as though they understand the fundamental principles or characteristics of reality quite well; they just do not like reality one bit. It is, for example, a reality whose justice is at best incomprehensible in human terms, at worst actively hostile to human justice. How is one to live in such a world? the poets ask. Their answer, to put it simply (and it is not always this simple: often this fundamental reality is so at odds with human reality that the poets get confused), is to construct a social order that can provide humans with support and comfort in the face of these circumstances. J. Peter Euben argues in his recent *Tragedy of Political Theory* that the purpose of tragic drama, particularly of Aeschylus' *Oresteia,* is to collectivize suffering.[46] I understand his claim to mean that tragic drama is about how men and women might best shepherd themselves in the face of a hostile world and a hostile ultimate reality.

Their project does not, as the poets recognize, work very well. Which does not mean that it is not the most important human project but simply that it is very difficult. It does not work very well because the hostile reality is within, not just without. (In *Heidegger and Modernity,* Luc Ferry and Alain Renaut suggest that the unconscious is a key dimension of Being.[47]) Humans cannot insulate themselves from a hostile fundamental reality, as this reality is also (but not solely) within humanity. This is evidenced in the fact that humans frequently act with all the caprice, envy, and jealousy of the gods, mediators of Being. What makes the poets antihumanists, of course, is that in the face of this reality it never even occurs to them that man's "*humanitas* or *Eigentlichkeit* lies in his capacity to wrench free of his determinations," as Ferry and Renaut define humanism.[48] Yet if they share this with Heidegger they share little else. Whereas Heidegger holds that the god is "near yet hard to grasp," for the tragic poets the reverse is true. The gods are all too present, all too near, all too intrusive. Not to open the self up to god but to construct a human world in the face of the inhumanity of the gods must be the real human task. This antihumanism keeps a place for humans—indeed, it makes them central.

Today it seems to be widely if often implicitly held that if human reason is not somehow the measure of reality, then there exists nothing else human that might take its place. This view is given added impetus by the insight, basically correct, that not only is reason not the measure of the cosmos, it is not the measure of human conduct either. Human beings do indeed seem neither to know nor to control their basic nature and desires, and reason frequently offers a defense against this insight. This, I take it, stands as the key insight of

postmodernism, what unites such diverse authors as Foucault, Lacan, Bourdieu, and Lyotard. Covering a variety of fields from sociology and history to
psychoanalysis, and a variety of methodological approaches from realism to
nominalism, these authors agree upon at least one thing, that "one has to dis-
pense with the constituting (*constituent*) subject, to get rid of the subject itself,"
so as to see history strictly as the maker of subjects, as Foucault puts it.[49] In a
related fashion, Lacan argues that the subject, at least insofar as it is conceived
as an autonomous actor, an ego, "is structured exactly like a symptom. Interior
to the subject, it is only a privileged symptom. It is the human symptom par
excellence, it is the mental malady of man." Bourdieu writes of "philosophy
without a subject," pointing out with great penetration how this postmodern
insight is prefigured in the structural sociology of Emile Durkheim and his
many followers. Lyotard, whom Sonia Kruks labels a "philosopher of desire,"
finds no subject at all, just an "inchoate and eruptive libido against which
consciousness could be only a moment of repressive unification."[50]

In fact, the tragic poets and the postmoderns share a great deal. Both agree
that man is the object, but not the subject, of his own desires. Vincent Descombes' claim, in "Apropos of the 'Critique of the Subject,'" that for the postmodern "it becomes conceivable that Romeo . . . is amorous without his being
the subject of his love," would have been readily understood by the tragic poets
(if they could have understood the jargon).[51] Indeed, this is the theme of many
tragedies, such as Euripides' *Hippolytus,* in which Phaedra is overcome with
desire in the form of Aphrodite, a goddess acting on her from without—a particularly acute way of expressing the otherness of desire. Similarly, the tragic
poets would have been quite familiar with the idea, expressed by Derrida in
"'Eating Well,' or the Calculation of the Subject," that responsibility has nothing to do with freedom—that is, with being a subject who might choose to act
otherwise. Rather, responsibility is thrust upon us by the very otherness of the
world (the topic of chapter 5).[52] It would be wrong to conclude that Derrida,
particularly, seeks to liquidate the subject. Nor do most of the twenty con-
tributors to *Who Comes after the Subject?* a recent volume on the topic. On the
contrary, Derrida seeks to redefine the subject, so as to understand it in terms
of its responsibility to the other. It does not take a great deal of imagination
to see a connection between this attitude toward the other and Heidegger's
attitude toward being.

So the tragic poets and postmoderns share much, but it would be a mistake
to ignore the difference between them. This difference stems in part from the
fact that the tragic poets were not faced with the "sovereignty of the subject" in
the first place. The tragic poets did not need to take the subject apart, as they
never assumed that any sane person might believe man to be an autonomous
reality. Other ideas separate the tragic poets from the postmoderns. Consider

Paul Valéry's statement that "My fate is more me than myself. A person is only made up of answers to a number of impersonal incidents," quoted by Sylviane Agacinski to illustrate the postmodern view of what comes after the subject.[53] Surely the tragic poets would have had no difficulty with the first sentence. With the second they might have had more trouble, depending upon how much one emphasizes the term *answers*—that is, how much creativity a person is allowed in constructing answers to events.

The poets believe in character. Not in the sense of a strong will that allows characters to control their desires, so-called good character. Rather, in the sense of a fixed disposition to act in a certain way, a stable constellation of traits. These traits may be overwhelmed by contingency. This is the theme of Euripides' *Hecuba,* in which Hecuba's nobility of character survives the loss of her husband, children, and country but not betrayal by her guest-friend, Polymestor. Traits and dispositions need not be immutable to be stable. Whereas character is usually stable for the tragic poets, nonetheless it contains qualities of otherness: it is given to us, not chosen, and often is conceptualized as a *daimon,* a spirit that accompanies us throughout life, neither subject nor object. Responsibility, from this perspective, has much to do with coming to terms with that otherness of character. In *The Differend* Lyotard seeks to "refute the prejudice anchored in the reader by centuries of humanism and of 'human sciences' that there is 'man.'"[54] The tragic poets, on the contrary, believe in man, whose basic qualities and character are fixed. To hold otherwise is itself hubris. Nevertheless, this "man" of the tragic poets is no sovereign subject, not even to himself. More often than not he is an object to himself. This tantalizing difference between the tragic poets and postmoderns makes it so fruitful to compare them.

How is all this connected to my attempt to "enlarge" psychoanalytic theory? The answer is simple. Although there have been profound advances in psychoanalysis since Freud, no one since Freud has put all the pieces together: psychoanalysis as an account of human nature (such a dangerous term these days), psychoanalysis as an account of civilization and its discontents, and psychoanalysis as therapy, showing how each operates according to the same basic principles.

The humane antihumanism of the tragic poets offers, I believe, a chance to begin to put these pieces together again in a new way. Not, to be sure, with the systematic regularity of Freud. The analysts I draw upon differ too much for that. In addition, so many different psychoanalytic theories have emerged subsequent to Freud, each with its own important piece of the puzzle to contribute, that an account of man, woman, and civilization based upon a single theory seems today both impossible and undesirable. This does not, however, mean that coherent stories are no longer possible. On the contrary, I believe that the tragic poets tell one such story: about what it is like to live as humanly as one can in a world in which even man himself is often hostile to his own humanity. This story illuminates, and is illuminated by, psychoanalysis, which is why I want to tell it. More than this: only a humane antihumanism is compatible, I believe, with the truths of psychoanalysis.

Confusion

PART 1

Greek Tragedy and the Dionysian Crisis

CHAPTER 2

Oh, blank confusion! true epitome
Of what the mighty City is herself.
—William Wordsworth, *The Prelude*

First I shall tell a story about the three poets and how they deal with the issue that since Leibniz has been called theodicy but which is better captured—because the Greeks did not assume that the gods were just to begin with—by the term *Dionysian crisis*. This story concerns the Greek anxiety that the Olympian gods, the sky gods, will finally prove to be no different from the Furies, the earth gods. Both are bloodthirsty, vengeful tyrants. As such this story concerns anxiety and confusion over the inability to distinguish good and bad, or to hold them separate. The chorus in *Antigone* states the proverbial wisdom: "the bad becomes the good to him a god would doom" (621–622). But if the gods themselves are bad, requiring that people do bad things, then what are people to do? Is it good to be bad, bad to be good? The iterations, and hence the possibilities for confusion, are endless.

One might call this the fundamental anxiety, at least of the Greeks and probably of ourselves as well: how to know good and bad and so hold them apart. Philoctetes puts the problem in terms every Greek would understand: "How can I reckon the score . . . when praising Heaven I find the gods are bad?" (Soph., *Philoctetes,* 451). The relation between anxiety about the goodness of the gods and what Klein calls paranoid-schizoid anxiety is apparent. How can people protect the good from the bad if they cannot even keep them straight? This, we recall, was Richard's problem. It was the problem of the poets as well. Furthermore, even if people come to know, as Euripides seems to, that the gods are generally bad and so no source of moral guidance, the question of whether they themselves might do better becomes more poignant. If the immortals are not good, how can a mere mortal be? Could a man really be superior to a god? Klein calls this depressive anxiety. No more fundamental barrier than this is confronted by the poets in their attempt to carve out a human and humane refuge in a fundamentally hostile world.

AESCHYLUS

Are the gods hostile to human happiness and good fortune? Or do they merely object to the greed and hubris that happiness and good fortune so often bring? Aeschylus' *Persians,* produced in 472 B.C. and possibly the earliest of his extant plays (depending on how one dates the *Suppliant Maidens*) gives both answers. The chorus speaks of crafty, deceitful gods who entice people into doing the sorts of things that the gods then punish. In a word, the gods practice entrapment. They pretend to befriend man but only in order to involve him more deeply in his own destruction (see 97ff, 157ff). Darius, however, attributes the punishments of Zeus to acts of hubris uninvited, as it were, by the gods, such as Xerxes' bridging of the Hellespont (see 740ff). Gilbert Murray refers to both views as part of "the Inherited Conglomerate," in which explanations of human disaster were manifold and not necessarily logically consistent.[1] This, though, should not cause us to underestimate the Greek desire for gods who are just. That too is part of the Conglomerate. Concerning the Greek gods, Dodds says: "Man projects into the cosmos his own nascent demand for social justice; and when from the outer spaces the magnified echo of his own voice returns to him, promising punishment for the guilty, he draws from it courage and reassurance."[2]

True enough. One must go on to ask, as the poets did, what happens when what returns to man is not justice but chaos and injustice? What happens when man looks around his world and finds that the arrogant prosper and the pious and temperate are led to disaster? What happens when, as Dodds puts it, "God's in his Heaven, all's wrong with the world"?[3] The poets confront this reality and the doubt and confusion that it raises. Why the tensions and contradictions of the Inherited Conglomerate were more easily tolerated in the archaic era, becoming a crisis only in the era of the three playwrights, will be discussed later in the chapter.

Aeschylus addresses this crisis in a sophisticated fashion, arguing, in effect, that as society develops, the gods too grow, becoming more just in human terms. This appears to be the theme of *Prometheus* (making some assumptions about the two lost plays of the trilogy), as well as of the *Oresteia* trilogy (*Agamemnon, Libation Bearers,* and *Eumenides*). It is the most optimistic teaching the poets have to offer. In *Agamemnon,* it will be recalled, Agamemnon returns victorious from Troy only to be murdered by his wife Clytaemestra, in part because he had sacrificed their daughter Iphigenia and in part because Clytaemestra is jealous that Agamemnon has taken a mistress. In *Libation Bearers,* Apollo orders Orestes, son of Agamemnon and Clytaemestra, to avenge his father's death. With his sister Electra he kills his mother, Clytaemestra, and her lover, Aegisthus. Almost immediately after the murders Orestes goes insane, believing he is being persecuted by the Furies, bloodthirsty monsters who punish matricide. (In this play, Orestes is the only one who can see them.) In the *Eumenides,* after finding that Apollo cannot save him from the Furies, Orestes goes to Athens, where Athene holds a trial over his guilt. The votes are even, and Athene sides with Orestes, freeing him. The play ends with Athene convincing the Furies to take up residence in Athens as servants of the law. They become Eumenides, "the kindly ones."

Aeschylus addresses the confusion of good and bad by confronting, rather than denying, the fundamental anxiety: that the sky gods, including Zeus and Apollo, are really Furies in disguise, bloodthirsty demons. Not every Greek writer faced this problem. Isocrates, for example, simply asserts that some gods are good, some bad. The gods, he says, are divided into "those who are the cause of good things for us and are called Olympians, and those who are set in charge of disasters and punishments and bear less agreeable names."[4] Plato's solution was more complex, involving the creation of a higher world of abstract standards, the Ideas, by which even the gods might be measured and stories about them bowdlerized. Socrates tells Euthyphro to "say what the holy is, and never mind if gods do love it" (*Euth.,* 11b). Such a strategy of transcendence was not available to the tragic poets. How, they seem to ask, can anyone say what is good who does not know whether the gods love it or not or whether their love for it can be relied upon?

Anxiety about the sky gods, preeminently Zeus and Apollo, fills *Agamemnon.* Even the famous affirmation of faith in Zeus invites doubt: "Zeus whoever [of whatever sort] he be" ("Zeus hostis pot' estin," 160ff).[5] Euripides' *Orestes,* widely recognized as a parody of Aeschylus' *Oresteia* (compare, for example, *Eumenides,* 657–670, *Orestes,* 550–560), echoes these lines: "We obey the gods—whoever the gods may be," says Orestes ("ho ti pot' eisin oi theoi," 418). Here there is no doubt who the gods are. They are evil beings, and in the line immediately preceding this Menelaus calls Apollo's order that Orestes kill his mother "callous, unjust, and immoral." With qualifications, my argument will be that Aeschylus and Euripides differ on this point less than is generally assumed.

Against this conclusion, one might argue that in the *Oresteia* the gods have realized a rough justice. The magnified echo of man's cry for justice has returned to him only slightly distorted. But consider the larger context, in which the justice of Zeus upon Troy cost the lives of thousands of innocents and the suffering of many thousands more. And Clytaemestra's murder of Agamemnon only continues a cycle of violence that will require still more human sacrifice. Is this even rough justice? One sees doubt and confusion in the chorus' claim that through suffering inflicted by Zeus may come grace or favor. "From the gods who sit in grandeur, grace (*charis*) comes somehow violent (*biaios*)" (180–

183). About this Winnington-Ingram says, "between the notions of grace and violence there is a clash: it is virtually a paradox." It is also, I would add, a sign of actual confusion, in which words themselves lose their meaning and become oxymorons—as Thucydides points out words do in moments of great anxiety (see *History,* 3.82). One is tempted to conclude, Winnington-Ingram continues, that "in *Agamemnon,* from 60ff onward, every reference to Erinyes [Furies] is associated, textually, with Zeus, every reference to Zeus with Erinyes."[6]

Anxiety about the goodness of the gods forms a useful analytic focal point because the gods are such ready recipients of projective identification, in which unmastered anxiety and confusion are externalized. But the confusion is evident in the more mundane concerns of the chorus as well, questions of whether the Trojan War was good or bad or whether revenge should be valorized or rejected (see 1560; compare with 580, 625). First one way they sway, then the other, depending in large measure upon whether the war or act of revenge was successful. Here is the nexus of the confusion of good and bad, in which good comes to be equated with sheer power, the power to keep at bay the bad (badness is often experienced, Klein tells us, as the fear of being vulnerable to persecutors). Through this way of thinking, to which the chorus is so susceptible, rampant aggression, violence, and hatred become good, as long as they are directed against badness. At the conclusion of the *Libation Bearers,* the chorus that had been goading Orestes to kill his mother finally begins to wonder if Orestes is a savior or merely a bringer of death. The answer, it seems, depends not so much on the rightness of Orestes' act as it does on its success in halting the cycle of violence (1065–1075). Or rather, rightness and success become one.

Look at it this way. From the very beginning of *Agamemnon,* the chorus has been anxious about the unfinished business that hangs over the house of Atreus: the murder and mutilation of the children of Thyestes by Atreus, Agamemnon's father (of these children only Aegisthus remains, and Clytaemestra has taken him as her consort); Agamemnon's sacrifice of his daughter with Clytaemestra, Iphigenia; the adultery of both Agamemnon and Clytaemestra; and Agamemnon's harsh, brutal treatment of the Trojans, as well as the fact that his is the only ship to return to Argos, all for the sake of a beautiful whore. The chorus has good reason to be uneasy. In such anxious circumstances one might expect the chorus to turn to the gods, except that the chorus grasps that the gods do not stand outside this cycle of violence but cause it. Artemis caused the sacrifice of Iphigenia (see 133–160, 203) and Zeus the destruction of Troy; soon Agamemnon will pay for the misdeeds of his father—apparently, so the chorus believes, another act of Zeus (see 1487). In general I have eschewed a literary approach to the plays, which makes an analysis of the internal symbolic code key. Such an approach to the first half of *Agamemnon* is revealing, however, focusing as it does on the complex and confusing symbolism, in which, for example, an image of eagles who have lost their young segues into the image of eagles devouring a pregnant hare (found at 49–55, 105–145).[7] We may read this symbolism at many levels, at one of which it is simply intentionally confounded and confusing and so reflective of the chorus' confusion, in this case over whether the acts of the Atreidae, who seem to be represented by the eagles, are just.

We survive in a world such as this, a world in which "truth and good are torn asunder," as the chorus puts it (623), in good measure by equating goodness with power, including the power to do great violence. Over and over this is the way the chorus resolves its doubts about Agamemnon's expedition against Troy (note 580, 625, 1560), Clytaemestra's slaughter of Agamemnon (see 1487, 1564), and Orestes' murder of Clytaemestra (in *Libation Bearers,* 1065–1075). If the violence succeeded, then the gods must have intended it, and therefore it is good. There is nothing here that is not Zeus. The problem, of course, is that such thinking quickly leads us to confuse good and bad, for we must deny what we know to be true: that certain acts of brutal violence are bad, no matter how successful. Not only that, but in equating success, violence, and goodness, we are tempted to reverse goodness and badness, so as to preserve the equation in all circumstances.

The association of the Furies with the sky gods continues in the *Libation Bearers,* where Orestes calls upon Zeus to "send up from below a late-punishing doom" (382). There was at this time a cult of Zeus Chthonios, a nether Zeus, the Zeus of the dead. Thus, in Aeschylus' *Suppliant Maidens,* the chorus threatens that if they do not win the Olympian gods to their side, they will hang themselves, and so become suppliants of "him of the earth, the host of many guests, the Zeus of the dead" (156ff). Similarly, their father, Danaus, refers to a second Zeus who judges the dead in Hades (see 229–230). But which is the real Zeus? That, of course, is the problem. Orestes has turned to this aspect of the Inherited Conglomerate, as does Clytaemestra in *Agamemnon,* when she dedicates the third wound inflicted on her fallen husband to the Zeus beneath the earth who keeps corpses safe (see 1385ff). The sharp distinction between sky gods and earth gods, such as that asserted by Isocrates, looks more and more like manic denial (the gross idealization of the good to isolate it from the bad), for Zeus can be found aligned with both. Conversely, it is no accident that the *Eumenides* opens with the Furies at the very heart of Apollo's sanctuary. It is just where they belong. Similarly, the Furies are not mistaken when they respond to Apollo that it is not the blood they have shed that contaminates the omphalos, the sacred stone that represents the navel of the universe in Apollo's temple, but the blood he has demanded (at 160–170).

It is Aeschylus' greatness that he does not deny this confusion. He recognizes it, seeking to resolve it not by a mere reassertion of the paranoid-schizoid distinction (all sky gods are good, all earth gods bad) but rather by a higher level of integration. That seems to be the purpose of the *Oresteia*. Says Winnington-Ingram, upon whom I have drawn heavily in this section: "The trilogy is haunted by polarities—light and darkness, day and night, good and evil, hope and fear. . . . But the polar opposites refuse to be kept apart (any more than the two worlds of gods): always the worse encroaches on the better—always until the closing scene."[8] Recall Meltzer's characterization of Richard's anxiety in similar terms, when he could not prevent the destructive and "Hitleresque" part of himself from encroaching upon his goodness. The result was confusion, not integration, in which Richard did not know who was his friend. Klein dealt with this anxiety by attempting to bring Richard into contact with his own hatred and aggression, so that he might gradually become convinced that they need not overpower his love. Only this preliminary sorting out allows the integration of love and hate at a higher level. Aeschylus proceeds in a similar fashion. Or, as Winnington-Ingram puts it, "*Eumenides* sorts things out which have been fused in the earlier plays, only that they may be harmonized at a higher level."[9] Yet in the end the question remains whether this harmony does more than simply cover up a deeper confusion.

Eumenides achieves harmony by having Athene persuade the Furies to transform their ways without abandoning their avenger's role. There is still a place for fear, trembling, and revenge—but that place becomes contained within a civilized society and serves it. Apollo threatened the Furies—force against force. Athene persuades them to help civilization, by containing their rage within the institutions of justice. From now on revenge will complement institutionalized, civic justice, not compete with it. In this way the cycle of revenge, fostered by the sky gods and the Furies alike, is broken by law. Aeschylus distinguishes the realms of sky gods and earth gods but not by denying or rejecting the truth represented by the Furies: that the mind of the past, as the Furies call themselves, can be contained and integrated but never transcended. The Furies move underground, but their power is not denied. They will sit on shining chairs and receive devotions from the citizens—a mark of respect as much for their primitive power as for their commitment to justice.

In a brief essay on the *Oresteia* written shortly before her death, Klein interprets the play as an account of Orestes' recovery from severe paranoid-schizoid illness, characterized by a virtually psychotic fear of persecution, the consequence of guilt over his matricide. His recovery is facilitated by Athene who, representing the good mother (or analyst, one might add), helps him to integrate his hatred and so to find a place for his Furies. Yet one wonders. Does this not seem a little too easy, too similar to manic denial? Certainly the final procession of the *Eumenides* contains manic elements, for the Furies are not merely tamed but rendered eternal allies of Athenian justice and goodness (see 1035ff). Before, they were devoted to blood vengeance, mutilating bodies, and sucking the blood of their victims. After their transformation they become the source of all goodness, protectors of good harvest, the lives of young men, and the safety of Athens. Were an analyst to make a comparable claim about her success in overcoming her patient's paranoid-schizoid anxiety we would wonder at its truth, knowing that the cure can never be as perfect as this. Against this criticism of Klein (and Aeschylus too, perhaps), one might focus on the closeness of the vote, in which Orestes is acquitted only by the intervention of Athene, for reasons that hardly seem compelling. She always takes the side of the man. About this Klein says: "I would conclude that the opposing votes show that the self is not easily united, that destructive impulses drive one way, love and the capacity for reparation and compassion in other ways."[10]

Nevertheless, the transformation of the Furies seems too complete: from Furies they become "the kindly ones," Eumenides, protectors of Athens. Though the term *Eumenides* never appears in the play itself, it is generally held that this was indeed the title which Aeschylus gave to the play. What is not clear is whether this term was commonly applied to the Furies at this time. In any case, it captures not so much the spirit of integration as the spirit of utter transformation and denial. Indeed, the more one thinks about the resolution, the more problematic it becomes. Too complete and perfect in some respects, it remains inadequate and confused in others. Often it is argued that the Furies represent preoedipal morality because they value ties of blood over ties of marriage, which is why they punish matricide but not a wife's murder of her husband. Apollo, on the other hand, represents a more advanced oedipal morality, that of the marriage bond, upon which developed civilization depends. Yet Apollo's defense of Orestes is based upon his assertion that father, not mother, is the real parent. "The parent is he who mounts." The mother is only the nurse (660). This, of course, does not make Apollo the defender of oedipal morality at all. He has simply redefined parenthood. Even if one assumes that oedipal morality signifies an advance over that of the Furies, Apollo does not represent it. Quite the contrary—he degrades the marriage bond, turning it into a transaction between strangers, one of whom provides a temporary home for the father's seed, as a person might leave property on deposit with another (see 658–659).

It might be argued in response that although Apollo speaks for the defense, Athene saves Orestes and finds a place for the Furies. Thus, her position should be taken as the final one, especially as the last third of the play is devoted to her confrontation with the Furies, Apollo having decamped. True enough, but consider again the grounds of her preference for Orestes:

It is my task to render final judgment here. This is a ballot for Orestes I shall cast. There is no mother anywhere who gave me birth [Athene was born from the head of Zeus; he had swallowed her mother, out of fear she would give birth to a son stronger than himself], and but for marriage, I

am always for the male with all my heart, and strongly on my father's side.
So, in a case where the wife has killed her husband, lord of the house, her
death shall not mean most to me.
(735–740)

Athene represents a man's ideal of what every woman should be. Along with
Apollo, son of Zeus, she embodies the principle of patriarchy. What she does
not represent, at least in this passage, is an advancement in civilized morality
but only a shift in the preferred targets of revenge: from men to women. One
might argue that at least she has tamed the most primitive forces, the Furies.
But has she really? Is not the morality of Apollo equally primitive, equally
vengeful, but just a little easier to take, especially if one is a man? All this
has not escaped the attention of feminists such as Kate Millett, who argues
in *Sexual Politics* that Athene is an accomplice in the triumph of patriarchy:
"Athene born full-grown from the head of her father Zeus marches on, spoiling
to betray her kind. . . . [The *Oresteia* ends with] five pages of local chamber
of commerce rhapsody." Disagreeing with Millett, Anne Lebeck argues that
Euripides treats this triumph with tongue in cheek, using "wit and humor" to
capture the "paradox and parody" of the resolution, which is no genuine resolution at all but a way of raising unsettling questions in an indirect fashion, by
only pretending to resolve them. Millett takes Aeschylus too literally.[11]

D. J. Conacher argues that the transformation of the Furies is neither sudden nor complete. Early in the play Aeschylus characterizes them as instru-
ments not merely of vengeance but of the discipline necessary to preserve
civilized society (see 494–516). This role remains even after their transformation, which is why some, such as Hugh Lloyd-Jones, argue that the Furies
are not transformed at all. "When the Erinyes become Eumenides, there is
not the least question of their giving up their function."[12] (This is, of course,
what makes the tragedies so interesting: completely opposite interpretations of
seemingly straightforward passages are common.) In addition, one might argue
that although Athene gives an apparently stupid reason for her preference for
Orestes, this reason does not affect her subsequent plea to the Furies to transform their ways. Her argument has nothing to do with Orestes, who has left
the stage along with Apollo, and everything to do with the need to contain the
retributive violence of the Furies within the rule of law (see 795ff). Furthermore, even though the Furies are, *pace* Lloyd-Jones, utterly transformed into
the kindly ones, Athene's attitude toward them is not: when the Furies talk
of brutal vengeance, she talks of the rule of law; but when the Furies become
manic caretakers of Athens, source of all goodness, she reminds them of their
retributive role (at 925–995). It is in her role of the great persuader, who can
hold good and bad together without confusing them, that Athene triumphs.

This, though, does not make the grand resolution of the play any less false. It only makes it more poignant, as at least one of the characters seems to know that life is not so simple.

A Kleinian perspective on Greek tragedy may be fruitful, but this perspective must not be equated with Klein's own interpretation of the *Oresteia,* which seems insufficiently vigilant against the dangers of mock reparation and manic denial. Rather, Klein's analysis of the human propensity under the pressure of anxiety to confuse good and bad, a propensity that often expresses itself in superficial attempts to harmonize them, proves more helpful. I believe this best accounts for the unsatisfactory treatment of marriage in the *Eumenides.* Marriage cannot be rendered a mature union until it is free of the threat of the furies—in this case the man's fear that his wife is the fury that he once feared his mother to be. Aeschylus does not confront this anxiety, nor, apparently, does Greek culture. Or perhaps he did at least once, in the *Suppliant Maidens* trilogy, of which only the first (at least it was probably the first) of the three plays remains: *Suppliant Maidens, Aigyptioi, Danaids.* Once thought to have been among Aeschylus' oldest extant works (the *Suppliant Maidens* is now generally dated to the mid-460s; the *Oresteia* was produced in 458 B.C.), the trilogy seems to have involved another grand resolution along the lines of the *Eumenides,* complete with trial. Although no one knows whether the trial was of the suppliants for murdering their husbands, or of one of the suppliants, Hypermestra, for disobeying her father and *not* murdering hers, it seems to have been the point of the trial, and the trilogy, to defend the harmony of a marriage based on persuasion, rather than on force (see, for example, *Prometheus Bound,* 858–870; fragment 125 Mette; *Suppliant Maidens,* 1052–1071). One reason, therefore, to remain vigilant against mock reparation is better to appreciate the real thing when it comes along, as it occasionally does—perhaps in this lost trilogy.

Did Aeschylus, in the *Oresteia,* intend to leave his audience in doubt and confusion, albeit in such a subtle way that they would hardly know where these feelings came from? Or did he choose in the end to reinforce the audience's manic defenses against their own doubts? Perhaps this lies behind the almost religious appeal of his work. We experience its grandeur as uplifting because it reinforces our defenses against our own doubt and confusion about the goodness of the cosmos. We cannot know the answer to these questions, and perhaps it does not matter anyway. What is clear is that the grand resolution of the *Eumenides* reveals itself as remarkably superficial, only thinly covering the deepest confusion and doubts. My own opinion is that there is little difference between Aeschylus' resolution and the deus ex machina favored by Euripides in *Orestes* and *Electra.* Both impose an actual resolution so implausible and unsatisfying that the psychological effect is more unsettling than cathartic. That this is so often missed in Aeschylus demonstrates not only how grand and noble form can obscure this effect but also our great need for resolution and clarification, even when upon closer examination that desire looks like manic denial. Although Bennett Simon in *Tragic Drama and the Family* recognizes that the resolution of the *Oresteia* is a "perverse solution," he is not as critical of it as I am, because he seems to believe that the audience would have been able to use the false closure as material with which to construct their own genuine resolution.[13] I think it more likely that this perverse solution would have fed the audience's manic denial.

It is risky to turn to the fragments of lost plays to prove anything, in part because they can support almost any interpretation. (Actually, the term *fragments* is misleading; it refers not to pieces of otherwise lost text, but to any ancient reference to now lost plays.) I have run this risk once already, however; the second time is always easier. The fragments of the two lost plays that together with *Prometheus Bound* apparently comprised Aeschylus' Prometheus trilogy (*Prometheia,* as it is called) suggest that the *Prometheia* concluded with the same type of grand resolution one finds in the *Oresteia,* so that by the end of the trilogy Zeus and Prometheus, implacable opponents in *Prometheus Bound,* are reconciled. Unfeeling Zeus comes to pity Prometheus, and both become more flexible in their positions. Prometheus is released, but to allow Zeus to save face he agrees to wear the symbol of his chains forever in the form of a garland.[14] Assuming that these fragments give an accurate picture of the *Prometheia,* it looks like Aeschylus' penchant for the implausible resolution of opposites was not exhausted with the *Oresteia* (most hold that *Prometheus Bound* was written well after the *Oresteia,* probably in the last two years of Aeschylus' life). It also appears that Aeschylus took these implausible resolutions seriously, but that cannot be determined. Certainly Prometheus running around wearing a garland might be seen as an instance of the parody to which Lebeck refers. It is, in any case, wise to remain skeptical about such grand resolutions. The greatest danger is not so much that we shall fail to appreciate their grandeur (generations of critics have seen to that) but that we shall overlook the skeptical Euripidean message contained within the noble Aeschylean form.

SOPHOCLES

Dodds argues that Sophocles was "the last great exponent of the archaic world-view."[15] Perhaps he was, as long as one appreciates the doubt and confusion at the heart of this worldview. This too is part of the Inherited Conglomerate. One sees this doubt and confusion even where one might not expect to, in *Ajax* for example, often seen as an early work (445–440 B.C.) that stands particularly close to the archaic ideal. In *Ajax,* Athene once again intervenes in the affairs of humans, driving Ajax insane so that he kills and tortures animals thinking they are the leaders of the Greek army, who humiliated him by depriving him of the honor of Achilles' armor. Doubly humiliated, he kills himself in shame to save what is left of his honor. The Greek army wants to refuse him burial, but Odysseus intervenes, saying, in effect, that revenge must halt before the grave. Ajax's failure is generally seen as the failure of *sophrosune* (self control) to temper the quest for *arete* (excellence). For Ajax had earlier rejected the help of the gods, who in the end destroy him. Yet in rejecting the gods, Ajax is hardly behaving as an archaic hero would. "Nothing could be less characteristically Homeric," as Winnington-Ingram puts it.[16] To characterize this play as archaic in outlook would be too simple.

Note the lesson that Ajax draws from his humiliation. He speaks of yielding (*eikein*) to the gods, and reverencing (*sebein*) kings (666ff). "Surely he should have reversed the verbs," says Winnington-Ingram.[17] In the guise of re-stating what was probably the most familiar moral lesson of that era—practice sophrosune, avoid hubris—Sophocles suggests a far less elevated lesson: beware of the gods as you would a powerful and dangerous animal. Not because it is good or just, but simply because it is powerful and dangerous. Much of Sophocles' work has this character. Using traditional forms and structures and apparently delivering traditional moral lessons, Sophocles actually raises grave doubts about that same tradition.

It is in this context that we should regard Kitto's famous account of Sophoclean *dike,* a term only misleadingly translated as "justice."[18] For Sophocles, dike is a universal principle of recoil, given in nature. We can understand it, but not change it. In this regard, dike resembles physus, even though it is nominally nomos. In fact, the nomos-physus distinction is quite complex, corresponding hardly at all to our distinction between natural and social laws. Nor should we regard Sophocles' running together of nomos and physus as proof that the tragic poets were less philosophically sophisticated. Both Plato and Aristotle join these principles, arguing that good customs (nomos) rest on nature (physus), which is the point, after all, of the *Republic,* as well as of Aristotle's *Nicomachean Ethics.* Sophocles' view of dike as nomos-like reflects an emphasis that differs from that of the philosophers, but it would be mistaken to regard his view as fundamentally opposed to theirs, a naive conflation of natural and social laws.

The principle represented by *dike,* recoil, most concerns acts of violence: as one sows, so shall one reap. Expressed in scientific terms, which seem especially appropriate to Sophocles' way of thinking, the principle of dike reads simply "for every action there is an equal and opposite reaction." In this principle, suggests Kitto, one finds an echo, albeit often vague and distorted, of the cry man makes to the heavens for justice. It would be foolish to deny the centrality of such a concept in Sophocles' work. Certainly Creon, in *Antigone,* suffers from such recoil. He denies burial to the dead, and sends a dead man's sister, Antigone, to be buried alive. In so doing, he reverses the natural order, for which he is punished by the deaths of his son and wife. So too does Ajax deny the natural order, the power of the gods. And Oedipus suffers from the sins of his parents, perhaps, or from his hubristic confidence in his own reason.[19] But what did Antigone do to deserve her fate? Or is she just another disposable instrument in the service of the destruction of the hubristic Creon, as Oedipus is an instrument in Laius' destruction? At one point the prophet Tiresias suggests just this: that Antigone has become a virtual Fury sent to destroy Creon (see *Antigone,* 1075). Not only does it begin to look like dike is incompatible with human justice. Its operations begin to seem almost incomprehensible, even though it is generally held that Sophocles set out to make the incomprehensible gods comprehensible, if not fair. In another era this becomes the view that it is better to live in a world ruled by an unjust god than one with no god at all. Even injustice is better than chaos and confusion. In fact, with Sophocles one actually gets all three: injustice, chaos, and confusion. Today we look too hard for clarification from the tragic poets. Perhaps we demand too much of them, overlooking their willingness to confront confusion—and to live with it.

The reaction of the chorus to the fate of Oedipus in *Oedipus Tyrannus* is instructive in this regard, for Sophocles probes at truths that the chorus, like the ideal audience with which it is frequently identified, cannot yet grasp. Beginning to fear the truth about Oedipus, the chorus can recite only traditional pieties about how gods punish hubristic, arrogant tyrants. Going further, the chorus challenges the god, saying that they will not worship Zeus unless he acts justly to punish the guilty tyrant (see 860–919). The chorus just does not get it. It has no adequate categories for Oedipus. Whatever else he may be, Oedipus is not the arrogant, hubristic tyrant to whom the chorus refers, but a benevolent ruler, praised by all for his wisdom, decency, and pity. (Even by a strict definition of the term—"a nonhereditary ruler"—Oedipus is no tyrant: he has, of course, inherited his throne from his father, though he does not yet know it.) Rather, Oedipus is *agos,* that wonderful Greek term that means both "cursed" and "sacred," but more cursed than sacred. Or rather, to be cursed by the gods is to be sacred, in the sense of belonging to the deity. Creon's characterization of Oedipus as "this cursed, naked, holy thing" captures this status (1425). Believing himself to be protected by his reason but in fact utterly exposed to the gods, Oedipus thinks that he is acting according to his own plan when in fact he is fulfilling theirs, a plan that has nothing to do with justice.

Or at least not with a civilized justice that refrains from punishing sons for the sins of their fathers.

"We are you Oedipus" (or "Oedipus, you are my pattern"), says the chorus toward the end of the play (1195). By this it intends to convey the conventional wisdom, "Call no man happy before he is dead," as life is full of reversals, for Oedipus and for us all. In fact, Sophocles seems to intend a double meaning. "We are you Oedipus," in the sense that we are all agos, naked before the gods, belonging to the deity but in no position to take any comfort from this. In suggesting that it is man himself who is agos, Sophocles pulls back the corner of a curtain, showing man to be more exposed to the divine than he understands and more than he cares to know: exposed to a world of forces that care nothing for justice and pity, at least not as these are understood in the polis.

Introduced toward the conclusion of *Oedipus Tyrannus,* the theme of Oedipus as agos forms the leitmotif of the subsequent *Oedipus at Colonus.* About this play C. M. Bowra says: "at the end of *Oedipus at Colonus* no unresolved discords remain, no mysteries call for an answer."[20] All is resolved, and Oedipus is recompensed for his suffering, showing the gods to be just in ways that humans can understand. "Because his sufferings were great, unmerited and untold, Let some just god relieve him from distress," says the chorus (1565). Apparently this is what happens. Yet, perhaps things are not as clear as this. Set about twenty years after the events of *Oedipus Tyrannus, Oedipus at Colonus* concerns the apparent apotheosis of Oedipus. After his twenty-year exile, Oedipus, accompanied by Antigone, arrives at the Attic deme of Colonus, where the oracle of Apollo prophesied that he was to die. The chorus of men of Colonus wants to expel him as polluted and Creon wishes to abduct him, for he is now a man blessed by the gods, but Theseus, king of Athens, allows him to die untouched, in honor and glory, in the grove of the Furies at Colonus.

Yet the events of the play are not really straightforward. In particular, there is confusion over what finally happens to Oedipus. In the end he simply disappears. Does he go up or down, join the sky or the earth gods? "We turned around," says the Messenger, "and nowhere saw the man, But only the king, his hands before his face. . . . Then very quickly we saw him do reverence to Earth and to the powers of the air, With one address to both" (1650ff).

Why even consider that Oedipus might have joined the earth gods? Because as much as he loves his daughters, he is filled with unquenchable rage against his sons, for reasons that seem to go beyond their apparent complicity in his exile. To Polynices he says,

> For this I pray.
> And I cry out to the hated underworld
> That it may take you home; cry out to those

> Powers indwelling here; and to that Power
> Of furious War that filled your hearts with hate!
> (1390ff)

"Is it too much to say," asks Winnington-Ingram, "that Oedipus earns his status as a chthonian power by acting like the unpersuaded Furies of the *Oresteia*?"[21]

Read with a focus on the play of passions, the most striking thing about *Oedipus at Colonus* is how the intensity of Oedipus' love for his daughters is matched by an almost incomprehensible hatred of his sons. How can a man who loves so much hate so much? Apparently in both Oedipus excels the common man. Oedipus' passions are organized along strictly paranoid-schizoid lines, his love and hate being totally divided: his love for his daughters seems to depend upon his hate for his sons and vice versa.

> If I had not these daughters to sustain me,
> I might have lived or died for all your interest.
> But they have saved me, they are my support,
> And are not girls, but men, in faithfulness.
> As for you two, you are no sons of mine!
> (1365ff)

Behind this apparently rigid and stark separation of love and hate, however, is a hint that the distinction may not be so clear: the daughters are like sons, yet the sons must be destroyed. Oedipus was of course always filled with rage. In *Oedipus Tyrannus* this rage seemed to be the stereotypical anger of the autocrat used to having his way. Here it seems more, a rage so intense that it cannot be contained but must spill over to those he loves.

Consider that in sending his sons to death, he is dooming his beloved daughter Antigone at the hands of Creon as well. Sophocles makes it clear that we should see that connection and so remember his *Antigone,* written about forty years earlier. First, he has Polynices ask his sisters to provide a proper burial if his father's curses are fulfilled. Second, Theseus promises Antigone safe-conduct to Thebes so that she may attempt to prevent their fratricide (see 1408–1410, 1770). To be sure, Oedipus did not intend his beloved daughters to die. But his rage is so extreme that it cannot be contained; it must spill over contaminating those he loves. This is reflected in Oedipus' own mysterious, ambiguous death. Only apparently an apotheosis, his disappearance may just as well have sent him to the underground world of the Furies. The play is purposefully unclear on this point.

> But some attendant from the train of Heaven
> Came for him; or else the underworld
> Opened in love the unlit door of earth.
> (1660ff)

Recall that the grove to which Oedipus came to die, and which the chorus was afraid he transgressed, was the home of the Furies. Much of the play is built around the paradox between the quiet beauty of the grove and the "fearful goddesses, daughters of Earth and Darkness" who inhabit it (39). One sees this paradox in Oedipus' prayer to these "Queens of dread aspect": "Come, sweet daughters of primeval Darkness . . . have pity" (109–110). And perhaps they do—for one of their own. Nothing could be further from the truth than Bowra's claim that at the end no mysteries call for an answer. Sophocles gives us the form of reconciliation and clarification but not the content. Those who are overly impressed by grand form, Sophocles' famous tense and ordered calm, are likely to miss this.

Likely to miss this too are those like Heidegger, who at the conclusion of "What Is Metaphysics?" cites *Oedipus at Colonus* as the last gasp of early Greek openness to Being. Heidegger is not entirely wrong, of course. The puzzling fate of Oedipus does represent a glimpse behind the curtain into a more fundamental reality. Just not one that is hospitable to humans. Indeed, this reality remains so inhospitable that its presence in the world is likely to create and reflect the gravest doubts and confusions in people's minds, so that they risk destroying what they know to be good. Consider in this regard Sophocles' *Women of Trachis* (probably produced circa 440 B.C.), a play whose conclusion is frequently compared to the end of *Oedipus at Colonus*. *Women of Trachis* draws upon the tradition of Heracles' apotheosis, in which he dies only to be carried to Olympus by Zeus, reconciled with Hera, and married to her daughter Hebe. In Sophocles' version, however, Heracles is a brute, the play ending not with his apotheosis (only his exit to the place where his apotheosis was said to occur) but rather with his son Hyllus' curses upon Zeus for the god's ruthless cruelty. The play concludes with the famous lines "and there is nothing here that is not Zeus."

About this conclusion the translators of a recent version state that the play ends with a "suspension of final judgment" about the justice of Zeus and the correctness of rewarding such a man-brute as Heracles with divinity.[22] *Oedipus at Colonus* may arguably be claimed to end with a "suspension of final judgment," but not *Women of Trachis*. There the judgment is as clear, harsh, and brutal as are the Greek gods. Why this desire to see ambiguity where it is not? Perhaps because with ambiguity remains hope: hope that the gods, and ourselves, are not as they so clearly appear to be. It is, of course, not merely among literary critics that one finds such fondness for ambiguity. It may well be that at least some highly abstract philosophical systems also employ ambiguity for this purpose: to hide or disguise, perhaps even from the creators of the systems themselves, some unpleasant truths about the world and perhaps too the implications of their own thoughts. So Luc Ferry and Alain Renaut seem to argue in *Heidegger and Modernity*.

EURIPIDES

"Tragedy without affirmation" is how Kitto characterizes Euripides' work. Perhaps a more accurate characterization of it would be tragedy with transparently false affirmation, in which the god in the machine provides a resolution so obviously implausible and false that it simply heightens the truth that in this world there is no resolution at all. Yet even this is not the whole story. *Orestes* offers perhaps the most extreme example of transparently false affirmation. Unlike Aeschylus, Euripides represents Orestes and his sister Electra as depraved, degenerate murderers and kidnappers. Instead of coming to terms with his guilt over his murder of Clytaemestra, Orestes seeks to escape from Argos by taking Helen, recently of Troy, hostage and threatening to kill her. This, Orestes and Electra manage to convince themselves, will cause them to be received as heroes, for everyone hates Helen for the misery she has caused. To this plan Electra adds that they should either kidnap or kill Hermione, daughter of Helen and Menelaus, in order to make good their escape, or at least to cause Menelaus to suffer. Trapped on the roof of the palace of Agamemnon in the midst of their escape, they are rescued by Apollo who, among other things, deifies Helen and marries Orestes to Hermione. About this play J. Peter Euben says: "the *Orestes* confounds the moral universe of the *Oresteia*. . . . To be unsure about the existence, let alone moral place, of the Furies *and* Apollo is to undermine the divine boundaries of the *Oresteia*."[23] I would put it slightly differently. In the *Orestes,* the doubts about the gods implicit in the *Oresteia* are acted out in strictly human terms, so that Orestes himself becomes little more than an avenging Fury.

Euripides, it is often argued, brings the gods down to earth, rendering them little more than alienated, objectified passions. Perhaps this is true, though far too much ink has been spent on the question of whether Euripides is an atheist, and I shall not pursue the issue here. More interesting is whether Euripides believes that man might someday civilize the gods . . . and his own passions. "O Phoebus [Apollo], your holy word was brute and ignorant," says Orestes in Euripides' *Electra* (970). True enough, but can man do anything about it other than suffer? Regarding this question and in fact most of the questions he confronts, Euripides gives two answers. One answer dominates. It is found in *Helen, Ion,* the *Bacchae,* and most of his other plays—that people must suffer the brutal and brutalizing confusions of the gods. The other answer, far less central, is that people might civilize the gods. More on this solution shortly.

Helen draws upon a popular countermyth, mentioned in Plato's *Republic* (586c) and elsewhere, which claims that Helen was not really abducted to Troy. Angry at Paris, Hera gave him only a simulacrum of Helen, while the real Helen hid out in Egypt. In the play, Menelaus stops by Egypt on his return from Troy and is most surprised to find his wife there, for he too had been tricked by the illusion. Together he and Helen devise a plan to rescue her from the son of the Egyptian king, who desires her. They escape, slaughtering fifty Egyptians in the process. Charles Segal sees *Helen* as a virtual epistemological treatise on the difficulty of distinguishing appearance and reality. Not entirely wrong, his account misleads because it suggests that Euripides is a precursor of Plato: "Euripides, like Plato, suggests that the ultimate reality may consist in a purity and beauty that we reach through the violence and confusion of the *eidola* [Ideas] that deceive us with their false gods."[24]

Cedric Whitman makes a similar argument, suggesting that the air (folds of *aether,* lines 44, 584, 605) that conceals and transports Helen, as well as serving as the substance of her illusion, seems to represent a higher purity and truth.[25] Both accounts, but especially Segal's, serve *themselves* as *dei ex machina,* in which Euripides is saved in the end from his own confusion to become a philosophical precursor to Plato. Such a view may make us feel better but it does a disservice to Euripides, who is more interested in the truth—even if this truth offers only confusion—than in resolution. In fact, the play shows how confusion can pile upon confusion until nothing is clear. Perhaps, the play suggests, Helen never existed. Thousands died for the sake of an illusion, for nothing. Or perhaps she did exist: a beautiful whore. Thousands died for something worse than nothing, for evil. As Winnington-Ingram suggests, perhaps Helen is herself a Fury, her beauty an invitation to destruction.[26] Or perhaps she existed, beautiful and innocent: a victim. But would that mean that those who died at Troy died meaningful deaths? Not necessarily. All these questions and more run together in the play. And there are no answers, only more confusion, in which a ritual cleansing turns into a slaughter (see 1575–1620). Gunther Zuntz argues that the key problem of the Euripidean age was not entirely different from our own. How is man to live in a godless world? "Different individuals had different answers, and Euripides gives them all."[27] Similarly, what is real and what mere appearance? Euripides again gives all the answers. Which means he gives none at all.

Yet to put it this way could be a little misleading, were it taken to suggest that Euripides is merely a theorist of confusion, of chaos. Like Aeschylus and Sophocles, he deals with a particular confusion and the anxiety it generates: the confusion of good and bad, generated by the failure of paranoid-schizoid defenses to hold the two distinct. These defenses fail, in good measure, because the culture failed to provide adequate moral support. One sees a wonderful simile for this failure and confusion in *Ion.* Ion was born of Creusa, who was raped by Apollo. Ashamed, Creusa exposed Ion, leaving him to die. Apollo, however, sent Hermes to rescue his son, and have him brought up at Delphi. Twenty years later, Creusa and her husband, Xuthus, come to Delphi to pray for a child. Apollo tells Xuthus that the first person he sees after leaving the temple will be his child, and of course the first person is Ion. Creusa is enraged, fearing that this stranger will inherit everything, and plots to kill Ion by poisoning him. For this purpose she carries two drops of Gorgon's blood, given to her by her father. One drop fosters life and cures disease. The other kills.

OLD MAN: Do you carry them apart or mixed together?
CREUSA: Apart. For good and evil do not mingle.
(1016–1017)

A perfect expression of the paranoid-schizoid defense, the defense nonetheless fails, as Creusa attempts to administer the poison to one whom she loves but does not recognize, her confusion overcoming her ability to hold love and hate separate. Fortunately, Ion becomes suspicious, mother and son are reconciled, and the play concludes with lots of questioning and doubt (and only the most transparent reconciliation) about the goodness of Apollo who caused such things to happen.[28]

How is one to survive in a world of such confusion and doubt? Like Dionysus, rather than like Heracles, it appears—hardly a comforting conclusion. Heracles, in Euripides' play of the same name, is driven mad by Hera. He is vulnerable because he is such a straight arrow, such an easy target. His identity, although not richly textured, is crystal clear for all to see—and for Hera to exploit. He is a warrior, the most admired hero among the Greeks. Utterly predictable, he would never, for example, feign madness as Odysseus did to avoid going to war. Thus, all Hera need do is convince him for one brief moment that his loved ones are his enemies. Heracles will do the rest. Yet even in the aftermath of madness, when he considers suicide, he does not consider giving up the bow with which he has killed wife and children. His bow remains the symbol of his identity, painful as it is, and is more important to him than life itself (see 1375ff).

Contrast Heracles with Dionysus in the *Bacchae,* the god of shifting masks and countless names. Dionysus survives, indeed, he drives *others* mad, because he has no identity, because he is slippery, constantly changing shape and form. Who could turn him against himself, the usual means by which the gods destroy a man (see Sophocles' *Antigone,* 621–622), when it is unclear who "he" is? Even his sexual identity is traditionally ambiguous. Heracles destroys fearsome beasts. Dionysus destroys those who fail to recognize his divinity, which defines his own narcissistic grandiosity, what he truly cares about. Recall that in the *Bacchae* Dionysus comes to Thebes in anger because his mother's relatives do not believe that his father was Zeus. Dionysus drives the female population of Thebes into a frenzy as punishment. When the young, rational, and very conventional king of Thebes, Pentheus, seeks to have him arrested, Dionysus bewitches the king, causing him willingly to lose his identity in the belief that he is achieving his freedom (see 810–845). Dressed as a woman, Pentheus goes out to spy on the Bacchae. The madwomen, including his own mother, Agave, tear him to pieces. In the end, his grandfather, Cadmus, and Agave are exiled, Cadmus transformed into a serpent whose sufferings (he believes) shall never end (see 1360).

It should not be overlooked that Dionysus and Pentheus are cousins. Their mothers are sisters, daughters of Cadmus. Perhaps Dionysus and Pentheus represent the unintegrated portions of a single personality. Yet if this is the case, they are two halves that do not make a whole. Almost every bad thing that one could say about Pentheus could be said of Dionysus as well. When the chorus accuses Pentheus of ferocity, blood, and violence, or with being inhuman are "they not in fact abusing Pentheus for the possession of Dionysian traits of character?"[29] Neither, as Euben points out, respects the bonds that unite families and cities.[30] Once again, the gods provide no alternative to human confusion; they just add to it.

Surely Euripides is not arguing that one must become like Dionysus to survive. Nevertheless, in his last play Euripides seems to be suggesting that the world is so confused, appearance and reality so confounded, good and bad so mixed up that they cannot be sorted out. Anyone who tries to use reason or the authority of the state to make sense of things, as Pentheus does, will simply be destroyed. There may be other ways to survive in such a world than that of Dionysus. But Dionysus is the consummate survivor, for he cannot be pinned down. Even more, in a world of confusion and unclear boundaries, he is king—the theme of the *Bacchae*. One is reminded here of Christopher Lasch's account of the *Culture of Narcissism*. In such a culture, the narcissist is sovereign. Knowing no loyalty to anyone or anything other than him- or herself, standing for nothing but his or her own glorification, substituting glittering appearance and charm for depth and seriousness, the narcissist is perfectly equipped for life in a bureaucracy or a large corporation. Who says the Greek tragedies are not still relevant?

Each of the protagonists in the *Bacchae* claims to be wise (*sophos*). The Bacchae assert their own wisdom, understood as the avoidance of excess, including an excess of self-control (see 385ff). Yet they rejoice in rending animals and revel in the dismemberment of Pentheus. Pentheus and Dionysus each claims to be wiser than the other (see 655–658). And even though Pentheus purports to represent the principle of reason, by any standard he is less rational than Dionysus, who unlike Pentheus remains calm, in control, and able to plan ahead and act accordingly. Euripides intends no irony when Dionysus says about Pentheus, "calmly will I bear with him, however high his rage; for it is a wise man's part to practice an even-tempered self-control" (640).[31] Even Tiresias claims to be wise, which is surprising, for in Greek thought acceptance of the conventions of tradition is generally opposed to cleverness, whereas Tiresias would equate them (see 200–203).

So, what is wise? What is rational? What works? Apparently nothing, unless the strategy of Dionysus remains the best: to stay calm, cool, collected, but all in the service of one's narcissistic grandiosity. This is what psychoanalysts call narcissistic rage: a cold, calculating rage that can wait calmly for revenge and then take it with no mercy and no pity.[32] But this seems to work only for a god, who has the power to enforce his rage. For men and women who live in the polis the best strategy seems to be that of Tiresias, who acknowledges the power of Dionysus while hoping to contain it by worshiping the god within the bounds of tradition and ritual. Tradition and ritual, such as the festivals of Dionysus, at once respect the god's power and contain it within established institutions. Yet it is no accident that Euripides portrays Tiresias as more than a little ridiculous, and that Cadmus, who follows the same strategy as Tiresias, is not protected by it at all, perhaps because he is not a true believer but only a conventional one. To ritualize the powers of Dionysus and so contain them may represent the best man can do, but it is neither very dignified (it is appeasement of the powerful because they are powerful), nor likely to be very effective.

Only in a chronological sense is the *Bacchae* Euripides' last word. One might just as well read his *Iphigenia in Tauris* (probably a late play, circa 414–410 B.C., as dated by meter) as his final statement. *Iphigenia in Tauris* represents Euripides' other answer to the question of how to live with the gods' confusions and brutalities: by civilizing the gods. Humans can do better than the gods. The plot is based on the assumption that Iphigenia was not sacrificed by her father, Agamemnon. At the last minute the goddess Artemis, who had demanded the sacrifice, whisked Iphigenia away to Tauris, in barbarian Scythia, where she came to serve as Artemis' priestess, preparing human victims for sacrifice. One day Orestes appears in Tauris, still hounded by the Furies. Sent by Apollo, who set as a condition of his liberation from the Furies that he return to Attica a statue of Artemis that fell to Tauris, Orestes is captured and prepared for sacrifice by Iphigenia. At almost the last moment they recognize each other, and together they devise a daring escape by sea, taking the statue of Artemis with them. But wind and seas turn against their ship, and they are about to fall into the hands of the Taurians, when Athene intervenes: the statue is installed in a shrine in Attica, with Iphigenia as its priestess, and Orestes is finally freed of his Furies.

Iphigenia is herself remarkably confused about Artemis. "No! I will not believe it of a God!" she says when confronted with the paradox that a goddess who is protector of virgins, young mothers, and baby animals demands human blood. "She so delicate in all these ways will yet demand the blood of human beings on Her altar-stone." Perhaps, wonders Iphigenia, "people, being murderers themselves, are charging Thee with their own wickedness" (380–390). But no, Artemis really is this way, and Iphigenia's lot is bound up with the confusions of the goddess: she must cleanse and purify those who will be killed for Artemis' sake. In fact, not Iphigenia alone is confused about Artemis. In myth Artemis was closely identified with Hecate, a virtual Fury, armed with a scourge and accompanied by a blazing torch and terrifying hounds. A single statue combining the images of both was common image, serving to represent a crossroad. Perhaps Euripides means to suggest that Orestes was sent to recover this image. It would make psychological sense.

In Euripides' version, Orestes has neither been cleansed nor restored to sanity by his trial at Athens (references to Aeschylus' *Eumenides* abound), for some of the Furies refused to go along with the verdict. As a result, Orestes must undertake further penance, restoring the statue to Athens that had fallen into barbarian hands. Psychologically speaking, of course, the statue had not fallen into barbarian hands, it had been there all along, in the barbaric practices of bloody revenge and human sacrifice. In restoring the statue of Artemis to civilized hands, Orestes is civilizing the goddess herself, recognizing her barbaric aspect but containing it within human customs, much as occurs in the *Eumenides*. "And let this be the law," says Athene, regarding how Artemis is to be worshiped in Attica:

> When they observe
> Her festival, the priest shall hold,
> In memory of you [Orestes], the sharp blade of his knife
> Against a human throat and draw one drop
> Of blood, then stop—this is no disrespect
> But a grave reminder of Her former ways.
> (1455–1460)

Here, of all places, in what has been called a light romantic comedy, one finds arguably the most successful resolution of the problem faced by all three poets, the difficulty caused by projection of human confusion into the gods, from which it is subsequently reintrojected, causing still more confusion. Most successful, in part, because *Iphigenia in Tauris* involves less manic denial, and more open recognition of confusion, than either Aeschylus' *Eumenides* or Sophocles' *Oedipus at Colonus*. The gods too get confused and blinded, as we do, says Orestes in *Iphigenia at Tauris*. Rather than listening to gods, oracles, or dreams, we should trust our own good sense about right and wrong, imposing these on the gods if need be (see 570–580). Cedric Whitman calls this development the full circle of myth, in which Euripides retells stories about the gods on a human scale in such a way as to retain something of the order, wholeness, and completeness of the original mythic vision. It is, however, an almost strictly human order, with all humanity's faults, including the fact that for mortals, unlike immortals, "the way of purity lies through violence and suffering."[33] Orestes, for example, was willing to murder the barbarian (but actually pious and prudent) King Thoas, in order to purify Artemis and himself of blood-guilt.

Whitman is correct; the optimistic, humanistic strain in Euripides should not be overlooked. Nevertheless, Whitman is too sanguine. The fact that Euripides creates a human order (in which the gods depend upon man's goodness, not vice versa) renders that order enormously susceptible to confusion and reversal, as the violent means of purification and renewal come to contaminate the end itself. Why this is so is explored more fully in the next two chapters. Whitman's statement reflects the problem, not just the solution. Even in *Iphigenia in Tauris,* only a god's intervention can straighten things out. Can we really expect, Euripides seems to be asking, man to perform this task for himself: to be his own deus ex machina? Not even in this most optimistic of Euripides' plays and, hence, not very often.

One might well conclude that Euripides accepts only mock reparation that knows and shows itself as such. It remains reparation but only of the truth about the confusions of men and gods, which is best "repaired" by ceasing to tell lies about itself. Against this conclusion it has been argued that the implausible, unsatisfying resolutions characteristic of so many Euripides' plays, particularly *Orestes,* represent not merely a knowingly and intentionally false note, but an instance of art reflecting upon itself—that is, showing us that the play was only a play, a play about a play.[34] Perhaps, but even if this interpretation proves correct, it signifies the end of tragedy. Once tragedy is no longer primarily about the polis but about itself, it becomes an escape. From what? From truths so simple that it is hard to see how they could cause confusion. In *Orestes,* for example, everyone, even Orestes, agrees upon two things: Orestes was wrong to kill Clytaemestra, and Apollo is a brute (see, for example, 285ff, 325ff, 395–396, 417–418, 500ff, 1667–1670). Then why the confusion? Sometimes confusion serves as a defense not just against paranoid-schizoid anxiety but against depressive anxiety as well, as Klein calls it: that people can recognize right and good and what deserves to be protected and still be unable to do anything about it.

CULTURAL ORIGINS OF THE DIONYSIAN CRISIS

Too much time and energy has been spent trying to figure out the relation of tragedy to the cult of Dionysus. Even the Greeks puzzled over it. The claim that tragedy has "nothing to do with Dionysus," as the proverb puts it, was already being debated in the fifth century B.C. To be sure, it appears that tragedy—at first, of course, just the chorus—originated at festivals dedicated to the god Dionysus and continued to be presented in Athens at state-sponsored festivals in his honor: the Great Dionysia in March, and the Lenaea in January, with further productions being staged at the rustic Dionysia. Nevertheless, the link between the tragedies that have come down to us and the cult of Dionysus remains tenuous and apparently seemed so to the Athenians as well.

To be sure, the two share an intellectual relation that can be readily re-constructed today. Tragedy is Dionysian because it concerns the discrepancy between appearance and reality: between word and deed, intention and result, and so forth. In this sense it deals with a theme embodied by Dionysus, the god of changing appearances and countless identities. To this currently popu-lar interpretation (which fits the deconstructionist thesis about texts having no fixed identity or meaning) I can add the one considered in my analysis of the *Bacchae*. With its highly stylized representation of the most primitive passions, tragedy represents the strategy of Tiresias, being an attempt at once to acknowledge and to contain the forces represented by Dionysus by trans-forming them into ritual. Friedrich Nietzsche's study of tragedy, considered at the end of this chapter, lends some support to this interpretation. In the end, however, this is not a terribly important issue, tending to confuse historical origins with intellectual reconstruction. Historically, Vernant correctly notes, the most important thing about Greek tragedy is that it was new, born with the democratic polis. Its significance does not lie in its origins, however, but in its subjection of the myths of heroes to the standards of the polis. Or, as Vernant, following Walter Nestle, puts it, "tragedy was born when myth began to be assessed from a citizen's point of view."[35]

Adopting this theme as his motto, Vernant interprets it to mean that the myths of heroes came to be assessed by the standards of law and individual responsibility that had arisen in the Athenian polis. Tragedy, he says, "con-fronts heroic values and ancient religious representations with new modes of thought that characterize the advent of law within the city state."[36] He might also have said, along the lines of A. W. H. Adkins, that tragedy represents the confrontation of the heroic interpretation of arete with one less disruptive to the polis, emphasizing cooperation and *sophrosune,* "prudence." Indeed, this is how Adkins interprets Plato's politics: as making arete safe for society.[37] Although this interpretation of tragedy would not be false, it would miss a key point. The "citizen's point of view" should not be idealized as that of truth, jus-tice, and the Athenian way. Rather, the citizen's point of view is that of Plato's Glaucon and Adeimantus, citizens overwhelmed by fear and doubt regarding traditional values who anxiously wish that they were not. (Chapter 6 will consider Vernant's definition of tragedy from a different perspective, in which the citizen's point of view is that of pity.)

In Plato's *Republic*, Glaucon and Adeimantus represent the Greek in the street—or at least the average young aristocrat. Attracted to sophists such as Thrasymachus, they are nonetheless unable to go along with his ethical naturalism, as it is sometimes called today: justice is the interest of the stronger. On the other hand, they find the traditional pieties about justice thoroughly unconvincing. The best life, they hold, is to appear to be just, but actually to be unjust. Such a life would combine the pleasures of a good reputation with the material rewards of injustice. This is how the world actually works. At the same time, they are troubled by these circumstances, almost desperate in their desire that Socrates show them why this is not the best life but hardly ready to listen to inspiring speeches. Indeed, Adeimantus warns Socrates that one thing he will not believe is that the gods reward justice. We are all adults here, says Adeimantus, and we know that the gods can be bribed. Commit many large injustices, make lots of money, and in your old age build a temple to the gods. They will forgive anything. They demand respect, not justice (*Rep.* 366a–d).

The remainder of the *Republic* concerns Socrates' attempt to address the doubts of Plato's elder brothers. So do most of the tragedies, though of course the answer of the poets is different. Are Glaucon and Adeimantus confused in the sense characterized in the previous section? Perhaps not quite, for they are creations of a philosopher. They are unhappy and anxious about the nature of the world and of the gods. They want the appearance and reality of justice to be one. But they seem quite convinced that they are not. In this sense they are less confused than anxious and unhappy. Any teacher of undergraduate students today will recognize this characterization—it is that of the average student. Glaucon and Adeimantus are suffering, it seems, from what Klein calls depressive anxiety: the fear that man's greed, envy, jealousy, and wickedness are so great that he can never protect and live up to the values he cherishes. In fact, man is so bad that he has even contaminated the gods, who demand nothing more than honor, at best merely the appearance of justice. In this sense Plato's older brothers capture perfectly what I have called the Dionysian crisis that so dominated Greek culture: the fear, not always conscious, that man is so bad that he cannot help but contaminate and destroy everything good. Only the rigid separation of good and bad prevents this pollution, but the Greeks did not see this separation holding any more, projecting its failure onto the gods.

The breakdown of this separation leads to confusion and reversal, coupled with heightened doubts about whether people can act more virtuously than the gods, even should they be able to distinguish good from bad. This depressive anxiety in turn leads to more confusion, as people choose to reverse good and bad in order to preserve their belief in their own goodness. I shall explore further how this process works in chapters 3 and 4. Herein, then, lies the Dionysian crisis, which I understand to be an explanation of a problem in Greek culture rather than a historical explanation of the fact that Greek tragedy is associated with the cult of Dionysus.

Why did the Dionysian crisis become so acute at the time of the rise of Athenian democracy? Certainly the explanation cannot be simply that the Greeks came at that time to doubt the justice of the gods. They had done so since the archaic era, as we saw in the discussion of the Inherited Conglomerate. The doubts about the gods expressed in Aeschylus' *Persians* (472 B.C.) are exemplary. What happened to intensify these doubts, so that they became so anxiety-provoking? Most important, and encompassing, was the rise of the polis, whose walls (the polis was originally not just a city but a citadel) represent humanity's attempt to exclude the caprice, jealousy, and anger of the gods, only to find that it could not: these things stem from within, not without. A large-scale phenomenon, the crisis was intensified by a number of social changes, including the development of writing. Contrary to Nietzsche, the plays are not best seen as spontaneous expressions of Dionysian wonder. In them the Dionysian element becomes more controlled: every word uttered by the chorus has been written down and memorized, for example. Writing allowed a level of intellectual control and reflection impossible in an oral tradition. Drawing upon Eric Havelock's famous work on the literate revolution, Segal argues that the advent of written drama means that "the clearly delineated roles and stable, univocal meanings of a traditional aristocratic society, with its emphasis on face-to-face contact, have been lost; instead, words and modes of behavior become paradoxical, and familiar boundaries no longer hold."[38] Segal here defines the Dionysian crisis in one sentence. Writing allowed a more reflective questioning of tradition than ever before, enabling both poet and philosopher to establish distance from it. Havelock explains the dilemma beautifully in his *Preface to Plato*. He defines the adoption of writing as the Preface, for it allowed the distance necessary for genuine criticism (Socrates is, as always, the great exception, though it should not be overlooked that we know of him only through the writings of others). The poets too were writers. But writing did not, of course, cause the Dionysian crisis. Rather, writing allowed the poets further to problematize what was already in doubt and confusion.

Where did Greek doubts come from? From myriad sources: the rise of a literate culture; the destruction inflicted by the heroic and agonal culture when it was transplanted to the polis; the rise of sophistic that heightened the doubts of young men like Glaucon and Adeimantus; the bloody, fratricidal civil war in Corcyra, which Thucydides implies was only an exaggerated version of what had been taking place in Athens even before the outbreak of the Peloponnesian War (see *History*, 3.83); the failure of democratic leadership after the death of

Pericles; the slaughter of the Melians (often cited as the inspiration for Euripides' *Trojan Women*); the hubris of Athens' invasion of Sicily, which led to the destruction of the Athenian empire. Such turbulence confounded the hope, expressed so nobly in Aeschylus' *Oresteia* and *Prometheus,* and by Euripides' *Iphigenia in Tauris,* that man might civilize even the gods, showing them what is truly good through the example of the just polis. In this hope the tragic poets come close, albeit just for a moment, to humanism as moderns understand it: that people might come to order the world in terms of human principles. The hope is expressed inconsistently in the tragedies, however, in good measure because the tragic poets recognize that the passions embodied by the gods are also within us, not simply without.

One sees a revealing instance of this in a surprising place: the famous "ode to man" in Sophocles' *Antigone* (at 332ff). At first its praise seems unambiguous: of all the wonders of the world, it claims, man is most wonderful. He crosses the stormy waters in his magnificent ships, causes the earth to yield its crops, tames the beasts, and with language and thought creates the polis that shelters him from the contingencies of nature. Even disease is subject to his medicines. Only death he cannot control. Yet a closer examination reveals the ambiguity of this praise, an ambiguity that extends beyond the ode's caution that man's cleverness may be used for ill as well as good (see 365).

It has been widely noticed that the adjective employed to praise man, *deinon,* means not only "wonderful" but "terrible, fearful." "Monstrously great" might be a better translation, suggests George Steiner.[39] Man, Sophocles seems to be saying, can control everything but himself, his own passions. This interpretation is reinforced by the unusual word Sophocles employs to characterize man's civic and legal temper that builds cities: *orgas,* which also signifies "ungovernable rage" (see 280, 355, 957, 766). Martha Nussbaum argues, along lines also suggested by the Frankfurt school of critical theory in its critique of the dialectic of Enlightenment, that man directs his rage at a sparse world that causes him to suffer and die. Progress is motivated by this rage, a desire to take revenge against a harsh and unresponsive nature for the suffering it causes us.[40] True enough. The problem is that this orgas does not remain directed merely towards external nature. The temper that builds cities also destroys them from within, by promoting *stasis* (factional conflict) and hubris. Man becomes the sacker of his own city. In a related fashion, the word *thought* in the ode (*phronema,* 354), so central to man's achievement, also signifies "pride," precisely the sense in which it is employed to characterize Antigone's stubbornness (459).[41] Nor are these paradoxes strictly internal to the ode. Considered in the context of the entire play it becomes clear that Sophocles' praise of man is ambiguous, even ironic. Man exerts control over the beasts and the waves, but he cannot control his own temper, which is more than enough to destroy him, as Creon reveals so clearly.

Nor—and this is perhaps the most important point—does man know the limits of the control he does exert. For instance, Creon seeks to extend sovereignty beyond the grave to encompass the dead, which marks the realm of the gods. In this extension even the most fundamental distinctions become confused, as Creon buries the living (ordering Antigone walled up in a tomb to die), and refuses burial to the dead. The shelter that the city promises is denied to those most in need of it: the dead, and those who mourn them. Even the words employed in the "ode to man" take on an ironic meaning in the course of the play, as the image of the sea, the subject of man's control in the ode, returns in subsequent odes to characterize the helplessness of irrational suffering (see 584ff, 953ff, 966ff). Finally, Creon comes to characterize his own disaster as a harbor (at 1284).[42] Similarly, the animals and birds that were the subject of man's control in the "ode" become images and messengers of the violation of a divine order, as Tiresias hears bird cries he has never known, an augury of disaster (see 1000ff). Even the conquest of disease comes to be questioned, as the city itself becomes "diseased" and "polluted" as the result of Creon's acts (1015).

One might argue that Creon represents harsh, calculating, instrumental reason, whereas Antigone typifies the claims of nature and earth, like the mother bird's, who laments her empty nest (see 423–425). True enough, but the poets are nothing if not subtle, and although Antigone speaks for nature (or rather, for the cosmos, which includes the gods), she does so in a way that mimics its most rigid and inflexible aspects, such as the unyielding rock she seems to compare herself to, rock that is not worn away by tears (see 826–827). Needed is a mode of response that mimics the more flexible and vital aspects of nature, while leaving place for human reason—a reason that knows its place.

In spite of the element of manic denial in the "ode to man," presumably intended by Sophocles to confront reality in the course of the play, it would be mistaken to argue simply that the ode is a lie, mere denial. The Athenians, for example, had hardly conquered disease, as the plague was to remind them so dramatically a little over a decade after Antigone was produced. Nevertheless, the ode is partly true. Man has achieved these things in some measure. But precisely its partial truth highlights the anxiety, confusion, and depression that hide behind the ode, and are revealed in the course of the play. The ode is ironic, evoking anxiety and tension not merely because it is hubristic but because the control that man has achieved over the external world means nothing if he cannot control himself.

The polis (and it is this that the ode idealizes: not man, but man the citizen of the polis) represents an attempt to transcend the caprice of the gods and the hostility of the world to human purposes. Within its walls, man may be more just, humane, and compassionate than the gods, a frequent theme of the plays. Often, for example, a character argues in a thoroughly nonhubristic way that man is nobler than the gods. In Euripides' *Heracles,* Amphitryon, Heracles' nominal father, says to Zeus, the actual father, that "I, mere man, am nobler [have more arete] than you, great god," because I respect what belongs to others, and care for those I love (340ff). Similarly, the final speech of Athene, in Euripides' *Suppliant Women,* seems intended to show her as less generous, and less caring, than Theseus, just as "Artemis was less noble than Hippolytus, Aphrodite than Phaedra," as Kitto puts it.[43] Theseus, mythical king of Athens, frequently represents the ideals of the fifth-century B.C. Athenian polis.

The attempt fails. The polis cannot insulate man from the caprice of the gods because the caprice works through human nature: it is already within. The hope that the polis might become a refuge fails, just as the walls of Troy failed to keep out the clever invader, who knew how to tempt those within to their own destruction: with promises of easy peace and sudden glory. In fact, the term "caprice of the gods" is probably too tame. What is within is rage, jealousy, envy, greed for honor and glory—all qualities frequently attributed to the gods. Yet the Dionysian crisis was heightened precisely because a world less capricious, more just and caring than that ruled by the gods became a conceivable if impossible goal. Man hoped that he might do better than the gods. In failing, he could no longer take the moral ambiguity of the gods for granted as he once had. The heightened disjunction between hope and ideal on the one hand, reality on the other, gave rise to the crisis.

Is not the Dionysian crisis similar, which does not mean identical, to that confronted by postmodernists today? Doubt about the justice of the gods is perhaps not as pressing for us as for the Greeks. The crisis of reason's relation to social progress presses harder, for the hopes of the Enlightenment were so great and lasted so long. World War I, World War II, the Holocaust: it is almost impossible not to implicate reason itself in the calamities of this century. This insight did not, of course, begin with the postmodernists but with Max Horkheimer and Theodor Adorno's *Dialectic of Enlightenment* in 1947. Since then, more than one enlightened, tolerant liberal democracy has kept the caprice of the gods at bay only by engaging in an orgy (one way the term *orgas* comes down to us today) of rage against those who remain outside. Reason and enlightened civilization as an orgy of revenge against outsiders, who differ either in sex, race, religion, or degree of sanity: is this not the view of Michel Foucault? Finally, although insight into these unpleasant truths may be liberating, it may also be quite confusing, for one may not see what might take the place of the previous order when virtually every practice seems implicated in the crimes of reason. Perhaps because they were not as disappointed about the failure of reason as modern man (they never expected so much from it to begin with) the tragic poets had less difficulty in imagining humane alternative principles for civilization—responsibility and pity.

The polis seeks to wall out not merely the caprice of the gods. It would also

They also appear in the words of Paul Shorey, who has written of the works of Sophocles as "the supreme embodiment in literature, as the Parthenon is in art, of the unique harmony of beauty and reason that it is the note of the Greek genius in its prime." Similarly, A. C. Person extols Sophocles' "flawless moderation which is truth to life itself."[47]

Without a doubt there are powerful Dionysian aspects to Greek tragedy. They are found, however, not merely in the chorus. Indeed, no one living has ever heard the "dithyrambic chorus" whose musical ecstasy Nietzsche views as Dionysian. In fact, the term *Dionysian* could be a little misleading, were it taken as suggesting that the Greeks celebrated and reveled in the confusion and loss of boundaries found in so many of the tragedies, finding relief there from the burden of civilization. Rather, the Greeks suffered horribly from this confusion. Nor did they suffer quietly. It led them to do horrible things to relieve the tension, such as the ritual slaughter of the bull that turns into the slaughter of fifty innocent Egyptians in Euripides' *Helen*. This is the topic of the next chapter, in which ritual is seen as a generally ineffective antidote to confusion.

Nietzsche's mistake, surprising in some respects, stems from his desire to see Greek tragedy as an expression of *health,* of a "healthy pessimism" so in love with life that it can confront the horror and suffering that goes with it. "Is there a pessimism of strength?" he asks. "An intellectual predilection for the hard, gruesome, evil, problematic aspect of existence, prompted by well-being, by overflowing health, by the *fullness* of existence?"[48] From this perspective tragedy becomes the *Heilslehre* for the truly tough, a therapy for the strong. When the going gets tough, and man wants to escape to a more pleasant world, the art of Greek tragedy "approaches as a saving sorceress, expert at healing. She alone knows how to turn these nauseous thoughts about the horror or absurdity of existence into notions with which one can live: these are the *sublime* as the artistic taming of the horrible."[49]

In spite (or perhaps also because) of his debunking of the sweetness-and-light perspective on Greek tragedy, Nietzsche views tragedy as therapy, designed to make us feel better. To be sure, it is a therapy that freely admits the horror and absurdity of existence, but it is still therapy, designed to make a tough life easier to take. In this respect his view does not differ much from that of idealists like Kitto who see the beautiful and noble form of tragedy as offering recompense for the suffering it portrays.

I propose that we read Greek tragedy more radically than Nietzsche. That we see it as an account of the "horror or absurdity of existence." Period. What is this horror or absurdity of existence? That the most powerful forces in the cosmos, the gods, cannot be counted on to help us know good from bad. Indeed, they are likely to deceive us, with the result that we are unlikely to know the good until we have destroyed it, and so have ourselves become bad. We live in a world whose fundamental reality is hostile to human happiness and fulfillment. And this hostility works itself out by confusing us about what constitutes genuine happiness and fulfillment, at least until it is too late to change our direction. Here is the real meaning, and the real terror, behind the proverb that those whom the gods would destroy they first make crazy—that is, unable to distinguish good and bad. Tragedy's strength lies in its ability to tell this truth. It does not lie in its ability to tell this truth in a way that also provides comfort by transforming it into beautiful form. Nor does the truth of the poets lie in their pursuit of what Heidegger calls "der Spur zum Heilen" (the track of healing), which takes us close to Being and so makes us whole. Not only is this view similar to Nietzsche's (a point frequently commented upon) but it is similarly wrong: an apparently tough-minded approach that in the end looks for the poet to save us, rather than simply to tell us the truth.

Beautiful form lies, taking away some of the horror by transforming it into shining beauty, a point the Frankfurt school was always aware of in its aesthetic theory. For this reason Adorno argues that there can be no poetry after Auschwitz.[50] About this he may be mistaken; even grief has its limits. But it may be correct to say that there can be no truthful lyric poetry (the type of poetry Adorno had in mind) *about* Auschwitz. This seems to be Herbert Marcuse's position in *The Aesthetic Dimension*.[51] What then is the function of beautiful form, the famous tense and ordered calm, as well as the beauty of the choral odes? At its worst it serves to reinforce the defense of manic denial, so that goodness and power become one. Aeschylus runs this risk, though perhaps he is more subtle and paradoxical than we can readily appreciate today. At its best, particularly in Sophocles, beautiful form is the sugarcoating on the pill, designed to get us to swallow it before we know how bad it truly tastes. Or as Rainer Maria Rilke puts it, "Beauty is nothing but the beginning of terror that we are still just able to bear."[52] Although one might argue that this is what Nietzsche means, it is not what he says. What Nietzsche says is that beauty makes suffering easier to bear, which is not Rilke's point. In a word, the poets are not therapists but artists. It is the task of artists to tell the truth, even if so doing requires truth be disguised so that others will listen. One must not, however, think that the sugarcoating, the beautiful form, is more important than it is. It is what is inside that counts.

It is of interest that Nietzsche seems to misunderstand Euripides so thoroughly, arguing that Euripides killed tragedy by transforming it into a virtual philosophy. "Aesthetic socratism" is how Nietzsche characterizes Euripidean drama.[53] How could Nietzsche be so wrong about Euripides? In part the answer is surely that Nietzsche's distinction between the Apollonian and the Dionysian has become a straitjacket, so that Euripides' deemphasis of the Dionysian chorus and increased emphasis on the complexity of the plot (presumably the realm of Apollo) require the conclusion that he is some sort of rationalist. That Nietzsche was a slave to his own categories cannot be the only reason. There must be another, and one can at least surmise that it is simply that Euripides is neither healthy nor therapeutic, and Nietzsche chose not to see this. Nor are Aeschylus and Sophocles, but the mirror that Euripides holds up to the reigning cultural crisis reveals an image both starker and more threatening than that of the other poets, in part because there is no escape into beautiful form or noble characters but only the transparent reconciliation of the deus ex machina. For all Nietzsche's infatuation with the Dionysian, he seems only to want it in controlled doses, confined to the chorus. Once confusion comes to dominate the plot as well, leaving nothing to contain itself and implicating Apollo as much as Dionysus, Nietzsche will have nothing of it. Indeed, Nietzsche apparently employs some defensive confusion and reversal of his own, calling the most Dionysian poet the most rational. (Actually, this is part of a tradition which regards Euripides as a rationalist because he challenges the gods. Such a narrow focus leads this tradition to downplay other sources of irrationality in Euripides' work: the sources within man.)

Nietzsche is, of course, not the only famous drama critic who appears to regard tragedy as therapy. Today it is often held that this is Aristotle's view. Aristotle declares that tragedy is a form of action which serves by means of pity and fear to bring about "the *katharsis* of such emotions" (*Poet.*, c6). By *katharsis* Aristotle is often thought to mean something like "purgation": through the vicarious experience of such emotions, the individual is relieved of their intensity within himself. The tragedies are like safety valves, releasing pent-up emotion in the audience. Although it would be foolish to deny that tragedy serves this function, I shall argue in chapter 7 that *katharsis* is better understood—etymologically as well as aesthetically and psychologically—as *clarification* of the emotions: truthtelling about the passions, including the confusion and disruption they bring. From this perspective, Aristotle lends little support to Nietzsche's therapeutic approach to tragedy. On the contrary, Aristotle bolsters my view that above all the poets are artists, concerned to tell the truth. Not necessarily factual truth but universal truth, the type that renders poetry superior to history, as Aristotle puts it (see *Poet.*, c9).

If tragedy is not primarily about purgation, neither is ritual, though ritual has much in common with tragedy. Indeed, one might regard tragedy as an instance of ritual (one meaning of *katharsis* is "ritual purification"), though this classification turns out to be too simple. Ritual, especially blood ritual, seeks to restore the paranoid-schizoid separation between good and bad, love and hate, care and rage, that seemed to be falling apart under the Dionysian crisis. In this sense ritual embodies not merely tragedy without the beautiful form, without art. Rather, ritual represents tragedy in the absence of truthtelling, which is one reason Cadmus does not get off lightly in the *Bacchae*. Ritual seeks to restore the paranoid-schizoid distinctions without first telling the truth about their confusion and reversal.

Even should the thoughtful reader agree with the foregoing analysis, he or she may well be asking, "What has all this to do with psychoanalysis?" Everything, I would argue. Psychoanalysis concerns mental conflict: the way in which emotions in conflict, such as love and hate, divide the self, conflict the self, confuse the self. No principle is more central to psychoanalysis, and it is on precisely this that the chapter has focused: the way in which these conflicted, confused emotions are projected into a larger world, that of the gods, and experienced there. We cannot look into the psyche of the classical Greek. We *can* look at the projections of that psyche into the culture, drawing conclusions about both from theories concerning their relationship.

William Arrowsmith argues that the psychology of Greek tragedy is not individualistic but modal, concerned with generic types, not individuals. In fact, all psychology, or at least all psychological theory, is modal. Consider, for example, Freud's theory of the Oedipus complex, an account of a generic pattern that is, after all, resolved uniquely by every individual and every family. Nevertheless, Arrowsmith's point seems basically correct. "Modal psychology can be, I am convinced, no less complex and sophisticated than modern individual psychology."[54] Arrowsmith is basically correct because what he is really writing of with the term *modal psychology* is not a different type of psychology, but a different application: to cultural types. This is how the poets applied their psychology, which is a key reason that they lend themselves to psychological study. The psychologically minded critic is elaborating the poets' modal, or cultural-typical, psychology, not merely imposing his own, though of course the critic must actually do both, as I pointed out in chapter 1.

Not only this. What makes the tragic poets such good psychologists is the way in which they portray external conflicts so as to represent internal ones. It is frequently noted, for instance, that protagonists in Greek tragedy fight not their opposites but their doubles. Prometheus is as rigid and unyielding as Zeus, and Tiresias, spokesman of the gods, says to Oedipus, "You do not see how much alike we are," referring to the anger each feels when his authority is threatened (Soph., *Oedipus Tyrannus,* 338; see also 405). The way in which the cousins Pentheus and Dionysus are mirror images of each other has already been mentioned. So too with Creon and Antigone. What this means, and allows, is that the tragic poets can represent conflicts within an individual as conflicts between people, or between people and gods, which is of course what we do also: we project internal conflicts into others (projective identification) and fight them there. In analyzing these conflicts we can psychoanalyze the characters, who are not so much individuals as embodiments of representative patterns of emotional conflict. The stylized gestures, the masks, and formal language of tragedy suppress individuality, with the result that we can see the conflict of emotional forces even more clearly, as though they were no longer contained within individuals but living a life of their own within the culture. In fact, this is much the way Melanie Klein views psychic conflict, as I have argued at length elsewhere.[55]

Am I arguing that culture is a mirror, if sometimes a magnifying one, of the psyche? Certainly this is part of the story. The other part is that culture is itself psyche. Through cycles of projective identification with gods and other cultural ideals and their subsequent reintrojection into the projectors, culture comes to act like psyche, albeit often in an exaggerated fashion. For example, as people pool their anxieties about distinguishing good and bad in the culture, and the culture only intensifies this confusion, culture itself will reinforce individual anxiety rather than ameliorate it. This does not mean that culture lives a life of its own, acting as a group mind. Cultural forces are psychological forces, becoming such via projection and introjection. Analyzing such cultural artifacts as tragedies is not merely a way of gaining access to the individual Greek psyche. It *is* psyche. Not the individual psyche in all its idiosyncratic richness and not necessarily an average psyche, if there is such a thing. Rather, culture as psychological defense will reflect, often in exaggerated form, the modal, and generally the most intense, psychic conflicts and defenses of its members.

What makes the concept so complicated is not so much the relation between psyche and culture as the fact that the tragedies are art: not merely modal psychology but also critical reflections upon it. Ritual in tragedy, to take one example, is not the same thing as actual ritual studied by anthropologists. Ritual in tragedy already has an additional meaning, that given it by the poet, who is at once a member of the culture and its critic. In studying ritual in tragedy, the topic of the next chapter, this must be kept in mind.

Death

PART 2

Failure of Blood Ritual in the Tragedies

CHAPTER 3

In vain do they strive for purification by besmirching themselves with blood, as the man who has bathed in the mire seeks to cleanse himself with mud.—Heraclitus, fifth fragment

It is easy to overlook how central the idea of pollution (generally *miasma* but occasionally *mysos*, as in Sophocles, *Oedipus Tyrannus*, 137) is to the tragedies. We readily recall the centrality of pollution in *Oedipus Tyrannus*. That is what the play is manifestly about: the pollution of the plague that is destroying Thebes echoes the incest of Oedipus. It is easier to misjudge its importance in *Antigone*. Yet the pollution caused by the unburied body of Polynices is as central to *Antigone* as incest is to *Oedipus Tyrannus*. What differs is that here a protagonist denies not merely his own pollution but also the very possibility of pollution itself. "No mortal being can pollute the gods," Creon says (1044). The play serves to demonstrate the costs of such manic denial. One reason modern critics underestimate the centrality of pollution in the tragedies generally is that pollution is not a contemporary idea. We understand and recognize Greek doubt about the gods, even if it takes place within a polytheistic system. Indeed, it is so familiar that it is frequently analyzed under the heading of *theodicy,* a modern if possibly misleading category. There is, however, no modern category for the Greek concept of pollution, though we might link it to our concerns about environmental pollution. Rather, we seem to associate pollution with "primitives" and the like, which we regard as the realm of the anthropologist.

In fact, there is a modern category that captures the concept of pollution quite well. That category is psychoanalytic and concerned with the phenomenon analyzed in the preceding chapter: the contamination of good by bad, of love by hate. Ritual is an attempt to reestablish firm boundaries between polarities, generally by reinforcing paranoid-schizoid distinctions. Pollution, in other words, may be categorized as a form of paranoid-schizoid anxiety over breaching the distinction between good and bad. Ritual is the paranoid-schizoid defense, aimed at restoring the breached boundary. This definition fits well the concept of pollution held by anthropologists such as Mary Douglas and Victor Turner, who see it in terms of anomaly and ambiguity: something is where it does not belong.[1] Or as William James puts it, dirt is simply matter out of place. In a word, pollution is contamination of good by bad, precisely what the Kleinian account of paranoid-schizoid distinctions also concerns.

Though this contamination may take several forms, the most important as far as blood ritual is concerned is the confusion of love and hate, care and destruction, or violence and reparation, in which violent hatred and aggression come to be defined as good only as long as they are directed at what is bad. In the *Republic* (332b), Polemarchus says that we ought to harm our enemies. That is what justice truly is. One problem with such a view is that it invites self-deception: whatever is the object of my aggression and violence must therefore be bad. This is also how the Nazi doctors defended their horrendous acts, according to Robert Jay Lifton. Rather than containing hatred and aggression, such a viewpoint risks transforming the whole world into something bad in order to justify one's own violence. Plato seems to recognize this point when he has Socrates respond to Polemarchus by demonstrating that something that is truly good will never make something else less so. "In short," asks Socrates, "will good men use their goodness to make others bad?" "That cannot be so," Polemarchus is forced to respond (335d). Though Plato and the poets soon diverge, on this point they agree: to harm and victimize others is bad not simply because of its effects on others but because of its corrupting effect on the victimizer's psyche.

POLLUTION, GUILT, AND RITUAL

My concern in this chapter is with a particularly dramatic form of pollution and ritual: pollution by blood or violence and the blood ritual that seeks through imitation and reversal to limit the contamination. First, however, it may be useful to consider a physical account of a blood ritual, in order to understand how bloody such rituals truly were. Though the Greeks believed that it perverted the sacred to kill a man who sought refuge at an altar, many of those same altars were perpetually stained with the blood of sacrificial animals. On vase paintings the white-chalked sides of the altars are almost always shown stained with blood (see too *Iphigenia in Tauris*, 75). Pausanias (5.13.11) tells of an altar made from the blood of the sacrificial victims, which had apparently been mixed with their skeletal remains.[2] That these opposing uses of their altars did not appear contradictory to the Greeks needs explanation. I draw upon Walter Burkert's account in *Greek Religion* of blood ritual, although the references to comparable blood rituals in Greek tragedy are mostly my own.[3] Burkert describes an average blood ritual, so to speak. Although the Greeks distinguished between strict blood rituals (*sphagia*) and those in which the animal was subsequently eaten (*omophagia*) this distinction is not crucial here.

The day of the ritual is set apart and those involved wash themselves and dress in clean clothes, often wearing a garland woven from twigs. The animal chosen to be sacrificed must be perfect, and it too is adorned and its horns gilded. A procession escorts the animal to the altar; ideally the animal goes willingly. Many legends concern the way an animal presents itself for sacrifice when the time comes. One sees a reflection of this sacrificial ideal in Euripides' *Iphigenia in Aulis,* in which Iphigenia's final willingness to be sacrificed is valorized by the chorus (at 510ff; see also Eur., *Hecuba,* 545–580, which idealizes Polyxena's similar willingness. In Aeschylus' account of the Iphigenia story, on the other hand, Iphigenia is simply gagged, so that she cannot curse her father's house; see *Agamemnon,* 235). Once the animal arrives at the place of sacrifice the priest draws a circle around it, rendering it sacred. Everyone stands around the altar, and lustral water is sprinkled over the hands of the participants and the animal. Often the animal is given a drink, so that it may appear to nod its head, seeming to assent to its own sacrifice. The sacrificer uncovers his knife, concealing it while approaching the victim.

The slaughter follows. Smaller animals are raised above the altar and the throat is cut, the blood washing over the sacrificer and the altar (see Aesch., *Eumenides,* 283). An ox, on the other hand, is felled by a blow from an ax, and an artery in the neck is cut. At the fatal blow the women cry out in shrill, high tones, as they do in Aeschylus' *Seven against Thebes* (at 269). The blood is collected in a basin, and sprayed over the altar. "To stain the altar with blood (*haimassein*) is a pious duty," says Burkert. The animal is then skinned and butchered, and the inner organs, especially heart and liver, are roasted on the fire of the altar (see Eur., *Electra,* 780–835). The heart may be torn still beating from the body, but to keep the skull intact is a sacred duty (see, for example, Soph., *Women of Trachis,* 781–782). Depending upon the details of local custom, as well as on the nature of the particular ritual, the entrails are generally eaten first and the inedible remains consecrated to the gods, often by being burned on the altar fire. Only then is the meat consumed. It did not escape the notice of the Greeks that even though the sacrifice is performed for the god, the god receives almost nothing: only bones and smoky fat.

There are, as one might expect, numerous variants of such rituals. In one such, a funeral sacrifice, the blood is allowed to flow into the ground, satiating the dead with blood, *haimakouria.* In Euripides' *Hecuba* (see 90–100, 125–127), for example, Achilles' ghost cannot be laid to rest until it receives fresh blood. Says Arrowsmith, "It characteristically wants the vigorous blood of the young Polyxena, not that of the old Hecuba. Indeed, the persistent theme of *youthful* sacrifice in Euripides rests . . . upon the refusal of the chthonic powers to be appeased by anything less vital."[4] In sacrifice prior to battle, the sacrificer cuts the throats of the animals (herds of sacrificial animals are driven along with the army for this purpose) in view of the enemy, as in Aeschylus'

Seven against Thebes (see 40ff). In all such sacrifices, however, the blood is not incidental, but central. As Burkert puts it,

> The shock of the terrors of death present in the warm flowing blood strikes home directly, not as some painful adjunct, but as the very centre towards which all eyes are directed. . . . Greek tragedy surrounded its own scenes of uncanny violence and necessary destruction with the metaphors of animal sacrifice almost as a standard accompaniment and frequently described and played out scenes of sacrifice. Without doubt both poet and public experienced what Walter F. Otto has called the "violent drama of the animal bleeding to death . . . the expression of a mood whose grandeur is paralleled only in works of high art."[5]

Burkert's study is part of a valuable structuralist anthropological literature on Greek blood ritual, complementing the work of René Girard, Marcel Detienne, and Jean-Pierre Vernant. Nevertheless, it must not be forgotten that in studying ritual in Greek tragedy one is not studying ritual per se but its use in a work of art. Consequently, the symbolism of blood has a double meaning, an importance both in the ritual act and in the play, which may not be the same. As a rough generalization, one may say that in actual rituals the blood of the sacrificial animal has a quasi-magical ability to cleanse guilty blood (it takes blood to cleanse blood) or guilt. An extreme form of this psycho-logic is found in a fragment of an uncertain play, probably by Aeschylus, which refers to how a man who has committed murder by treachery may cleanse himself by tasting and then spitting out the blood of his victim (fragment 192 [354]). In general, the tragedies criticize this logic, demonstrating instead how bloody sacrifice only perpetuates the cycle of violence. Indeed, ritual's most striking aspect in the plays is its perversion, the way in which a ritual designed to cleanse blood and stop the cycle of violence leads only to more bloodshed. Often this perverted ritual involves human sacrifice, as if murder could halt murder.

The poets are critics of blood ritual, though it is certainly not the case that every blood ritual in the tragedies is part of a critique. At one level the criticism leveled against blood ritual attacks its superficiality: the ritual tends to value clean hands over a clean heart. In contemplating Clytaemestra's murder, Orestes says that although he will kill his mother, time and ceremonies of purification will wash the stain clean (see Aesch., *Libation Bearers,* 965; also *Eumenides,* 283) We know, of course, that the matter is hardly this easy; Orestes' guilt runs far deeper. In Euripides' *Orestes,* Menelaus claims that his hands are clean. "Your hands, yes, but not your heart," responds Orestes (1602). Yet superficiality does not constitute the poets' fundamental complaint against ritual, especially blood ritual. To see this it is useful to look at what might be called the foundation myth of blood ritual and animal sacrifice: the story of

Prometheus, who tricked Zeus during a sacrifice. This myth reveals the deceit—ultimately the self-deceit—at the heart of all blood ritual. Whether such deceit is always bad will not be addressed here. Certainly Euripides regards the ritual-based solution to dealing with the forces of Dionysus as disingenuous, which is why, I earlier speculated, Cadmus does not get off lightly in the *Bacchae*.

The founding myth of blood ritual, Prometheus' deception of Zeus, comes to us originally from Hesiod's *Theogony* (535–616). Gods and mortals have quarreled and in a gesture of apparent good will to Zeus on man's behalf, the Titan Prometheus sacrifices a great ox, distributing the pieces of the animal into two piles, one for each of the participants in the quarrel. In one pile he hides pieces of meat within the belly of the ox. In the other he wraps the bones of the ox, covering them with fat so that they look like meat. Then he asks glorious Zeus to choose between them. Zeus, who is not deceived, nonetheless takes the bones and fat (probably to entrap Prometheus, and man) and is enraged. For this reason he withholds fire from man. From this it happens, says Hesiod, "that on earth the human race burns white bones for the Immortals on altars exuding the perfume of incense" (556–557). Otherwise expressed, from this it happens that man sacrifices to the gods just those parts of the animal that he neither needs nor wants. What appears to be a sacrifice is an insult. Blood ritual was born in deception. But a strange deception it is: of all-knowing Zeus, who cannot really be deceived, by merely clever Prometheus. The real deception, it seems, is of the self: of man by man. What exactly is the deceit involved? What truth is being hidden?

Given the self-deceit at the heart of blood rituals aimed at cleansing pollution, it is surprising that Dodds should argue that pollution is a concept associated with the beginnings of guilt cultures rather than with the more primitive shame cultures.[6] One would have thought pollution to be the form that anxiety takes in a shame culture, in which morality is strictly external: what one does or does not do matters, not what one intends. In such a world, clean hands are enough. Or rather, clean and dirty hands are all there is. A. W. H. Adkins' argument that the so-called Greek shame culture is actually better understood as a "results culture" reinforces these reservations.[7] For it is the prime characteristic of a results culture that only consequences count. Good intentions, good will, and a good effort mean nothing. There can be no valid excuse for failure (except perhaps death), not even such a forceful reason as being vastly outnumbered in battle. Once again, if only results count, clean hands are enough. The state of one's heart hardly matters.

In spite of these reservations, Dodds's claim that pollution is a concept associated with the earliest stages of a guilt culture is instructive. Consider, for example, his observation that pollution plays a relatively small role in Homer, who tells the tales of a shame culture. In Homer's brief account of the Oedipus myth, Oedipus continues to reign in Thebes after his incestuous guilt is discovered. Eventually he is killed in battle and buried with royal honors (see *Odyssey,* 2.275ff; *Iliad,* 23.679). There is, says Dodds, no trace in Homer of the belief that pollution was either infectious or hereditary, and the simple Homeric purifications performed by laymen are a far cry from the elaborate rituals of the poets. From these and other considerations, Dodds concludes that in the concept of pollution one sees faint beginnings of the concept of sin, that is, of guilt understood as a condition of the psyche. The fear that one could be contaminated by a chance contact or polluted by the forgotten offense of a remote ancestor segues into the fear that one may be guilty through thought or intention, not simply deed. Both pollution and guilt concern invisible contaminates of purity. In this way they differ from shame, which requires that baseness be exposed, observed. Invisible shame, unknown to actor and observer alike, is a contradiction in terms. Beyond this, perhaps, one may not fruitfully go. Shame and guilt are modern concepts, pollution (*miasma*) and ritual purification (*katharsis*) those of the Greeks, and neither goes into the other without remainder. Nevertheless, the assumption that pollution is a primitive form of guilt can help us better understand the problem of blood ritual, by providing a link to the psychoanalytic study of guilt.

The Kleinian tradition makes a distinction between primitive and more mature forms of guilt that can illuminate the relation of pollution and guilt. Unlike Freud, who made no qualitative distinctions among types of guilt, Klein distinguishes between guilt associated with the paranoid-schizoid position and that associated with the depressive position. Paranoid-schizoid guilt takes the form of fear that we will be harmed by the harmed object: fear of retaliation. Often too it takes the form of anxiety for the self, as in "I have harmed the person I love and depend upon; now I am alone in the world. How shall I survive?" When projected into the culture, paranoid-schizoid guilt is expressed in the morality of the *lex talionis,* "an eye for an eye." Paranoid-schizoid guilt is defended against by splitting. Good and bad are held rigidly apart, in the hope that good will be strong enough to defend itself against retaliatory attacks by the bad. We see this, argues Klein, in the *Eumenides,* where Orestes seeks refuge with Apollo and subsequently clings to the statue of Athene in the hope that the gods' goodness will protect him from the wrath of the Furies.[8] Here we see another problem with paranoid-schizoid morality: its tendency to define goodness as the power to protect.

Depressive guilt is different, for it expresses genuine concern that one has harmed a loved person or endangered something good. It is called depressive because it is associated with the fear that one is not good enough, or strong enough, to protect the loved person from harm—that is, from one's own badness. Depressive guilt reduces the splitting of good and bad, allowing the subject to recognize that the harmed bad object is also the loved good object. In other words, depressive guilt is an expression of emotional development. Klein reads the *Oresteia* as an account of the transformation of Orestes' guilt from paranoid-schizoid to depressive. At first, Orestes is mad, his guilt strictly paranoid; he fears that his furies will rend him limb from limb for his matricide. Later, however, with the help of Athene, he and Athens find a place for the Furies—deep underground to be sure. Nevertheless, from their new home the Furies serve civilized justice under law, rather than oppose it. Klein interprets this resolution as an account of the transformation of Orestes' guilt, his recognition that good and bad mother are one allowing him to find a place for his own badness that is not completely split-off and isolated from his goodness.

Blood ritual represents an expression of paranoid-schizoid guilt aimed at preventing the pollution of the good self by the bad. Its goal is to contain the violent and hating self lest that self spill over and contaminate everything, including loved ones. Finally, ritual seeks to prevent retaliation by Furies or other avengers of the dead and damaged. Though generally not couched in psychoanalytic terms, many anthropological studies of blood ritual support these conclusions. In *Violence and the Sacred,* René Girard states that "all concepts of impurity stem ultimately from the community's fear of a perpetual cycle of violence arising in its midst."[9]

Conversely, ritual serves to break this cycle, primarily through finding a scapegoat: originally a person (called a *pharmakos*), later a sacrificial animal. The blood of this sacrifice, Girard goes on to argue, symbolizes perfectly the psychological issues at stake. Blood represents the life force that can be drained and in this process spill over onto others, contaminating them with death. Originally a liquid, able to penetrate virtually any boundary, it quickly congeals, its stain difficult to remove. What was once contained within the form of the body pours out and becomes formless. Because of its changing, liminal character blood comes to take on the magical, symbolic burden of duality: it contaminates, but it may also cleanse. Such dualistic symbols are common in ritual and magical thinking: the knife that heals; the fire that destroys and purifies; the blood that pollutes and purifies.

This imagery stems from the deepest layers of the mind, what Freud called primary process thinking, the kind of thinking that occurs in dreams. One sees this even in the Greek term *pharmakon,* which means both a medicine and a poison. *Pharmakon* is closely related to *pharmakos*, the "scapegoat," one who is sacrificed in atonement for others. In "The Antithetical Meaning of Primal Words," Freud points out how many words, particularly those like *cleave* that evoke primal experiences, have opposite meanings (in this case "to cling to" and "to sever").[10] This dualism reflects the workings of the unconscious mind, particularly as revealed in dreams, in which identical things may be rendered as opposites and opposites as identical. Which is why, of course, the confusion and reversal that I have written about may be so profound, tapping the deepest layers of experience and thus placing so much pressure on conscious distinctions that these distinctions become perverted and twisted.

A particularly dramatic example of the paranoid-schizoid defense against confusion occurs in Euripides' *Ion,* in which two drops of Gorgon's blood, ostensibly the same substance, have opposite properties and must be kept separate lest something terrible happen. Noted earlier, the example is worth elaborating in the present context.

> "How is it to be used? What power has it?" asks Creusa's servant.
> "One drop fosters life and keeps away disease," responds Creusa.
> "What action does the other drop have?" the servant asks again.
> "It kills—a poison from the Gorgon's snakes," says Creusa.
> "Do you carry them apart or mixed together?" asks the servant.
> "Apart. For good and evil do not mingle," Creusa responds.
> (1010–1018)

Blood ritual addresses precisely this anxiety: that bad blood has contaminated good, and the boundaries between them must be restored. It does so not merely by an act of imitative violence nor one of scapegoating. Rather, it restores the boundaries by a re-creation of violence within strict limits: within the sacred circle, the framework of ritual, with special clothes and knives, all of which serve to reassure the doer of the violence and the community that observes the ritual that violence can be contained. Ritual is limited to an attack on the bad and will not become so extreme as to spill over onto the good.

The participants in the ritual seem to say, "The violence we have committed or observed (or merely imagined) threatens to destroy the entire community and all that we care about. Let us reenact this violence in a highly circumscribed fashion, so that we may convince ourselves that it can be contained within limits. In particular, we shall focus upon, and control, the spilling of blood, that symbol of the contained becoming uncontained. In letting the blood fall onto the altars, and even onto ourselves, we shall demonstrate to ourselves that what is apparently uncontained and unstructured is actually controlled by the ritual itself." In a word, ritual reinforces psychological defenses aimed at reestablishing firm, paranoid-schizoid defenses against violence, rage, and hatred that threaten to spill over to contaminate the good.

More general studies of rituals of purification support these conclusions. Victor Turner, in *The Ritual Process,* argues that in spite of the reversal and confusion associated with ritual (he points to Carnival in India, in which the latrine cleaner becomes king for a day), its goal is always to establish firmer boundaries between things that should be held separate.[11] Similarly, in *Purity and Danger,* Mary Douglas argues that pollution punishes a symbolic breaking of what should be joined, or a symbolic joining of what should be separate. Conversely, ritual seeks to preserve order, structure, and boundaries, even if doing so requires disorder, even reversal.[12] Blood ritual in particular involves precisely this. Rigidly controlled reenactment tries to contain the violence that has broken through—violence that otherwise threatens to shatter all boundaries, destroying the community and everything good within it.

Like many anthropologists, Douglas is hostile toward psychoanalytic interpretations of ritual. Thus, she criticizes Bruno Bettelheim's *Symbolic Wounds,* which explains Australian and African circumcision rituals in terms of male envy of female reproduction: the bleeding wound of the circumcision imitates menstruation. Against this interpretation she sees the body as representing society itself, so that the circumcision ceremony creates a symmetry of the two halves of society. Male and female are fundamentally alike—both bleed.[13] Douglas may well be correct, but like many critics of psychoanalytic interpretations, she objects not to a psychoanalytic view as such. Rather, she objects to, without being clear about it, a particular form of psychoanalytic reductionism that reduces everything to sexual desire and envy. Only put aggression, hatred, violence, and the guilt and anxiety that they engender at the center of psychoanalysis, and many of the standard objections to "psychoanalytic reductionism" disappear. In fact, my argument resembles hers: in blood rituals the participants projectively identify the human body (or its animal surrogate) with the social body, so that when violated the one serves as substitute (scapegoat) for the other, a body that would otherwise be divided and destroyed by the participants' own penchant for indiscriminate civic violence (what the Greeks called *stasis*).

Such an explanation need not regard ritual as an epiphenomenon, mere evidence of unconscious processes. Rather, through cycles of projection and reintrojection, culture and ritual come to take on a life of their own. The answer they provide for human needs and conflicts comes to structure those needs and conflicts themselves. By using ritual and culture to reinforce their own psychological defenses, individuals make these defenses their own. Culture penetrates psyche as much as psyche penetrates culture. A psychoanalytic study of culture need no more reduce culture to psyche than psyche to culture. Rather, it will identify the cycles of projection and introjection that constitute both.

One should never underestimate the effectiveness of paranoid-schizoid defenses, especially when they are institutionally reinforced, as they are in ritual.[14] Nevertheless, blood ritual and paranoid-schizoid defenses remain fundamentally unstable, for they are vulnerable to confusion and reversal. If one is unclear about which objects demand care and respect and which violence, then the ritual reenactment of violence designed to demonstrate that it need not spill over and contaminate the good may only intensify one's anxiety. Overwhelmed by doubt and confusion, one fears that perhaps the bad object has been protected and the good destroyed. Additionally, ritually reenacting violence serves to create a more violent world: blood spilled in ritual is still blood, ritual violence still violence. To live in a world of blood-stained altars means one inhabits a world infiltrated and contaminated by violence, from which there seems no escape but only more violence, as though violence were the only defense against violence. This *is* confusion and reversal. Under such circumstances the culture appears more psychologically ill than its members. But not for long. Soon cultural confusion and anxiety will intensify individual doubts by providing only failed and ineffective defenses against them. These anxieties define the Dionysian crisis.

WHY DOES RITUAL SO OFTEN BECOME PERVERTED?

In *Violence and the Sacred,* Girard writes of a "sacrificial crisis" in which the loss of distinctions and boundaries within the community leads to loss of distinction between pure (that is, sacrificial) and impure violence. As a result ritual becomes ineffective.[15] The similarity of this concept to what I have called the Dionysian crisis is apparent. One difference, however, lies in Girard's use of the idea—he makes *sacrificial crisis* in effect a term of literary criticism, treating the loss of distinctions as given, sui generis, an instance of the denial of otherness. The Dionysian crisis, on the other hand, concerns the origins of that loss of difference (understood as the confusion of good and bad) in real historical events, from the literate revolution to the failure of the polis to wall out the passions of the oikos and the caprice of the gods. The poets too are concerned with the failure of ritual. The perverted ritual provides their key theme, one in which the ritualistic attempt to break the cycle of violence fails, indeed is rendered a mockery, leading only to more violence. Below I examine several of these perverted rituals and try to assimilate the poets' treatment of blood ritual without too much forcing to my own.

In Aeschylus' *Agamemnon,* Clytaemestra defends her murder of her husband, Agamemnon, to the chorus in terms that suggest she regards it as a blood ritual.

I struck him twice. In two great cries of agony he buckled at the knees and fell. When he was down I struck him the third blow, in thanks and reverence to Zeus the lord of dead men underneath the ground. Thus he went down, and the life struggled out of him; and as he died he spattered

me with the dark red and violent driven rain of bitter savored blood to make me glad, as gardens stand among the showers of God in glory at the birthtime of the buds. . . . Were it religion to pour wine above the slain, this man deserved, more than deserved, such sacrament. He filled our cup with evil things unspeakable and now himself come home has drunk it to the dregs.
(1372–1398)

Clytaemestra has turned the tables on Agamemnon. Where once he sacrificed his daughter Iphigenia to the knife, now he shall be sacrificed. Where once he bloodied the Trojans, now he shall be bloodied. A rough justice has been achieved, even if Clytaemestra's motives are hardly pure. Yet this is not all that has occurred. In committing this violent act (perhaps in order to commit it), Clytaemestra has transformed murder into a ritual sacrament, leading precisely to the confusion of pure and impure violence to which Girard refers. Sometimes it is suggested that Agamemnon's willingness to step upon the precious household robes was itself an inverted sacrifice, a sacrilege, requiring another inverted sacrifice to set it straight (see, for example, 915–958). Perhaps, but only in grammar and mathematics do two negatives make a positive. In the tragedies, two inverted sacrifices just lead to more.

The psychoanalyst Janine Chasseguet-Smirgel writes of how the pervert comes to terms with his perversion by idealizing it.[16] Her point is that our ideas about what is good and bad are often so powerful that sometimes the only way we can do bad is by an act of psychological reversal, in which we convince ourselves that bad is good. Robert Jay Lifton makes a similar point regarding the killing-healing reversal he found among the Nazi doctors. To enable themselves to participate in the murder of the Jews, many doctors convinced themselves that it was a healing act: in killing the Jews they were healing a sick society, as they would remove a cancer. In this context Lifton refers to Douglas' *Purity and Danger*, arguing that the killing of the Jews itself became a perverted ritual, "a fierce purification procedure," in which the Jews became the human sacrifice.[17] The Judeocide became a ritual because ritualizing the killings seemed to promise that they could be contained, confined to the bad (the Jews), so as not to destroy the good (including the values of human decency) or redound on the aggressor. In fact, such ritual containment rarely works, at least not on such a horrific scale. Ritual becomes not containment but confusion (itself a defense, albeit a more desperate one), both for Clytaemestra and the Nazi doctors. Bloody murder poses as a ritual sacrifice, designed to purify what has been contaminated by the violence of the ritual itself. Conversely, ritual sacrifice becomes a way of justifying murder.

In Euripides' *Heracles*, Heracles returns from his twelve contests (*althloi*, often but misleadingly called his "labors"). Though most are not described in the play, the audience would have been aware of the deaths that Heracles had earlier caused. Heracles was among the most well-known and popular mythical figures among the Greeks, as well as one of the most brutal. An incomplete list of those he killed includes: the Nemean Lion; the Lernaean Hydra; the centaur Chiron (actually, the immortal centaur suffered perpetual agony from Heracles' poisoned arrow until he traded places with Prometheus and mercifully died); Hippolyta, queen of the Amazons; Diomedes, fed to his own carnivorous horses; Geryon, a three-bodied monster; Eurytion, a giant herdsman; Orthus, a two-headed hound; Cacus, a fire-breathing monster; Eryx, king of the mountain of the same name; Alcyoneus, a giant and brigand; Ladon, the serpent who protected the apples of the Hesperides; the giant Antaeus; King Busiris of Egypt; and Cycnus, the guest-murderer.

Upon arriving home after the last of his twelve contests, which required his extended presence in Hades, Heracles finds that Lycus, an old rival, has usurped his place in Thebes and is planning to kill Heracles' children so that they will not take revenge. Lured into Heracles' palace Lycus is quickly dispatched by Heracles. The chorus of Theban elders is ecstatic, and Heracles commences his ritual of purification intended to cleanse himself of the blood he has shed during his labors. Suddenly Madness appears, sent by Hera to destroy Heracles. Convinced that he is back at his bloody labors, Heracles hunts down his children and wife, killing them with his bow, believing them to be his old enemies.

At one level, Heracles is simply driven mad by a goddess who hates him. Yet Greek heroes generally contribute to their own madness, as the cases of Ajax and Orestes reveal (see too fragment 160 of Aeschylus). What has Heracles contributed? Blood. He has spilled so much blood that it can no longer be contained by ritual. The violence Heracles has unleashed is so massive that it overflows the ritual designed to purify him, contaminating all around him. Ritual purification and violence are reversed by the force of the violence itself. The paranoid-schizoid separation of good and bad can no longer hold, as good is itself sacrificed to bad. As Heracles' father asks him after the slaughter, "My child, what happened to you? How could this horror have taken place? Was it perhaps the spilt blood that drove you mad?" (965ff). A short while later Heracles, who has begun to return to sanity, asks, "Where did the madness overtake me? Where did it strike me down?" His father replies, "Near the altar, where you were purifying your hands over the sacred flames" (1143ff).

Yet this is not the whole story of Heracles. After recovering from his madness and learning the truth Heracles feels deeply polluted, hiding his head beneath his robes so as not to contaminate his friend Theseus. "Flee my foul pollution," he says (1233). In response Theseus, whom he had rescued from Hades, answers, "Where there is love contagion cannot come" (1234).[18] Theseus' love convinces Heracles to live, to endure his pain, and even to retain his bow, the symbol of his identity as a warrior. "You saved me then," says Theseus, "and now I pity you." Later Theseus tries to take Heracles' hand, and Heracles cautions, "Take care. I may pollute your clothes with blood." Theseus responds, "Pollute them then. Spare not. I do not care" (1398ff). Theseus is not hubristic, nor does he reject the very idea of pollution, as Creon does in Sophocles' *Antigone*. Rather, Theseus knows that shared pollution is a psychic concept, the blood Heracles would stain him with merely a symbol. As such it can be overcome with an emotion, with love. More generally, Theseus represents a mature, depressive response to pollution, which seeks not to wall it off but to contain it with love. Though the thematics are less grand, the presentation less noble, the resolution less encompassing than in Aeschylus' *Oresteia*, *Heracles* concerns much the same theme. Indeed, one might argue that *Heracles* handles the idea more successfully. Here, the love that heals is more real and personal than the distant benevolence for the male that characterizes Athene. Conversely, the resolution is less tinged with manic denial. Heracles' life will not be easy, his violence not permanently overcome by love.

The theme of Sophocles' *Women of Trachis* is strikingly similar. Once again Heracles has returned from his labors, having left his wife Deianira at home. In this play he brings home with him Iole, his lover. King Eurytus, Iole's father, had not wanted her to marry Heracles, and in revenge Heracles killed his son and destroyed his city. Deianira is understandably anxious about this new woman but graciously opens her home to her. Worried, however, about losing her husband's love, Deianira concocts a love potion from the blood of a centaur. Actually, the potion is a mix of the centaur's blood with the blood of the hydra, which Heracles had used to poison the arrow that shot the centaur (see 565–580). As in *Ion*, two kinds of blood are mixed, once again with disastrous results. Deianira smears the blood on a shirt that she gives to Heracles as a welcome home present. Putting on the shirt, Heracles performs his rites of purification, intended to cleanse him of the blood he has spilled in his labors.

This time the purification ritual is a fire ritual, and the ritual fire (called a "blood-flame," *phlox haimatera*, 766) activates the poisoned blood in the shirt. Not even different types of ritual purification can be kept distinct under the pressure of so much blood—everything becomes blood ritual. Heracles is consumed by a caustic fire (once again the means of purification becomes the means of destruction) and in horrible pain and agony strikes out at one more innocent man, the servant who gave him the shirt, smashing his head against a rock, so that it "pressed the pale brains out through his hair, and split full on, skull and blood mixed and spread. All the people cried out in horror" (780–782). Recall that the skull of the sacrificial animal ought to be kept intact, the sight of the brain being regarded as a desecration. Not even in his death-agony can Heracles refrain from the violence that perverts ritual.

As with so many of the tragedies, one can read much the same story in the play's imagery, which tracks the substantive events of the play. *Women of Trachis* begins with an image of the river Acheloüs seeking Deianira's hand in marriage, first appearing as a bull, then a serpent, then a man with a bull's face and a torrent of water for a beard (8–13). "I was being wooed by shapes," says Deianira (Williams and Dickerson translation). Terrifying to Deianira, these shapes nonetheless remain distinct. As the story progresses, however, the images of Heracles and the river meld into one, as the chorus describes their battle for the hand of Deianira (see 515–522). And although one might expect that any man who fights a river whose boundaries are as liquid as blood would meld with it, the same thing happens in Heracles' contest with the beastly centaur, Nessus. In the end the poison that kills Heracles is Nessus himself, eating away at Heracles from within, like the entity in the movie *Alien*: "The thing, again, again, it's pouncing, lunging in me, leaping, destroying. . . . It's eaten to inside me. . . . It's moved in" (1030, 1050–1055, Williams and Dickerson translation; see also 987). The point, of course, is that the beast is always within, residing there from the beginning, in Heracles, Deianira, the polis, and us all. This is why blood ritual is bound to fail: the strict paranoid-schizoid separations it represents are compromised by the confusion within. In the end there is only one kind of blood, that released by violence.

Euripides' *Electra* contains yet another account of ritual gone wrong. Orestes and his friend Pylades find Aegisthus, consort of Clytaemestra, and usurper of the throne that belongs to Orestes, on his way to perform a blood ritual. He plans to slaughter a bull at the shrine of the nymphs, so that they will protect him from Orestes. Aegisthus does not recognize Orestes and invites him to participate in the sacrifice. After slashing the bull's throat, Aegisthus asks Orestes to skin it and remove its organs. During this sacrifice, "Aegisthus scooped the prophetic viscera up in his hands. The liver lobe was not there. Unhidden, the portal-vein and gall-sac showed disaster coming at him even as he peered. His face darkened, drew down. [Orestes] watched and asked, 'What puts you out of heart?' 'Stranger, I am afraid. Some ambush is at my door'" (825ff). Orestes responds that a king can hardly be afraid and asks for a knife to complete the evisceration. While Aegisthus is leaning over the soft organs of the bull, sorting them out, Orestes takes the knife and drives it into Aegisthus' spine, killing him.

Once again, blood ritual not only fails to prevent violence, it is transformed into violence: the sacrificer becomes the sacrificed. *Electra* concerns the deceptiveness of appearances. Children of noble families are cowards, cowards have courageous sons, and Electra's poor, farmer husband acts with nobility. So where does truth lie? Inside the body, it appears, in the soft, fleshy organs that are such a central image in the sacrificial death of Aegisthus. Those familiar with Klein's account of the origins of the epistemophilic instinct, as she calls it (that is, the desire to know), in the young child's sadistic curiosity regarding its mother's insides will not be surprised by this imagery.[19] Here Euripides appears to be saying that to find the truth one must kill the body. Yet, if this truth is that such sacrificial violence only perpetuates violence, then one learns it only through an action that belies its intent. One must be violent to learn that violence cannot halt violence; by then, however, it is too late. Here is the heart of the Dionysian crisis, which is revealed by Euripides to be not merely confusion but a double bind, a Catch-22—a dilemma that only the gods could resolve, were they not so often its cause. Or as Orestes says of Apollo, who has ordered him to kill his mother, "O Phoebus, your holy word was brute and ignorant" (970).

Euripides' *Helen,* also concerned with the deceptiveness of appearances, has as its climax a blood ritual that quickly turns into a slaughter, though in this case not of the sacrificers. In this version, Helen never went to Troy (Paris unknowingly stole only her image), and hid out in Egypt, where she waited for Menelaus to find her. Menelaus stops in Egypt on his return from Troy and recognizes Helen, but they cannot leave together, for Theoclymenus, the son of the Egyptian king, has designs on her. In order to escape they fake a funeral at sea for Menelaus, during which they sacrifice a bull. Disguised as a castaway, Menelaus cuts the throat of the bull, praying that he and Helen will be freed. "And as he spoke, the blood rained on the water, favoring the stranger's prayer." The other Greek castaways on board Theoclymenus' galley unsheathe their swords, quickly slaughtering the fifty Egyptian oarsman. "The ship ran blood; but there was Helen cheering them on from the stern: 'Where is the glory of Troy? Come on, show it on these barbarians.'" The last line of the Egyptian servant, the only man to escape death, who describes this to Theoclymenus, is simply: "man's most valuable trait is a judicious sense of what not to believe" (1585–1618).

In this case the blood ritual does not turn on the sacrificers. It only intensifies the violence, so that the sacrifice of the bull segues into the sacrifice of the fifty barbarians. In this regard the blood ritual has accomplished its paranoid-schizoid purpose: it has intensified violence, but it has also contained it, so that only the bad and base (barbarians) are slaughtered. Yet something different is going on as well. Herodotus (whose work was published in full not much more than a decade before this play was produced in 412 B.C.) tells a similar story, in which Proteus, King of Egypt, intercepts Paris and Helen on their way to Troy, keeping Helen in Egypt for safekeeping. The Greeks did not believe the Trojans when they said Helen was not there and fought the ten-year war which they finally won. On his way home Menelaus stopped by Egypt and collected Helen, after disgracing himself and Greece by an illicit sacrifice involving two Egyptian boys (see *Histories,* 2.112–120).[20]

Does Euripides mean to suggest that the sacrifice he writes of is an equal disgrace? Does he implicitly draw upon a mythical-historical tradition of a disgraceful sacrifice committed by Menelaus to make a criticism of blood sacrifice in general? Probably. But what about the final words of the Egyptian servant? What should one not believe? That the escape of Helen and Menelaus represents a clever and glorious victory rather than one more pointless slaughter to add to the ten years of pointless slaughter at Troy. Yet in the end, as is usual with Euripides, the god in the machine, Castor, deifies Helen, sends Menelaus to the island of the blest, and concludes, "heaven never hates the noble in the end. It is for the nameless multitude that life is hard" (1677). The only way this resolution makes any sense is that it makes no sense and is not intended to. Everything is disordered and confused. The gods reward not goodness, and not even piety, but merely the simulacrum of nobility. Blood sacrifice is a disgraceful practice that only calls forth more violence. But in a world so disordered and chaotic, in which men kill each other for ten years over literally nothing—an illusion—what difference do the lives of fifty Egyptians make? What difference does anything in life make?

Here is the Dionysian crisis compounded with the deepest cynicism. But perhaps *compounded* is not quite the right word. For it is the nature of extreme confusion over good and bad that it eventuates in cynicism, cynicism serving as a defense against the despair and anguish behind the confusion. In their hearts and deep in their psyches men and women want to cherish and protect the good. Cynicism thus serves as a defense against profound depressive anxiety: fear that one is neither smart enough to know the good nor strong enough to protect it from one's own violence, as well as from that of others. Isn't this just what *Helen* is about?

RITUAL OR REASON?

Although the Greek concept of pollution is today an alien one, this is perhaps not our gain. Nor has the fear of pollution disappeared. Public reaction to AIDS and references to the "epidemic" of drug abuse testify to that. Although understanding guilt as a condition of the will has obvious advantages, it does not truly capture the primitive, often unconscious experience of being corrupted by badness. *Guilt* and *pollution* are not, of course, mutually exclusive. One may feel both. The term *shame* comes closer to the concept of pollution, except that shame generally concerns baseness rather than badness. The advantage of the concept of pollution is that it connects the deepest intrapsychic experiences with their social expression. Psychology has long had difficulty doing this: social psychology tends to be trivial, and depth psychology, such as Klein's, is often isolated from the social. The concept of pollution, although it taps the deepest levels of experience, is nonetheless social, its key attribute being its contagiousness: pollution may be spread to others. Conversely, pollution's spread may be halted by a relationship characterized by care, concern, and decency. Pollution is object relational, as the psychoanalysts put it; it concerns people's relationship to others, not just to themselves.

Seemingly among the most primitive of Greek experiences and concepts, fear of pollution overlaps closely with what Kleinians call paranoid-schizoid anxiety—the fear that our badness will overcome our goodness. This connection is no accident. Precisely because pollution is such a primitive concept, it finds its echo in depth psychology. Not because ontogeny recapitulates phylogeny, but because the organization of the psychological defenses of the ancient Greek differed from ours, so that these primitive experiences within us all were more likely to be projected into the culture and experienced there as cultural confusion, the Dionysian crisis. Why? The complete answer must wait until chapter 5, which concerns the coherence of the Greek psyche. The key point here is simply that a loosely organized individual psyche interacted with a culture that encouraged the acting out of paranoid-schizoid defenses in ritual over repression.

Charles Segal is not the first to contrast the ritual-based solution to the problem of civilization with that of Freud. As Segal puts it,

> The Greek solution to the problem of civilization, the ritualizing of violence and aggression, is almost the opposite of the solution proposed by Freud. Freud would have man accept his aggressiveness as a fundamental part of himself and deal with it through the integration of his ego, insofar as this is possible. Freud's solution has its analogue in the post-tragic period of fourth-century Athens, that is, the period when the ritual and sacral solution to the problem of violence begins to break down, to be replaced by the Socratic notion of self-control (*enkrateia*) and the inward mastery of passion by reason described in [Plato's] *Republic*. In this perspective one of the fifth century's great achievements would be the creation of a form that sublimates into the highest art man's harsh and painful confrontation with his own savagery.[21]

Segal's comments are revealing and concealing in almost equal measure. A society based upon blood ritual does represent a solution to the problem of civilization different from that posited by Freud and Plato. Blood ritual defends against aggression by an extreme form of splitting and displacement (projective identification), whereas Freud would turn people's aggression back against themselves in the form of the harsh and punitive superego. Although Plato's concept of reason differs radically from Freud's, the harshness with which Plato would have the rational part of the self subdue the desiring self is similar. One sees this, for example, in Plato's *Phaedrus* (253d–254e), where the ugly, wanton horse of desire is jerked to a halt so violently by a combination of reason and *thumos* (spirit) that its mouth and jaws drip with blood, forcing its body into submission. Plato's *Republic* contains a similar model of the psyche, in which reason and thumos once again join forces to curb the many-headed beast of desire (see 439d–441a, 588c–e). The "ritualizing of violence and aggression" is not absent in Plato's psychology but it is directed against one aspect of the self by another. This is the real meaning of self-control in Plato's account.

Contrary to Segal's interpretation, Freudian repression of aggression does not simply consist of teaching people to master their impulses through insight and emotional integration. That is a nice story, it is what much popular psychology would have us believe, but it is not what Freud said. Freud said that civilization depends upon the superego's transformation of the aggression against others into aggression against the self. Here is the origin of guilt and the malaise of civilization. In *Civilization and Its Discontents,* Freud asks

> What means does civilization employ in order to inhibit the aggressiveness which opposes it, to get rid of it, perhaps? What happens . . . [is that man's] aggressiveness is internalized; it is, in point of fact, sent back to where it came from—that is, it is directed towards his own ego. There it is taken over by a portion of the ego, which sets itself over against the rest of the ego and super-ego, and which now, in the form of 'conscience,' is ready to put into action against the ego the same harsh aggressiveness the ego would have liked to satisfy upon other, extraneous individuals. The tension between the harsh super-ego and the ego that is subjected to it, is called by us the sense of guilt. . . . Civilization, therefore, obtains mastery over the individual's dangerous desire for aggression . . . by setting up an agency within him to watch over it, like a garrison in a conquered city.[22]

Segal is not, however, mistaken to see that in important respects Freud's solution is similar to Plato's. They agree on the harshness with which to subject the psyche. In the *Republic,* as in the *Phaedrus,* Plato divides the mind into three parts, reason, spirit, and desire, comparing spirit with the guardians of the city ("reason's natural militia" [*phulakes*]), who will watch over desire, "like a garrison in a conquered city" (*Rep.,* 439d-444d). It is no coincidence that Plato and Freud employ the same simile, modeling the psyche after a repressive military regime. Of course, Freud read Plato, but, more important, their ways of thinking about rational self-control are similar. I have compared Plato and

Freud on this point in two recent books, so I shall not pursue it further here.[23]

In this context, it may be instructive to reinterpret the Oedipus complex, not because doing so will show Sophocles to have intuited something that moderns like Freud understand better, but because doing so may enrich our understanding of Freud. For it is frequently argued by supporters and detractors alike that Freud took from the Greek myth merely a name, rather than a concept or even a metaphor. If, however, we understand the Oedipus complex not simply as an account of a little boy's love for his mother, but as a study of the harsh repression necessary to maintain civilization itself, then the relation between Freud's term and the tragedy by Sophocles becomes more complex and subtle. Via the Oedipus complex the little boy learns to direct back against himself the harsh aggression he would have otherwise visited against father, had father not been so strong, powerful, and perhaps loved as well. It is no accident that Freud's mythopoeic account of the primal horde as foundation of civilization echoes the Oedipus complex. In the primal horde the jealous and resentful male children kill and eat their fathers. Appalled at their aggression and loss, they establish among themselves a regime at least as harsh and anti-erotic as that of the father, like a garrison in a conquered city. Civilization is the individual's solution to the Oedipus conflict writ large.

Seen in this light, Sophocles' Oedipus may be interpreted as a man who tries to live without the superego, seeking to harness his anger and desire to his reason (an ego function), and so coming to dominate a world free of the prohibitions of society, much as the primal father does. For a while his attempt works, but in the end it must fail. Oedipus' reason, which seemed able to coordinate desires with opportunities for their satisfaction (the definition of ego[24]) was in fact only acting out an exceptionally primitive desire to reunite with mother, a desire so aboriginal that its realization was incompatible with his civilization, or, indeed, with Freud's or our own. Reason was always simply rationalization, the slave of desire in the guise of its master. The best evidence for this interpretation is the simplest: Oedipus is the man who tries to be his own father. That is, he tries to be his own superego, using wit alone to coordinate his desires with opportunities for their satisfaction. He cannot, because wit or reason or ego is captured and suborned by desire from the day we are born. Sophocles and Freud are not saying the same thing about Oedipus. Nevertheless, if we interpret (*enlarge* is the term I have used) Freud from a Sophoclean perspective—that is, a perspective that sees in the Oedipus complex an account of the hubris of reason—then they may be seen to share the same universe of discourse.

It is important not to read history backward, so to speak, and see the poets' critique of blood ritual as somehow preparing the way for the Platonic alternative. None of my comments on how the poets criticize the paranoid-schizoid defense associated with blood ritual should be read in this way. On the contrary, Segal's insights reveal the problem I seek to address: that the options for civilization are limited to the splitting associated with ritual or the repression associated with Plato and Freud.

The contribution of the poets, largely unacknowledged, is to have laid out a third path. I have not yet outlined this way, except to say that it depends upon the release of the civilizing emotions that are based upon pity. For this to occur, however, various barriers to pity must be removed, so that it may be released and educated. Prime among these barriers are the splitting and paranoid projection associated with blood ritual itself, in which the whole world is divided (often in a confused fashion) into proper and improper objects of violence. In such a world, pity for some is purchased at the price of the violation of others. Those familiar with Klein's concept of depressive integration, particularly the way in which the impulse to reparation is released by the replacement of paranoid-schizoid defenses with depressive ones, will understand the inspiration for my interpretation of blood ritual as a barrier to pity.

The paranoid-schizoid defense characteristic of blood ritual requires self-deception, as revealed by the mythic origins of blood ritual in Prometheus' deception of Zeus. Particularly important is the deception of the self regarding its own propensity to violence and hatred. "Our enemies are bad, and so deserve my violence" or "My violence is aimed at freeing us from badness and evil" are familiar expressions of such self-deception, which the poets endeavor to expose, in part because, *pace* Segal, they recognized the instability of ritual-based self-deception in the fifth century B.C.

The liberation of pity requires, as a first step, an end to such self-deception, so that the self begins to come to terms with its own hatred and aggression. Not, however, because the end of self-deception allows rational repression based upon true self-knowledge. This is Freud, and possibly Plato, but not the poets. For the poets an end to self-deception allows the self to experience its own pain and suffering in an unmediated (that is, unprotected by paranoid-schizoid defenses) fashion, so that it may learn the wisdom that comes from suffering. This wisdom releases pity, the topic of chapters 6 and 7. First, however, it is necessary to consider further the source of the rage and hatred against which blood ritual defends. A key source is fear of death. Or, rather, the fear of a meaningless, pointless death.

Tragic Discontinuity of Life and Death

CHAPTER 4

Death is another country.—Sophocles, *Antigone*

In *Alcestis,* probably Euripides' earliest extant work, Admetus, king of
Thessaly, equivocates to his friend Heracles over the question of whether
someone has died. In response Heracles says that over an issue like this
one cannot equivocate. Either one is dead or one is not. "Being and
nonbeing are considered different things" (528). Heracles is, of course,
absolutely right. Yet to live well one must grasp their continuity while
never denying their difference. One must live with death constantly in
mind, without being overwhelmed by it.

It turns out that Admetus' wife, Alcestis, has died. Death allows Admetus to choose a substitute, and Alcestis has voluntarily given up her life
so that Admetus might live, after his parents refused to give up theirs.
True to his friendship with Admetus, Heracles battles death, and returns
with Alcestis. Yet although Alcestis has returned to life, she cannot speak
for three days, in recognition of the fact that she owes something to
death.[1] As Heracles, that great conqueror of death (his prize of victory
for his twelve contests is immortality), puts it, "You are not allowed to
hear her speak to you until her obligations to the gods who live below are
washed away. Until the third morning comes" (1145ff). But what exactly
do we owe death? And why? These are the questions that Euripides
raises. True to form, he does not answer them, though the play contains
several interesting hints.

In letting his wife die in his place, Admetus hardly appears the most
admirable of men. As Richmond Lattimore puts it in the introduction
to his translation: "The theme of the drama is not 'if a wife dies for her
husband, how brave and devoted the wife,' so much as 'if a husband
lets his wife die for him, what manner of man must that husband be.'"[2]
Yet Admetus does not receive much criticism at the hands of Euripides,
for he has one overwhelming virtue. He is the world's best guest-host,
or *xenia,* treating all who come his way, no matter what their condition, with the greatest care and respect. Indeed, because he is such a
thoughtful host he does not name the person who has died, for he does
not want to dampen Heracles' spirits with news of his wife's death. Why
would this theme be bound so closely to that of the continuity of life and
death? Why would Admetus' virtue, carried to such extremes, mitigate

his selfishness in letting his wife die for him, as it seems to do? Today, at least, being a good host is hardly considered the most sublime of virtues. Euripides implies that we are all guests in a foreign land—this is what it means to live on earth for a short while. As such, we are terribly vulnerable to mistreatment by others, who may kill us, cast us out, or simply make us feel alienated and uncomfortable in our temporary home. Such is Creon, who just before sending Antigone to her death says, "She was only a stranger in our world, and her stay is over" (Soph., *Antigone,* 890, Braun translation). In a world with people like Creon, the perfect guest-host is not just being polite. He is serving life itself, whose temporary guests we all are. Therefore his life is especially worthy. *Alcestis* is often viewed as an inverted tragedy, in which the protagonist is quite ordinary, with the exception of one significant virtue that saves him. But what a virtue: to be the host of life.

Furthermore, Admetus is capable of learning, as he does throughout the course of the play. He learns how much he really loves his wife and how much he will miss her. He also learns that each man must die his own death. No one can do it for him (see 700ff). These two insights are related. Because Admetus comes to recognize that life without Alcestis is not worth living, he comes to accept the necessity of his own death (at 1080–1085). Through love of another, another who loves him so much that she would die for him, Admetus learns to confront his own death. "I lost myself when I lost her," he says (1082, Arrowsmith translation). In losing his wife and learning how much he loves her, Admetus learns that no one is replaceable, no one is interchangeable with another. Each life is uniquely its own, and so too is each death. His is not such an easy lesson. As Arrowsmith points out, much of life concerns the struggle by some to get others to die for them.[3] We may say that a soldier dies for his country, but "his country" is just an abstraction. He dies so that others may live as they wish. Because in the short run it is possible to get others to do our dying for us, the temptation is great, especially among those with vast power or those immersed in the many distractions of modern life, to act as if they could do so indefinitely. The result is chaos; increased anxiety over dying leading to a cycle of violence that can only heighten the possibility of one's own premature death.

Contrast the attitude toward death in *Alcestis* with that in *Antigone.* Creon buries the living, Antigone, and refuses to bury the dead, Antigone's brother, the fallen Polynices, thus getting it just backwards. More generally, Creon seeks to subsume death under politics, to make of it just one more political category robbed of its mystery and transcendence, as he would also subsume eros, his son's love for Antigone. As such, he is the ultimate totalitarian, seeking to include not merely family, private associations, and religion under the state, but even death itself. Yet Antigone's relation with death is also problematic. She seems death-drenched, too much in love with death. She offers many images of death as the bridegroom or the tomb as the marriage-chamber, too many to appear to be merely regretting the joys that she will not experience (see especially 890–930). She claims (in a passage no longer subject to serious dispute) that she would not die for a husband nor even children. She could find another husband or have more children (see 900–930). Only her brother deserves this sacrifice.

Although Antigone frequently refers to herself in images that confound marriage and death, it would be too simple to say that she has confused them, as the Nazi doctors confused healing and killing, or as Klein's Richard confused good and bad. Thus, it is also too simple to dismiss her as death-drenched. She is, but primarily because she lives in the world of a tyrant who reduces both love and death to affairs of state. Antigone is a woman with great potential to love and care for others and a great need to do so (she cared for her blind father, Oedipus, for about twenty years). She is, however, blocked and frustrated in her ability to realize this potential, both by the circumstances of her birth (she is a child of incest) and by Creon's tyranny. Out of love, Antigone defies Creon and buries her brother Polynices (see 910–930). The result, of course, is her own death, but only because Creon has confused love with obedience to political power (see 295, 569), so that Antigone's genuine love for another must result in her death. Antigone lives in a world in which love and death are confused, and this takes its toll on her ability to hold them separate without denying their continuity.

Richard Emil Braun argues that in serving love, Antigone actually serves the highest law of all, god's law. His strongest argument is that the chorus' praise to love (personified as *eros*) immediately follows Creon's sentence of death upon Antigone, as though to say that Antigone's love demonstrates its universal force, a power so strong that not even the tyrant can bend it to his will (see 780–805).[4] Yet as is so often the case in the tragedies, especially those of Sophocles, the chorus is confused, unable to make the proper connections, as when it calls upon Dionysus, of all gods, to save them (see 1115–1150). The gods do not love, at least not in the sense that Antigone does. They merely desire, primarily adoration and respect, and Dionysus wants these most of all. Love for another, such as Antigone offers, is the highest *human* law, the best thing, along with pity, that humans can offer. But its violation is not why the gods intervene to punish Creon. On the contrary, the speech of Tiresias, spokesman of the gods, does not justify Antigone; it does not even refer to her (see 985–1090). The gods desire that their realm not be transgressed. Antigone desires to show her love for her dead brother. Their concerns are parallel but never touch. To be sure, Antigone invokes the gods on behalf of her cause (at 450–470), but she does so because they are part of a public language that all can understand. Her motive remains private.

Yet to put it this way could be misleading, were it taken to suggest that

Antigone's is a motive confined to the privacy of her mind. Rather, she wishes to acknowledge and respect the connections that exist between her and her brother, and her and her family, connections so deep that not even death can sever them. This puts her in conflict with the tyrant, who regards all relationships as fungible in the service of the state. "There are other furrows for his plow," says Creon in a famously crass phrase regarding how his son should regard the death of his fiancée, Antigone (569). Antigone's family feeling, however, does not make her a spokesperson for higher law. On the contrary, she speaks for the oikos and its connections. But perhaps these connections of love and care, not the universal rights of man or the categorical imperative, are actually the best bulwark against tyranny. I will pursue this theme further in chapter 6. Certainly Creon is scared to death of the power of these connections, several times equating his tyranny to the proper rule of a husband over his wife (see especially 805ff).

Alcestis and *Antigone* are remarkably different in style and form. *Antigone* seems a perfect example of the ideal of noble simplicity, calm grandeur, though Friedrich Hölderlin is surely correct that a lot of wild passion and primitive God-events (*Gottesgeschehen*) lie behind the controlled Apollonian façade.[5] Conversely, *Alcestis* is sometimes regarded as a comedy, not merely because it has a happy ending but because of the buffoonery of Heracles. Yet frequently far too much is made of the outward form of the tragedies, and we should not let this obscure their main point. Each play deals with the same question, which both Creon and Admetus (at least at first) fail adequately to answer. What do we owe death? There is no more important question in all life than this. Recently a group of survivors of those who perished on Pan American Flight 103, which was blown up over Scotland several Christmases ago, couched their effort in these terms. They could not rest until they had paid their debt to the dead. But why? What does this mean?

Psychoanalysts have generally interpreted this question in terms of mourning. We grieve for the dead, we mourn, so that we shall somehow overcome our loss. Psychoanalysts differ on how mourning works, Freud holding that it is a process of reality testing in which the mourner must confront the loss over and over until he or she is convinced that it is real, and until he or she is convinced that the narcissistic satisfaction of being alive outweighs the loss. Klein, on the other hand, holds that mourning is also a process of reestablishing a secure relationship with the internal good object—that is, with images of the loved person, images that concern the relationship between that person and ourselves. Mourning is thus a doubly difficult task, in which we must accept the loss of the actual loved one while at the same time keeping alive his or her image within ourselves.[6]

In viewing the relation between life and death exclusively in terms of mourning, psychoanalysis is once again in danger of reducing a fundamental issue to a less crucial one. Mourning is important. But the relation between life and death concerns not simply how to come to terms with loss. For the tragic poets, coming to terms with death involves more than coping with the subjective experience of loss, the pain of which they hardly ignore. They care more, however, about how one acts responsibly to acknowledge and preserve, albeit in a new form, a real relationship when one of the partners is gone. In the poets' concern with death there is a devotion to the objective reality of relationships missing in most contemporary psychoanalytic accounts. Through properly acknowledging this relationship we pay our debt to death. This chapter concerns that debt and is written under the assumption that if we do not pay it we shall impoverish our lives. As the psychoanalyst Otto Rank puts it, the neurotic "refuses the loan (life) in order thus to escape the payment of the debt (death)."[7] Or as the chorus in Euripides' *Hecuba* puts it,

> And now you know:
> Life is held on loan.
> The price of life is death.
> (1028)

Insights such as these, shared by psychoanalyst and poet, suggest once again that one should not be too quick to speak of psychoanalytic reductionism. Rather, the reduction occurs in particular psychoanalytic theories. The unreductive account of Robert Jay Lifton, upon which I draw in this chapter, is thus well suited to explain the poets' perspective. By *well suited* I do not mean that Lifton's views are identical to theirs. I mean what Peter Winch means in "Understanding a Primitive Society": capable of providing a sympathetic translation. Nor is all of Freud's thought on this matter reductive, as when he writes of our civilized attitude toward death as "living psychologically beyond our means." For Freud, we should give death "a place in reality and in our thoughts which is its due."[8] By this Freud means that we should abandon all doctrines that deny the "significance of annihilation," for such doctrines are pure denial. Freud's, though, is not the answer, but only the question: What is the "significance of annihilation" for life?

DEATH AND RAGE

The Greeks—and this is part of their great attraction—raged against death. They took seriously Dylan Thomas' advice, "Do not go gentle into that good night. / Rage, rage against the dying of the light."[9] The Greeks loved the light, that image of life so central in the plays, as we see when Iphigenia asks her father, Agamemnon, who plans to sacrifice her, not to deprive her of the sweet light (Eur., *Iphigenia in Aulis,* 1218ff). And the Greeks raged against death, a conclusion that may seem surprising, given the Greek conventional wisdom reflected in the chorus of Sophocles' *Oedipus at Colonus:*

> Not to be born is best.
> The second best is to have seen the light
> And then to go back quickly whence we came.
> (1225ff)

In view of this conventional attitude, how can it be claimed that the Greeks loved life? The answer is implicit in Eugène Ionesco's question, "Why was I born if it wasn't forever?" [10] Such an attitude does not express a disgust for life. It says, as the Greek said, "I want to be happy, fulfilled, and satisfied, now and forever. If I cannot have this, then the hell with it." This attitude may be childish, even narcissistic, but it does not reject life, only its pain, central to which is life's brevity.

Similarly, one is struck in reading the plays by how much the Greeks want: not merely to be happy but to be happy throughout a lifetime, now and always. The weeping and wailing we have come to associate with the tragedies does not simply express what we have come to call a tragic view of life—that man must suffer and die, that he is a plaything of the gods, and so forth. Rather, it rejects the tragic view, or at least, it protests against it. Behind the weeping and wailing of the chorus (for generally it is the chorus) lies the desire that life be filled with happiness. "Call no man happy before he is dead," a saying attributed to Solon and invoked in the last lines of Sophocles' *Oedipus Tyrannus* (1530), captures this ideal (see too Aeschylus' *Agamemnon,* 930). Happiness (*eudaimonia*) should at least endure for a lifetime. If it does not, then it cannot be true happiness. One might also call this attitude immature or self-centered, and perhaps it is. But it is not resigned. Just the opposite: it embodies outrage at the suffering life inflicts upon us.

Although such rage is admirable, and probably necessary to enable one to deal with death, it is also terribly problematic. Transformed into violence, as it so often is, the rage only makes things worse, destroying the meaningful continuity of life and death, which comprises the only idea that can assuage the pain and terror of life in the face of death. In *The Broken Connection,* his most sustained treatment of this topic, Lifton tells the story of Jean D., a woman in her mid-thirties who had been disturbed by the thought that her husband was evil, that he was the devil, and that he would kill her. She also had the idea that her child was "the devil's child," but that she herself was God, a "reincarnation of Jesus." In the course of her therapy, she recalled a profoundly disturbing experience that happened when she was about twelve. Brought up as an unusually observant Orthodox Jew and never before having experienced any doubts, she was praying in the Synagogue on the Jewish New Year when "I suddenly thought, 'Fuck God' . . . and this idea stayed in my head [so that] . . . whenever I tried to pray, it would come back." Her omnipresent cosmology, shared by parents and relatives, was breaking down into disconnected nothingness. The result was enormous guilt, panic, and the eruption of "violent" imagery directed at god, which reflected, says Lifton, the threat to her symbolic existence. This imagery began with God, and soon gave way to the fear "that I would kill somebody . . . I'd heard on the radio about a fifteen-year-old boy who had killed someone just to see what it felt like to kill."[11]

Consider this sequence, says Lifton. The threatened collapse of Jean's vital cosmology was a symbolic death equivalent, for it would destroy any connection between her and the larger order in which her parents and relatives lived. The response was the eruption of violent and taboo thoughts, the self's first defense against an experience tantamount to a deadly attack. In turn this led to guilt, terror, and the fear of retaliation for her sin. Lifton defines Jean's guilt as "an image-feeling of responsibility for bringing about injury or disintegration or other psychological equivalents of death."[12] Even though such guilt has the quality of what Klein calls depressive guilt, Jean's response was strictly paranoid-schizoid: a fear of being attacked. It is, says Klein, common for depressive guilt to be experienced in this fashion, particularly for those developmentally on the cusp between the two positions—that is, those who experience care and concern, but lack confidence in their own reparative powers.[13] In making this connection my purpose is not to show that Lifton is "really" a Kleinian, for of course he is not. I wish rather to show that one should not exaggerate the problem of incommensurability between different psychoanalytic theories. Despite quite different theoretical commitments and terms, two analysts will frequently observe the same phenomenon in a similar fashion. Perhaps the various psychoanalytic theories are little more than glosses on (and sometimes, regrettably, defenses against) basic emotional reactions to events. Although such reactions are variable, they vary far less than the theories that explain them.

DEATH AGAINST LIFE

Jean's reaction to the breakdown of her vital cosmology sounds like nothing so much as the more anarchic plays of Euripides, thus revealing a key point. The breakdown of a vital cosmology—what I have called the Dionysian crisis—does not necessarily lead to lives of quiet desperation, the stars going out one by one. It can result in dramatic outbursts of rage and violence, fire not ice. Yet it would be mistaken to see the poets' struggle with the problem of life-death continuity strictly within the framework of the Dionysian crisis. The problem of life-death continuity, exacerbated by the crisis, possesses its own dynamics, characterized by a cycle in which violence intended to restore a sense of vitality and control over one's life (life equivalents, as Lifton calls them: images of life against death) creates an even more insecure and frightening world saturated with images of death. Violence, initiated to restore a sense of vitality against death, in the end serves not life but death. More than any other theme, the poets were concerned with cycles of violence, generally within families. The previous chapter considered mostly failed attempts to keep such violence from polluting the self. This chapter looks at how such violence destroys not merely life but the continuity of life and death and thus the meaning of both.

One sees this in Sophocles, in which the dead so often strike back to kill the living. Indeed, this theme is absent from only two extant plays, as Kitto points out, and they are late ones, *Philoctetes* and *Oedipus at Colonus*.[14] In the Homeric prelude to *Ajax*, Ajax and Hector, bitter enemies, exchange gifts. Ajax receives Hector's sword and eventually kills himself with it. Then Teucer tells how Hector was killed by means of the belt he had received from Ajax, emphasizing the parallelism of their deaths. To the dead Ajax, Teucer says, "Do you see how in time Hector, though dead, was to destroy you?" (1027ff). In *Antigone*, Antigone says of Polynices, "Ah, it is your dead hand that has taken away life from me" (871). In *Electra,* "The dead live. Those slain long ago will drain from their slayers blood flowing in the reverse direction" (1417ff). In *Oedipus Tyrannus,* Oedipus pleads with Creon to drive him into exile in Cithaeron, "which my parents, when they lived, appointed to be my tomb; that I may die at the hands of those who tried to slay me" (1451). And in *Women of Trachis,* death from the dead is the central theme, as the centaur slain by Heracles' arrow gives Deianira a blood-poison that will eventually kill Heracles, not just for the sake of the centaur's revenge but also for the Hydra's, another of Heracles' victims. It will be recalled that the Hydra's blood served as the poison on Heracles' arrow.

Kitto analyzes these reversals in terms of the principle of recoil, dike, so central to Sophocles' work. But another principle also operates—or rather, another dimension of recoil. Each play involves a confusion or reversal of life and death under the pressure of violence and hatred. Death is pursued with an excessive zeal, in the hope that it may bring or restore life. More precisely, the protagonists zealously pursue death in the hope that in controlling the deaths of others, or the circumstances surrounding these deaths such as the burials of Ajax and Polynices, they might control their own deaths. To cause another's death is to gain control over life and death itself. Or so it seems. One sees an echo of this in the psychology of blood ritual. One also sees it, says Lifton, in the psychology of many of the Nazi doctors, for whom omnipotent control over their "patients" seemed to help them defend against their own anxiety about living in a world saturated with death. As Lifton puts it, "From the standpoint of a life-death paradigm, sadism is an aspect of omnipotence, an effort to eradicate one's own vulnerability and susceptibility to pain and death."[15] Such a definition fits not merely sadism but the type of violent revenge found in the tragedies. Indeed, violence in the tragedies seems to be an attempt to achieve such symbolic life equivalents as power, vitality, respect, glory, honor—all those things that promise symbolic immortality, control over life that leaves something after death. Let us briefly review the examples of reversal in Sophocles in light of these considerations.

In *Ajax,* death is not given its due, as Agamemnon wishes to pursue his revenge beyond the grave by not allowing Ajax's burial (see 1225ff). Not giving death its due is, of course, what *Antigone* is all about. The dead are left unburied, and the living are buried, in an attempt to bring death itself under political control. The tyrant's *orge,* his rage, creates a world in which love can be pursued only by embracing death. This ironic reversal, as both Norman O. Brown and Herbert Marcuse have argued, marks not just the world of the tyrant, but much of our world as well.[16]

More than any other character in Greek tragedy with the possible exception of Euripides' Medea, Sophocles' Electra sounds like Lifton's Jean. Indeed, there are psychotic elements to Electra's hatred, in which she fantasizes that she and her sister Chrysothemis will be revered, honored, and feted if they kill Aegisthus, their mother's lover and usurper of Agamemnon's throne (see 950ff). In all likelihood they would have been destroyed had they tried. Electra's family, and above all her father, had been the center of her world. Not for nothing does Jung call the female equivalent of the Oedipus complex the Electra complex, even if this name sexualizes Electra's relationship with Agamemnon in a way that Sophocles does not intend. Sophocles suggests instead that Agamemnon's murder disrupted Electra's vital cosmology, the center and meaning of her life, and only the prospect of revenge gives her life vitality and meaning, indeed, has kept her alive all the years since the murder of her father (in Sophocles' version, Electra is past childbearing and marriageable age, see *Electra,* 165; *electra* means "unmarried"). As Electra puts it, only the death of Aegisthus "can bring me redemption from all my past sufferings" (1490–1491). Why? Only death, she mistakenly believes, can restore her to life, a life wasted in an obsession with revenge. Revenge, and the prospect of violence it promises, serve her as symbolic life equivalents, as if causing the death of another could restore the meaning of her own life.

Earlier I argued that the incest of Oedipus was a death equivalent, a return to the mother's womb. Now it is clear that virtually all of *Oedipus Tyrannus* is about the reversal of life and death—Laius tries to preserve his life by killing his son, and his son, all the while thinking he is pursuing life by leaving home and winning a kingdom, actually pursues the death intended for him long ago, albeit a symbolic one, marked by incest, blinding, and exile. Finally, we recall that Heracles' labors were actually contests aimed at overcoming death. In the course of these labors Heracles commits great violence (Homer calls him a "brutal and violent man, who did not scruple to do evil," *Iliad,* 5.403–404), which in both Sophocles' *Women of Trachis* and Euripides' *Heracles* serve not life but only death, for him or for his family.

The violent disruption and chaos caused by the pursuit of death in the name of life remain under control in Sophocles' work, in part the result of their subjection to beautiful form. A similar level of control is apparent in Aeschylus. The servant who cries in the *Libation Bearers* that "the dead are slaying the living" (886) states the problem that the *Eumenides* ostensibly resolves. One could not say this about most of the plays of Euripides, in which the pursuit of death in the name of life threatens to destroy all order. Consider Medea. She is scared to death, a point not always sufficiently appreciated. She is frightened because she is isolated. She has left her family in the east, and cannot return, having killed her brother to help Jason, her fiancé, escape. Weak and vulnerable in a strange land, an outsider, on the margins, and thus especially dependent on her husband's protection she fears the exile imposed on her, the humiliation it brings, and the weakness it forces her to confront. "You have a refuge," she says to Jason, "but I am helpless, faced with exile" (*Medea,* 610). *Isolation, weakness, vulnerability, humiliation, exile*—these are the terms she uses to characterize her situation. All, of course, are death equivalents. Through a horrible revenge she seeks to restore a sense of her own vitality and control—life equivalents. Or, as Medea puts it immediately after confessing her plan to murder her children, "Nobody shall despise *me* or think me weak or passive" (800).

Why does she kill her children? This was not her original plan, which was to "make corpses of three of my enemies, father, and daughter and my own husband" (373). Following Philip Slater, one might argue that because of the Greek system of weak and diluted marriage coupled with the subjection of women, she overly identifies her sons with Jason, her husband. The primary reason she kills her children, however, is that she determines that their murder will hurt Jason more than would death itself, and Medea above all wishes to inflict the maximum pain, to counterbalance her own. "How did they die?" she asks about Jason's bride-to-be and her father. "You would double my delight if they died in agony" (1130). The question thus becomes how to inflict this pain on Jason. To kill his children is worse than death because it means that nothing of him can continue after death. He may take longer to die than if she had killed him herself, but he will be doubly dead. Killing his children robs Jason of the chance to participate symbolically through them in the transcendent. This theme is reinforced by the appearance of Aegeus, suffering over his childlessness, to whom Medea promises children if he will provide her with a haven (see 650ff). Jason, on the other hand, will become a living corpse, who will "die without distinction," as Medea puts it (1386). Medea need not kill Jason to destroy him. She need only destroy his house and legacy (790).

Death of the Family

One sees the emphasis on family throughout the plays. The house, the family, becomes more real than its members, in part because it is more lasting. At the beginning of Aeschylus' *Agamemnon,* the house of Atreus itself seems to speak through the watchman perched on its roof, telling everything it has suffered. "The house itself, could it take voice, could tell the case most clearly," says the watchman (36–37, MacNeice translation). In the *Libation Bearers,* the chorus repeatedly emphasizes the liberation of the House of Atreus, as though it were the real protagonist (see 800ff, 819ff, 961–973). Aristotle says that tragedy is not about character but action and life (see *Poetics,* c6). Perhaps, but it remains the case that in many of the plays the family is the real actor. To kill it destroys the possibility of transcendence itself. Conversely, the *Odyssey* portrays the ideal image of the house defeating its enemies and retaining its continuity (see the appendix). Once again, the tragedies explore the anxiety, disorder, and confusion suppressed by the mythic tradition.

The relation between family continuity and death is the theme of the psychoanalyst Bennett Simon's *Tragic Drama and the Family.* The ancient Greek sought immortality, according to Simon, through the generations of family. Because the family itself contains so many destructive impulses and conflicts, so much guilt, violence, and ambivalence, however, its continuity is threatened from within. The entity that promises a type of immortality contains fragmenting forces that belie its promise. In fact, this aspect of tragedy is so central to Simon that he defines the tragic hero as one who risks all, including family and self, to propagate the family, even if he or she generally fails to do so.[17] One such hero, Clytaemestra, kills her husband, Agamemnon, in order to uphold a family principle: that its children not be sacrificed to the interests of the father. Conversely, Orestes seeks to uphold the male line of Agamemnon, even if doing so requires that he kill his mother, Clytaemestra. In fact, Simon must do a lot of twisting, pushing, and shoving to make many of the tragic protagonists fit into his mold of family propagators. Nevertheless, his basic point is valid. In order to save the family, many tragic protagonists end up annihilating it. In so doing, they subject themselves to a type of double death, doing to themselves what Medea does to Jason. In order to understand the dynamics of this process more fully, I have found it useful to return to Lifton.

Much of Lifton's work has been devoted to the psychology of mass violence.

Not only why some, such as the Nazi doctors, perpetuate it, but why survivors find it so difficult to come to terms with. A key reason, he argues, is that the mass violence threatens to destroy any continuity between life and death. Ordinarily, one can take consolation for one's own death—indeed, find meaning in one's own death—by symbolically participating, via projective identification, in persons, activities, and events that will continue after one is gone. One lives on in the memories of others, and in the lives of one's children, students, and so forth. One also lives on in projects one has begun that others will complete and in achievements that others will learn from, appreciate, and develop further. One lives on through rituals, in which future generations will share. Mass violence, such as the Holocaust or nuclear war, threatens to obliterate not merely one's life but any connection to these images of transcendence. It does so by threatening the future—by obliterating anything to which one might establish a symbolic connection. Like Jason, the survivor is not yet dead, but when he dies he will be doubly dead. One might argue that belief in a transcendent god, in whose goodness one may share, cannot be as easily obliterated. Lifton's studies do not always bear this out, and the Greeks had no such consolation.

My argument is that the poets regarded the obliteration and destruction of a family, such as the House of Atreus, in much the same way that Lifton regards mass violence, as destroying the continuity between life and death and so transforming the survivors into a type of living dead. In order to set this claim in context, it is useful to understand the precarious situation of the family in the late fifth century B.C. Since the reforms of Solon in 594 B.C. had removed judicial authority from the head of the family, the family had declined in influence at the expense of the state. As the historian Gustave Glotz put it, "At one blow the family system was shattered, undermined at its very foundations. The state was placed in direct contact with individuals. . . . Throughout the whole of the fifth century the last traces of family responsibility were being progressively abolished."[18] It is easy to overlook this in the tragedies themselves because one of the conventions of tragedy stipulates that it concern great, mythical families who precede the rise of democracy. In tragedy, these families are destroyed from within. In reality, in fifth century Athens the family was being destroyed both from within and without. The result was to separate the individual from his traditional roots, making the problems of death and transcendence ever more pressing.

Arguing that tragedy should evoke pity and fear, Aristotle claims that this is best accomplished by depictions of family violence. The best plots will thus not deviate from such traditional stories as the murder of Clytaemestra by Orestes (see *Poetics,* c14). Aristotle does not say why family violence evokes the strongest responses, he just assumes it. Or rather, he holds it to be a truth that has been discovered by trial and error and leaves it at that. "This then is the reason why, as I said before, our tragedies keep to a few families. For in their search for dramatic material it was by chance rather than by technical knowledge that the poets discovered how to gain tragic effects in their plots" (*Poet.*, c14). Perhaps now we have the technical knowledge to understand why family violence is so effective in evoking powerful emotions. Family violence distresses us because it involves not merely the destruction of loved ones but the destruction of family continuity itself, leading to a double death. But, as is usually the case with the Greeks, the survivors do not go quietly to meet the night. Like Jean, they rage and rage, in the vain hope that violence might somehow forestall extinction.

In some accounts, like Aeschylus' *Oresteia,* the rage is finally contained by finding a place for the displaced survivors within the larger family of the polis. In others—Euripides' *Orestes* springs to mind—anger transforms the survivors into virtual Furies who would destroy anyone left after the death of the head of the family. It is significant that Euripides' play opens with Orestes having been in a death-like sleep for six days since killing his mother. Only violence, directed first against his own paranoid projections, the Furies, and finally against almost all who have survived, seems capable of restoring his sense of vitality. Against such rage, neither polis nor family can defend itself, as Orestes seeks to burn down his ancestral house (see 1543). Only the gods can contain such rage, and then in such a transparent fashion that we know the resolution to be false. Aristotle calls Euripides the most tragic of poets, because no matter how faulty "his management of other points," his plays are always concerned with the violence occurring within a handful of families (*Poet.*, c13). Fifteen of the nineteen extant plays of Euripides involve the death, murder, or sacrifice of children.

Death and the Imagery of Transcendence

It is a striking thing, the way the dead are generally portrayed in the tragedies. They are so very, very dead (see Eur.: *Suppliant Women,* 760–945; *Trojan Women,* 640, 1150–1260; *Hecuba,* 205–210; *Alcestis,* 385, 915; Soph., *Electra,* 1130). This is something that cannot be shown simply with quotations. It is a feeling one has in reading the poets' accounts of various confrontations with the dead that the spirit (*psyche*) and physical body are so closely linked that the death of the body means the end of everything. In part the feeling has to do with the loss of continuity that occurs when not just an individual but a family or polis is destroyed. Thus, in Euripides' *Trojan Women,* Hecuba mourns the loss not only of her child but of all Troy, and with it any prospect of continuity, when she says: "The dead, I say, are as if they had not been born. . . . Polyxena is as dead as if she had never seen this life" (640). No sense that the child might live on in the memories of others is apparent. One cannot explain this attitude strictly in terms of the mentality of, say, the Holocaust survivor; it appears in domestic contexts as well, as when Admetus says regarding death, "*Then* and *now*: a gulf so great it seems two wholly different unconnected worlds" (Eur., *Alcestis*, 915, Arrowsmith translation).

As David Claus points out, there was a Greek tendency going back at least to Homer and still influential in the fifth century to render everything psychic corporal, making no clear distinction between them. For example, Greeks characterized most emotions in terms of their physical location in the body, as we speak of heartache. Thus, such Greek terms as *thumos, menos, kardia, noos, phren/phrenes,* what Claus calls soul words, referred to both a bodily organ and an emotion. Nor is it always clear which was the primary meaning, Claus suggesting that the ancient Greek did not make the mind-body distinction we do.[19] We see a reflection of this in Plato's *Phaedo,* in which the existence of the soul (always rendered as *psyche*) is never questioned by Socrates' interlocutors, in part because they identify it so closely with the body. They doubt only whether it can survive the death of the body. Perhaps it just goes up in smoke. Or perhaps it is like the tune from a musical instrument, not identical with the instrument but depending upon it for existence. In the Kerameikos Museum in Athens I found the following inscription on the tombstone of Ampherete, a relief sculpture of her and her grandchild made at the end of the fifth century B.C.: "I am holding here the child of my daughter beloved whom I hold on my lap. When alive we beheld the light of the sun, and now I am holding it dead, being dead myself." That's it, there is nothing more, nothing continues, nothing remains, nothing carries on. One tombstone proves nothing, of course. But it captures a way of thinking about the dead that is present in the plays as well.

Consider the modes of symbolic transcendence to which Lifton refers: membership in a continuing family, which may be extended to include polis or nation; participation in a religious tradition, which may or may not include a belief in life after death; creative activities that transcend the individual; acceptance of one's place in a larger natural order or cycle; and experiential transcendence, a sense of being one with the All, in which both time and death disappear, Freud's "oceanic feeling."[20] Only the first mode was available to the average Greek (or at least to the average Greek as he was portrayed in the tragedies, which is my concern), and it was limited to the immediate family—transcendence through symbolic identification with children and grandchildren. Furthermore, family offers an especially vulnerable means of transcendence, as Simon's *Tragic Drama and the Family* emphasizes.

Accounts of Hades in the tragedies, as well as elsewhere in ancient literature and iconography, are inconsistent. Nevertheless, most accounts have a common theme that changed remarkably little from Homer to the fifth century, according to Robert Garland in *The Greek Way of Death.* The dead in Hades are powerless, lacking in strength (*menos*); nor do they possess wits, even though soul (*psyche*) and image (*eidolon*) remain. This is supported by the fragment of a lost play by Euripides, the *Kresphontes*, which states: "For if he dwells beneath the earth, among those who are no more, he would have no strength." Or as Bennett Simon puts it in *Mind and Madness*, the shade that survives in Hades is the split-off, impotent self. Nor do the dead seem to retain their personality, a claim Garland makes largely on the basis of a grammatical analysis of terms used to refer to the dead. "Sterile, deadlocked in time, conscious of loss, out of touch with the world above, lacking the sinews and strength of the living, yet preserving everlastingly their wounds, their rancor, their hatred"[21]—these are the terms used by Garland to characterize the dead in Hades, terms which give the cliché "a fate worse than death" new meaning.

There are, to be sure, stories about life in Hades, including family reunions, and even sex among the dead (never do the dead bear children). Antigone, for example, hopes but is far from certain that she will see her mother, father, and brother in Hades (see Soph., *Antigone*, 898–900). The overall picture of Hades itself was inconsistent and vague, as Garland points out, and thus mirrored the Greek view of the life of the psyche in Hades. Far from a comfort, continued existence in Hades seems utterly terrifying, a summary vision of the most horrifying death equivalents the culture could muster (with, interestingly, one exception: the dead are not mutilated). This is perhaps why most Greeks by the late fifth century B.C. apparently disbelieved in Hades (see, for example, Plato, *Phaedo*, 70a; Eur.: *Trojan Women*, 636, 1248; *Helen*, 1421). To conceive of death as mere extinction may have actually represented cultural progress in coming to terms with its terrors.

Hannah Arendt argues that the Greek sought immortality in noble words and great deeds that would live forever.[22] Thucydides' account of Pericles' famous funeral oration, in which Pericles promises that the deeds of the fallen will live on in the memories of the citizens seems to support Arendt's view (see *History*, 2.43). But this view does not play a major role in the extant tragedies, except perhaps in Aeschylus' *Seven against Thebes*, that "strange, archaic play," as David Grene puts it, and Sophocles' *Ajax*. To be sure, in Euripides' *Alcestis*, as in other plays, the chorus refers to how a heroic deed, in this case the sacrifice of Alcestis, will cause her memory to live forever, "a song that does not die" (445). It should not be overlooked, however, that Alcestis takes no comfort in this (435–460). Nor does Antigone take any comfort in the praise and fame that the chorus tells her will be hers. Instead she responds with an image of Tantalus' daughter being covered by slowly petrifying rock and strangled by ivy (see Soph., *Antigone*, 815–830). Undying fame seems but cold comfort to those soon to die, serving more to ease the anxieties of those who will live a little longer. The ethic of immortal words and deeds to which Arendt refers is actually part of an older, archaic, heroic tradition, whose influence was much stronger on the form of the plays than on the content. Furthermore, even within the heroic tradition the promise of immortality seems often to have been less important than some moderns idealize it to have been. As Simon points out, when Odysseus visits the shade of Achilles in Hades, he finds that Achilles would gladly trade a mundane life as a serf for immortal honor. Not only that, Achilles' chief interest lies not in his own heroic reputation but the fate of his son (see *Odyssey*, 11:482–495).

Tragedy, as Vernant states, is about subjecting heroic tradition to the standards of the citizen. Such standards concern cooperation, *phronesis* (tempered prudence), self-restraint, and so forth, ideas absolutely essential to the construction of a civilized polis, as the case of Ajax demonstrates so clearly, but hardly the stuff of legend. Pericles' funeral oration may invoke this heroic tradition to some effect in wartime, but he is evoking the ideals of a lost and dying world, which in the fifth century provided no real alternative to the family for the carrier of the imagery of transcendence. Nor should it be overlooked that Pericles mentions neither a single name nor a singular heroic deed. A key reason is that the Athenian army's hoplite phalanx, which depended on group cohesion (each man protected the other with his shield) not individual excellence, made battle characterized by the conflict between heroes, like that in the *Iliad,* militarily obsolete. In Pericles' speech the dead soldiers are anonymous servants of the polis, remembered only by their families. This may be good for the polis, evidence that the socially disruptive agonal culture was on the wane, but it is not so good for the heroic tradition that Arendt evokes. Nor does it provide much cultural support for the construction of connections between life and death.

What about the famous mystery cults, it might be asked. Did they not promise immortality and thus allow the Greek to participate in some combination of Lifton's second and fifth modes of transcendence (participation in a religious tradition and experiential transcendence)? Certainly the mysteries were active at the time of the tragedies, having been a force since the sixth century B.C. This in itself suggests that the heroic tradition had been dying for some time, for the search for private salvation is incompatible with it. Although the mysteries of Eleusis are the most well-known, there were over six hundred cults, in addition to the Orphics. An important part of many, though hardly all, of the mysteries was the promise that death would lose its terror, the initiate being guaranteed a blessed life in another world. But the mysteries play almost no role in the tragedies, with the exception of Euripides' last play, the *Bacchae.* The Bacchic cult seems to have included a promise of an afterlife. An inscription whose date is about 400 B.C. concludes, "And then the subjects of the Chthonian King will have pity and will give you to drink from the lake of recollection. . . . And indeed you are going a long, sacred way which other *mystai* and *bacchoi* gloriously walk."[23] Nevertheless, the promise of an afterlife does not seem to have been central to the Bacchic cults, and once again it plays no role in Euripides' account. To be sure, it seems likely that the conventions of the tragic form, which (often quite anachronistically) placed contemporary events and conflicts within a mythic context, may have resulted in a down-playing of the significance of the mysteries in everyday life in the fifth century. With a little imagination, however, one can usually see the press of contem-porary events on the tragedies. Certainly the Peloponnesian War influenced many of the plays. But it is hard to see even the faint consolation of the promise of a blessed afterlife in the works of the poets. The view of Sophocles' Electra, that death is nothingness, dominates (*Electra,* 1130).

PAYING OUR DEBT TO DEATH

The Greeks, evidently, were relatively weak in the imagery of transcendence. The idea they cherished, family continuity, was vulnerable not only to natu-ral forces (one historian has estimated that of one hundred young men aged twenty, only twenty would survive until sixty years of age[24]) but to the intra-psychic forces analyzed by Simon: rage, ambivalence, guilt, and desire, as well as to the social changes in the status of the family highlighted by Glotz. Today the modern, rationalized world also lacks strong images for transcendence. As Jean Baudrillard puts it, the dead are thrown outside of the symbolic circu-lation of the group. Indeed, one might regard old-age homes and the like as de-signifiers, in which those soon to die are isolated, so as to deny them the symbolic significance that comes from standing one step closer to the death that we all face. The Greeks did not have this option. Death was omnipresent, far more frequent among the young than it is today, and far closer too, not tucked away in hospitals and retirement homes. The pressure to make sense of death was greater for the ancient Greek, for denial was more difficult, but the Greek culture lacked sufficient resources. Thus came all their rage and violence, as though they might conquer death by causing death—an especially profound and destructive confusion and reversal.

The situation of the ancient Greeks was thus similar to and different from our own. Similar, in the sense that they too were weak in images of tran-scendence; different, in that their image of death itself was overwhelming, in part because their culture provided far fewer opportunities for organized de-nial. Death remained an awe-inspiring event in the sense of the Greek term *deinos,* "wonderful," "fearful," and "terrible" all at once. The ancient Greek was under much more immediate pressure to come to terms with death than we are, which is evidently why denial and repression regarding death were not as common in their culture as in our own.

Generally the poets confine themselves to depicting the catastrophic consequences of this confusion, as though to say, "See, this is not the way; it can only make things worse, as though you were trying to heal man by killing him." Although the cultural resources did not exist for the poets to transform the meaning of death and so create entirely new connections between the living and the dead, this was perhaps an advantage. For it meant that they (and increasingly we) were forced to find the transcendent in the immanent. I shall call this the middle way, and in this vein consider Euripides' *Suppliant Women,* which is concerned with what we owe death and why. With their formulation of this issue the poets made their greatest contribution to the problem of how to connect life and death without denying their difference.

The history of Western thought since the poets, beginning with Plato and Aristotle and running through the Medieval Christian reception and transformation of these philosophers (like Thomism), has concerned transcending death via the soul's participation in universals. As Plato puts it in the *Phaedrus* (250a–252b), the soul always longs to return to the realm of true Being whence it came, there to consort with Being forever. The Greek poets had no such comfort. Increasingly neither do we in the modern, rationalized world. Freud would face annihilation heroically . . . and alone. The poets seek to render death in social and human terms. They do not wish to deny its otherness in order better to subsume it under politics, as Creon would, or even under social and sexual hierarchy, as Admetus would. Yet even these perverse strategies reveal a genuine need to confront and understand the otherness of death in human terms. The poets seek new ways to do this, ways that neither deny otherness or death nor simply rage against it. This is their task, and ours: to render death in human terms, without denying that it is the most inhuman thing in the world. In doing this the poets avoid the arrogance of humanism without becoming antihuman. They take a middle way.

Many have wondered what Alcestis might have said after her silence of three days, most suggesting that she would have mildly remonstrated her husband, who was already wavering in his promise never to possess another woman (in Eur., *Alcestis,* 1000–1120).[25] To see the issue in these terms is to view it in terms of what makes us most comfortable, because they are so familiar: the all-too-human tensions between husband and wife that remind us that life goes on. What else Alcestis might have spoken of is death, telling us its meaning in human terms, as only she who has experienced it could. But we shall never know. The closest we can come to rendering death in human terms is the funeral ritual (*kedeia*). The poets sought to reinterpret funeral ritual, finding in it sources of connection between life and death that did not depend upon the heroic legacy of noble words and great deeds. They did this even as they wrote of the deaths of heroes and the sufferings of those who loved them. Such ambivalence marks the pattern of the plays, in which heroic themes and figures are subjected to the standards of the polis.

Suppliant Women

Euripides' play addresses the question of what we owe the dead and why, for in paying this debt properly, neither ignoring it nor paying too much, as Sophocles' Antigone does, we construct a connection between life and death. To be sure, the question what do we owe the dead is not the same as what do we owe death, but it is close enough. The dead are death's representatives on earth, so to speak. In finding a place for the dead in our lives, we find a place for death too.

The play concerns the efforts of the mothers of the seven warriors who fought unsuccessfully against Thebes to convince Theseus, king of Athens, to force Creon, ruler of Thebes, to release their sons' bodies for burial. At first Theseus balks, as the seven were aggressors. But his mother, Aethra, convinces him to help, for in death it hardly matters who was right or wrong. Creon hesitates, and Theseus launches a successful attack on Thebes, forcing the return of the bodies for proper funeral rites. Because more men were killed in Theseus' attack on Thebes for the sake of the bodies, the question of what we owe the dead and why intensifies. Whatever it is, it is apparently worth more than mere life. According to this play we owe the dead proper funeral rites. In denying these rites, Euripides' Creon exemplifies the same hubris as does Sophocles' Creon, seeking to extend the control of the state, as well as its vengeance, to realms in which it does not belong. This, though, is only part of the story, the negative part, as it were, concerned with the failure to respect the boundary between the realms of life and death that treats death as just one more instrument of politics.

The other part is that we owe the dead proper funeral rites in order to enfold them symbolically in the continuity of life and death. Freud approvingly quotes the dramatist Christian Grabbe, who consoles his dying hero with the reassurance that "we cannot fall out of this world." Such consolation, continues Freud, invokes "a feeling of an indissoluble bond, of being one with the external world as a whole."[26] Yet death threatens precisely this bond. In death we risk falling out of the world forever.

Funeral rites serve to "hold" the dead in precisely the sense that this term is employed by D. W. Winnicott, an analyst influenced by Klein. Originally used to refer to the first stage of the child's relationship with its mother, holding (though cradling is the paradigm, holding includes all aspects of the mother's responsiveness) serves to contain the infant's anxiety. Even though the sources of this anxiety are virtually ineffable, it is believed that very early the young child experiences image-feelings of coming apart under the stress of his or her own rage and desire, the consequence of his or her nascent ego being weaker than his or her passions. Such image-feelings of fragmentation constitute the first, and probably the most profound, symbolic death equivalent. Through her holding, the mother in effect says to her young child, "I can contain your anxiety, rage, desire, and despair, even if you cannot." It is Winnicott's insight that far more mature, symbolically mediated interactions also constitute a form of holding, for example, an insightful, well-timed analytic interpretation that recognizes the analysand's deepest anxieties and responds to them. Conversely, when the analyst's attention lapses Winnicott says that "the mind has dropped the patient."[27] Similarly, a cultural ritual may be a form of holding, containing the members' anxieties by translating them into a shared language and so allowing shared defenses to be constructed against them.

If cradling is the first act of holding, funeral rites are the last. From the cradle to the grave we never outgrow the need to be held, though ideally more abstract, symbolically mediated forms of holding come to substitute partially— never completely—for the physical act. Through funeral rites we say to those who survive that they too will not be forgotten in death. They will not be allowed to fall out of the world. Just as we enfold the bodies of the newly dead in ritual, so too we shall enfold our memories of their lives into our own, so that the images we have of them do not fall out of the world either. With these rites we state that our minds will not drop the dead. Evidently no consolation to the dead themselves, these rites address the fears of those soon to die— that is, of us all. In this context, the "feeling of an indissoluble bond" to which Freud refers is the bond between life and death, the continuity of which Lifton writes. It is not indissoluble at all, however, but most fragile, which makes the rituals of death even more important.

Recently I attended a funeral that began with the cantor singing a five-thousand-year-old funeral dirge. The dirge served not simply to hold and enfold the deceased in our memories. It also enfolded the deceased together with the mourners in history, a history so ancient that it reached toward eternity. The song of the cantor was, I believe, as Dionysian as any Greek chorus, serving for a moment to take the mourners (or at least this mourner) out of the world, making the living and the dead alike participants in eternity. This too is holding, in which we reinterpret the relationship between the living and dead, adding one more soul to the account of eternity, while acknowledging that soon we too must pay our debt. Through rituals such as this each is given a place, even if the occupants are constantly changing, in the Great Chain of Being and Nonbeing.

A number of the funeral rites portrayed in the tragedies involve a physical act of holding or containing the body in much the same way our coffins and graves do. In Euripides' *Trojan Women,* it is of great significance for the participants that the body of Astyanax, Hector's child and Hecuba's grandson, be properly washed, wrapped, dressed, crowned with flowers, and laid on Hector's shield, as though the shield could protect him, even though it did not protect Hector (see 1110–1250). Make no mistake, this elaborate ritual has nothing to do with preparing the child for entry into the nether world. In her despair, Hecuba remains convinced that death is nothingness and such rituals "an empty glorification left for those who live" (1250). Rather, we enfold and hold them in ritual so that we might enfold and hold them in the continuity of our lives, so that in turn we might find a place for our own lives in a history that points toward eternity. Such rituals become empty only when this continuity is itself threatened, as it was for Hecuba's family. Yet even then—or rather, especially then—the funeral ritual becomes the most important act of the Trojan women, the only thing they can do rather than suffer.

Holding is symbolized in ritual by dramatic acts like laying Astyanax's body upon Hector's shield but also through the whole process of washing and wrapping the body, cleansing and covering it, and so protecting it, in the sense of shielding it from exposure. Doing this was common (see descriptions in Eur., *Hecuba*, 610; Soph., *Antigone*, 1203). As both Burkert and Garland emphasize, washing and dressing the body, then placing a wreath on its head, was at the heart of Greek funeral rites.[28] It is this, ultimately, that the funeral rite is concerned with, whether the body is then buried or burned. Why? So that the dead need not be ashamed, which means so that their nakedness and vulnerability will not be exposed for all to see. For who is more vulnerable than the recently dead, except perhaps those soon to die? Rather than having said, moments before his death, "My God, my God, why hast thou forsaken me?" some witnesses claim Jesus cried, "My God, my God, why hast thou shamed me?" (Mark 15:34).[29] To be hung on a cross and left to die represents one of the most shameful deaths imaginable, in the sense that the victim's isolation, vulnerability, weakness, and nakedness are exposed, just as if his body had been left for the dogs. It is no accident that those about to die ask that their shame be covered, their vulnerability concealed. This too is holding.

Washing the body, so important to Greek funeral rituals that Oedipus' body was washed immediately before his death for it would not be available to wash after (see Soph., *Oedipus at Colonus*, 1595ff), seems to have an additional significance, though one should be cautious in separating washing from the rest of the funeral rites. The Greeks, we have seen, viewed the dead in an almost uncanny fashion, finding difficulty in separating the spirit of the dead from its body. As important as the body was to the Greeks in life, so too was it in death. Overvaluing the physical body, though, seems to have made internalization of the dead (that is, internalization of symbolic images of the dead) particularly difficult. Elaborate funerary treatments of the body, designed to cleanse its wounds and purify it, may have made internalization easier. Although the dead body and spirit were still tightly bound, the body itself was rendered less gruesome and uncanny, its image less threatening to internalize (See Soph., *Ajax*, 910–925). Washing epitomizes this symbolism, but internalization is the task of the funeral rites as a whole. As Lifton puts it, "the great problem for survivors in all cultures is to convert 'homeless souls,' particularly those of the recent dead, into comfortably enshrined or immortalizing souls. Funeral ceremonies are rites of passage precisely for this purpose. *What is involved is the symbolic transformation of a threatening, inert image (of the corpse) into a vital image of eternal continuity (the soul)—or of death as absolute severance to death as an aspect of continuous life.*"[30]

Prometheus Bound

Aeschylus' *Prometheus Bound* is a founding myth, concerned not only with the founding of ritual or even with the founding of civilization, its most obvious concern, but also with the founding of a new relation between man and death.[31] What Prometheus gave to man is, of course, important. He gave fire, symbolizing not merely technology but also the social skills, such as justice, with which to build a city (the Greeks understood such skills as a type of technology, a *techne*). Prometheus' gift leads Herbert Marcuse to characterize Prometheus as "the trickster and (suffering) rebel against the gods, who creates culture at the price of perpetual pain. He symbolizes productiveness, the unceasing effort to master life."[32] Against Prometheus, Marcuse sets Orpheus and Narcissus, images of effortless joy and fulfillment. Equally important, however (and much less frequently remarked upon) is what Prometheus took from man: man's knowledge of the time of his own death. In its place he gave blind hope (see 250). Prometheus' subsequent gift of prophecy did not include restoration of this knowledge and is perhaps little more than an elaboration of blind hope (see 480ff). Because the gift of ignorance and blind hope belongs to the mythological tradition itself and is not just an invention of Aeschylus (although in Plato's *Gorgias* Zeus takes back the knowledge, 523d–e), it seems important to consider why it has gotten such short shrift.

The Greek poets, like the Greek historians (see, for example, Thucydides, *History,* 5.103), are ambivalent about the value of hope. They consider it necessary, yet it often leads man to self-deception and ruin. Their concern is seen in Sophocles' *Antigone* (615ff) but also in Hesiod, who leaves unclear in his *Works and Days* (95–105) why hope (*Elpis*) was left behind in Pandora's box. Is it because it is something good for man or something bad? Yet Prometheus' gift of a portion of blind hope seems strictly good. And it is only a portion. He takes from man knowledge of the hour of his death but not knowledge of death itself. Had he taken that, man would have been no more than an animal, akin to the scurrying ants that Prometheus compares him to before giving him his wits (see *Prometheus Bound,* 450). With the knowledge that he will die, man is raised above the animals and given the possibility to construct a symbolic continuity between his life and the lives of those who preceded him and those who will follow and thus to make his own life meaningful. Were he to know the exact time and circumstances of his death, man might well be too afraid, too discouraged, too paralyzed by its approach to construct a world of meaning in which he might symbolically participate even after his own death. Or as Port (so full of life, so soon to die) puts it to Kit in Paul Bowles's *Sheltering Sky*: "Death is always on the way, but the fact that you don't know when it will arrive seems to take away from the finiteness of life. It's the terrible precision that we hate so much."[33] Is this not Prometheus' greatest gift, to have taken away some of the finiteness of life, so that we might struggle with transcendence? Not fire, not technology, not even the civic virtues and skills necessary to build a polis. Rather, Prometheus offers us the combination of knowledge and ignorance that gives man the chance to make a meaningful world out of one that threatens to destroy the meaning and purpose of every man's life by killing him.

Seen from this perspective, *Prometheus Bound* provides a new standard from which to judge the achievements of society. Technology, material comfort, an extended and less painful life, even civic justice may be seen strictly as means, however valuable. The end is none of these things. The standard of achievement by which a civilization may be measured is how these achievements allow us to construct better symbolic mediations between life and death, for in these mediations the real meaning of life resides. I mean this quite literally. If we do not know the meaning of our deaths, we do not know the meaning of our lives. And if we do not know that, then what is the point? Of anything? Seen from this perspective, perhaps Western industrial civilization represents not civilization's peak but only its detour, for we have forgotten the goal and substituted means for the end.

Although the poets only begin to take advantage of the opportunity offered by Prometheus, they suggest a powerful critique of any social theory that does not make death its chief concern. Consider, for example, the thesis of Max Weber, who characterizes modernity in terms of its substitution of means for ends, so that in the end man comes to live in a world of icy polar darkness, an iron cage.[34] One lives in darkness because one does not know how to die. Or rather, how to live in the face of death. The means of living supplant the end of dying well. Sophocles' "ode to man" in *Antigone* argues that man can conquer all but death; but because he cannot conquer death he transforms all of his marvelous achievements into rage or denial against death, and thus spoils life itself. He seeks to turn death into one more social and political category, as Creon does. Marcuse appreciates the value of joy and eros as an alternative to labor and self-sacrifice, and in this sense generates a powerful critique of Weber, but he does not really address the larger problematic within which Weber's work, or indeed any comprehensive social theory, takes place: how is one to live well in the face of death? "For death is the final negativity of time, but 'joy wants eternity,'" says Marcuse.[35] True enough—for us, and maybe even more so for the Greeks, the want of joy for eternity being the source of their rage. Nevertheless, as long as he remains mortal, man must continue to find a middle way between negativity and eternity, a way characterized by the construction of symbolic mediations between life and death.

On the subject of a middle way Marcuse has little to offer, suggesting that in a world suffused with eros, death itself will lose its terror.[36] The resemblance of this solution to that of the Bacchic mystery cults should not be overlooked. If, however, Marcuse does not find a middle way, neither do most social theorists less profound than he. For all his concern with liberating men and women from Weber's iron cage so that they might construct meaningful lifeworlds together, Jürgen Habermas would leave the problem of consolation in the face of death to traditional religion. There is, for example, no discussion of death in Habermas' masterwork, *Theorie des kommunikativen Handelns,* which concerns freeing the lifeworld from the tyranny of what Weber calls *Zweckrationalität,* or means-ends rationality.

As though death were not the most important barrier of all to the construction of a meaningful life! Two of the most perspicacious social theorists of the day have little to say about the middle way but neither does Plato, nor the generations of Neoplatonists who follow, all of whom seek to transcend death. It seems that the middle way is accessible neither to philosophies of transcendence nor to social theory but only to a perspective as profound as that of the poets: one that seeks no escape from this world, while avoiding the reduction of life, as well as death, to strictly human categories.

What is so difficult, but so important, is to humanize death without denying its otherness, an otherness that renders it sacred. The poets' humane anti-humanism may not be essential for the task but certainly makes it easier. Antigone pays too much to death, or at least for too long. Creon would pay nothing, except as it serves the state, whereas Admetus would get others to pay his debt. The suppliant women and Hecuba, on the other hand, seem to know the price. Not simply because as the guardians of life and death in the oikos they stand one step closer to eternity, though this has been argued, Garland for one showing that Greek women were far more intimately involved with the details of funeral and burial than were men.[37] Rather, I argue that the compulsion to which Greek women's lives were subject did not support the illusion that they could somehow cheat necessity.

Life

PART 3

Responsibility without Freedom

CHAPTER 5

This saturation (no other word will quite do) of Greek tragedy . . . in
the idiom of necessity and force is, in my judgment, the single most
obvious (but quite unexplored) fact of Greek tragedy.
—William Arrowsmith

In Euripides' *Hippolytus,* Phaedra says that our lives are generally worse
than the quality of our minds (*phroneo*) warrants (375). This certainly
seems to be true in her case. She is driven mad with desire for her
step-son, Hippolytus, by Aphrodite, who seeks to punish Hippolytus
for rejecting the charms of love. As is so often the case in the tragedies, Phaedra is an innocent bystander, destroyed in the gods' pursuit of
another. One might argue that from a psychoanalytic perspective there
are no innocent bystanders, Phaedra least of all. Her own unconscious
desires get her into trouble, eventually causing her to leave a vindictive,
and untrue, suicide note, which claims that Hippolytus raped her. But
I want to argue that the Greek view has much to recommend it. To be
sure, Phaedra defines the mind that gets such a bad deal rather narrowly,
as similar to what we might call the conscious mind or ideal self. Her
view may be too narrow in some respects, yet it nonetheless captures an
important truth about how we experience our lives and our passions.

  Even those who consider it important to respect the difference between
the Greek view of the self and our own are often quite condescending
toward the former (unless otherwise noted, *Greek* refers to the view of
the poets, which I presume comes much closer to that of the Greek in
the street than does the view of the philosophers). Thus Jean-Pierre Vernant, deeply concerned with preserving fidelity to the text, writes that
"the very way that tragedy developed bears witness to the relative inconsistency of the Greek category of the agent and its lack of internal
organization."[1] Similarly, John Jones, who concludes that "it turns out
to be our bad luck that Greek tragedy is superficially intelligible in a
modern way," interprets Sophocles' Antigone in just such a modern way.
Her "apprehension of self in absent circumstances is . . . shifting and
feeble. . . . In short, she knows no adequate modern 'you' which would
give an adequate modern sense to the question: 'What would you do if it
were a husband or child lying unburied?'"[2] Even though Vernant's and
Jones's interpretations recognize the difference between the Greek view

and our own, they do not, I shall argue, respect this difference. Rather, they render the Greek view inferior, almost childish in its simplicity, narrowness, and lack of subjunctive imagination ("If I were in this position, then I would . . ."). Why? Primarily, it seems, because the protagonists of tragedy frequently fail to internalize responsibility for their own passions and desires, making excuses for them as though they were the acts of gods.

Accused of taking drugs and lying about it, Mayor Marion Barry of Washington, D. C., said, after being caught, "That was the disease talking. I did not purposefully do that to you. I was a victim." More than once Barry has been compared with a hero in Greek tragedy, a basically noble character with a tragic flaw. Ignoring for a moment the question of whether this fits *any* of the tragic heroes (today most agree that Aristotle meant just what he said when he characterized *hamartia* as a big mistake, not a flaw in character[3]), it may be useful to pursue this comparison for a moment. The locus classicus of the "that was the disease talking" excuse is Agamemnon's statement in Homer's *Iliad*. Agamemnon, it will be recalled, compensated himself for the loss of his mistress by robbing Achilles of his. "Not I," he states afterwards, "was the cause of this act, but Zeus and my portion, and the Erinys who walks in darkness: they it was who in the assembly put wild *ate* in my understanding, on that day when I arbitrarily took Achilles' prize from him. So what could I do? Deity will always have its way" (19.86ff).

Impatient modern readers, as Dodds points out in *The Greeks and the Irrational,* generally have little sympathy for Agamemnon's apology, seeing it as a gross evasion of responsibility. But it is no evasion of responsibility in the judicial sense. On the contrary, it is on these same grounds—that he was unfree, compelled—that Agamemnon offers compensation to Achilles.[4] "But since I was blinded by *ate* and Zeus took away my understanding, I am willing to make my peace and give abundant compensation" (*Il.,* 19.137ff; also see 9.119ff). The fact that he was unfree, compelled, seems to make it easier, not harder, for Agamemnon to accept responsibility. This is what moderns find so difficult to come to terms with. Were Marion Barry truly the tragic hero with whom he has been compared, one who accepts responsibility in the absence of freedom, he would have said something like, "That was not me. That was the disease talking. For this reason I take full responsibility, and shall spend the rest of my life in exile." Not because it really was not the disease talking but because it was.

Charles Krauthammer, psychiatrist and columnist, wrote a piece on all this, arguing that Barry's defense is hogwash. We are discovering genetic correlates of violence, he says, yet we do not let killers off the hook. "The principle is so elementary that, were it not so abused, I should be embarrassed to spend a thousand words defending it."[5] But elementary though it may be, he never tells us what this principle is. I am not sure that we know it. Or rather, I am not sure we know *why* we hold people responsible for acts done under compulsion. The poets knew.

Consider the case of a young man, one of ten thousand children born to cocaine-addicted mothers each year in New York City. Imagine that his mother is sixteen and continues to take drugs, having no idea how to meet his needs. His father is long gone. Imagine (and it does not take much imagination) that the schools and social services are so underfunded and overwhelmed that they can do nothing extra for this young man, nothing extra to meet his special needs. Imagine too that he has spent his entire youth in a run-down neighbor-hood, with few jobs, lots of drugs, and a few big-time drug dealers who seem to live like the people on primetime television. Finally, imagine that he gets caught up in drug dealing, finally kills someone, and is arrested and bound over for trial. What is a just resolution? Was this young man truly free to choose to do otherwise? Or rather, was his position not closer to that characterized by Homer, in which his portion (*moira*) was such as to put wild *ate* in his understanding? For me, he fits Homer's scheme. He was not free. Nonetheless, he is responsible for what he has done and should be punished. But that is not fair, it might be argued. In fact, it is tragic. Absolutely. That is the point. Tragedy means, above all else, that people are responsible without being free. Of all the definitions of tragedy, this is the only one that I accept, because this is the only one that fits all the tragedies and the only one that is true. It remains true even though it is also the case that those who allow young men to grow up like this—which means most of us—are also responsible.

MOIRA, DAIMON, ANANKE, RESPONSIBILITY, AND FREEDOM

Toward the close of Sophocles' *Oedipus Tyrannus,* after the suicide of Jocasta and Oedipus' self-blinding, the chorus asks "What madness came upon you? Who was the *daimon* that lept, with a bound exceeding the extreme, upon that *moira* of yours that was already a *daimon*'s evil work?" (1299–1302). To this Oedipus answers that many of his sufferings were the work of a god, Apollo, "But it was none other's hand that [blinded me]: it was I" (1331–1332). It is sometimes held that Oedipus is saying, in effect, that although Apollo caused his sufferings, Oedipus himself takes full responsibility for poking out his own eyes. This seems to be supported by comments in *Oedipus at Colonus,* where Oedipus suggests that in blinding himself he was too harsh on himself (see 438). Winnington-Ingram's careful analysis of the Greek text, however, shows that such a distinction is too sharp, too modern.[6] Nor should one overlook the most obvious point of all in this regard: that Tiresias, spokesman of the gods, predicts the events that unfold in the play that culminate in Oedipus' blinding:

"the eyes that now see clear shall see henceforward endless night" (*Oedipus Tyrannus*, 420–421, Storr translation). This too was part of the plan.

What distinction, then, is the chorus actually making? *Moira* is our "portion," or "fate." But not just ours. Zeus too is constrained by moira (see Aesch., *Prometheus Bound*, 520). *Daimon* also is a measure of man's fate. This can be seen etymologically, in which the root idea of *daimon*, *da-* (to share), relates to the whole cycle of words that since Homer's time refer to humankind's portion, share, or lot: *moira*, *moros*, *aisa*, *heimarmene*, and so forth. Nor is there any fundamental conceptual difference between *daimon*, *moira*, and such other familiar fate-words as *ananke* (necessity) and *tyche* (chance). But if a daimon is man's fate, it is more personal than these abstractions, like the daimon of Socrates that kept him out of trouble (see Plato, *Apology*, 31d–e; *Euthyphro*, 3b). As Joel Schwartz puts it,

> To the earlier religious poets a man's *daimon* was a distant and totally alien force that sprang from the blue and frustrated his intentions, his very personality. To Sophocles a man and his *daimon* are on much more intimate terms. It has attended him from birth and has from the beginning shared in constituting his personality: it does not "frustrate" his intentions because from childhood it has been active in shaping the entire range of characteristic responses from which his intentional acts derive.[7]

It is terribly important, however, to draw the right conclusions from this. A daimon is a different kind of fate, more personal, more akin to one's character. But that does not mean that with one's daimon one may transcend fate. It represents fate on a smaller scale, a human scale. It is "ethos anthropo daimon," as Dodds puts it, "no longer . . . an alien thing assailing their reason from without, but . . . part of their own being."[8] But still a daimon, still inescapable.

On this issue, especially, we must sharply distinguish the poets and the philosophers. Even for early philosophers such as Heraclitus, who states that no daimon leaps upon man to shape his character, character is man's daimon (fragment 119), a view quite the opposite of the view of the chorus in *Oedipus Tyrannus* quoted above. Similarly it would be an exaggeration to argue that Sophocles' view of daimon signifies the "discovery of mind," to use Bruno Snell's famous phrase. To be sure, something like this is the position of Plato, who argues that man chooses his daimon. For this reason he is in good measure responsible for his fate. Thus, in the myth of Er, Plato claims that each man, through the exercise of his rational will, chooses his daimon before birth. Lachesis, the allotting goddess, controls only the order in which men make their choice. And ananke, necessity, only seals these choices once made. Plato states: "It is not that a *daimon* will get you by lot, but that you will choose a *daimon*. Virtue owns no master. The responsibility is the chooser's. God is not responsible" (*Rep.*, 617d–e).

Aristotle's argument is related, if more down to earth. A man's actions depend upon himself, he argues, because action creates character (*ethos*), the core insight of his *Nicomachean Ethics*. A man's character may be flawed, leading him to do various bad things. But our participation in the development of our own character by the decision to develop or not develop good habits does not make us less responsible for our actions. "For in every domain, actions of a certain type produce a corresponding type of man" (*Nic. Eth.*, 1114a7–8). Once the character is formed, the subject is indeed constrained by it. Through his choice of habits, however, man has a substantial say in the formation of his character. Often this move—making man responsible for his own fate—is seen as the key achievement of the philosophers, the way in which they excel the poets. I argue that these issues are not so simple. (Nor should it be overlooked that Plato, at least, makes his claim as part of a pedagogical myth that is at least literally untrue.)

It would be mistaken to assert that the poets' position is simply the opposite of the philosopher's: that one's character is as much an act of fate as it is an act of Apollo. The mix, the interpenetration, of moira, daimon, ethos, and other factors noted below makes the poets' account so rich. In this regard their view also differs from that of Thucydides, who, although he may believe in religious power as represented by tyche, sharply distinguishes tyche from human nature, *anthropine physis,* and all that it causes. Clytaemestra, on the other hand, ten times claims responsibility for the murder of Agamemnon, and then characterizes herself as an instrument of an ancient curse (Aesch., *Agamemnon,* see especially 1379–1386, 1497–1504). Apparently there is no contradiction between the two explanations in her mind, which has led many to argue that there is an element of confusion in the poets' account in general. Divine and human responsibility often appear conflated, or "overdetermined," that "blessed word" as Winnington-Ingram puts it.[9] "Blessed" not merely because it locates the confusion in the poets, rather than in ourselves or reality, but also because it saves a place for human freedom. If the fate of Oedipus or Ajax is overdetermined, then part of the determination must stem from the choice of these heroes to be the type of people they are. Frequently this overdetermination is expressed in theories of double motivation, as they are called, in which the will of the gods and character are equally involved. Thus, what Agamemnon is "constrained to do under the yoke of Ananke [sacrifice his daughter Iphigenia] is also what he desires to do with all his heart and soul if it is only at this price that he can be victorious."[10]

To some free will is the most important issue. If Oedipus, for example, is not responsible for his fate, then he is not tragic but merely pathetic. And so are we all, mere playthings of the gods. Many find this conclusion unacceptable, arguing that Oedipus must have freely chosen to compound his moira by choosing to be the sort of angry, hubristic person whom the gods can turn against himself. Bernard Knox is the best-known exponent of this humanistic ideal. "For in the play which Sophocles wrote the hero's will is absolutely free and he is fully responsible for the catastrophe."[11] As William Chase Greene puts it, Sophocles "creates the tragedy of character."[12] The question then becomes, of course, does man choose his character? and I have argued that the poets' view is quite different from Aristotle's. As Winnington-Ingram puts it, "Ajax did not decide to be *omophron* [single-minded]: he was *omophron*. Antigone did not choose to be the daughter of Oedipus or to inherit the hardness which was both her death and her glory."[13]

Nor did Oedipus choose his rage. This, though, need only render these men and women pathetic if we equate responsibility with freedom. Only then does their lack of freedom make them mere objects, playthings of fate, rather than subjects. But who could say of Oedipus, Ajax, or Antigone that they are playthings of fate? Quite the contrary, their active agency is present in virtually every word they utter. This disjunction is ours, not the poets. In a similar fashion the modern interpretation of *hamartia* as a "tragic flaw" in the protagonist's character, rather than the objective mistake that Aristotle says it is, seems designed to rescue an element of freedom from the poets (see *Poetics,* c13). If the tragic catastrophe stems from a flaw in one's character, then the catastrophe appears more meaningful than if it were the result of a mere mistake, which could happen to anyone. If, that is, one has any say at all in deciding what sort of character to become.

What renders Oedipus, Ajax, and Antigone genuine subjects has nothing to do with the supposed fact that each is a basically noble character with a tragic flaw. They are subjects because each accepts the consequences of his or her character, consequences that are hardly trivial, such as permanent exile or death. Indeed, about the only Sophoclean protagonist to whom this characterization does not apply is Electra, who generally sees herself as a mere reactor, an agent of fate (see *Electra,* 620). It is no mere coincidence that she is also the most depressed of the Sophoclean protagonists. But if character is itself just another locus of necessity, then does it make sense to talk of the subject as one who accepts responsibility—that is, of the subject as one who makes a choice as to how to live with his character? The question arises, of course, because character seems so central to the act of choosing about such important things in the first place. Character, however, need not be all of one piece, as the postmoderns have emphasized. There is nothing contradictory about assuming an aspect of character that has a choice as to how to be with its own givenness— that is, a choice as to *how* to come to terms with its own fixity but not *whether* to do so. Only in logic, but not psycho-logic, must an entity be either identical or nonidentical with itself. Even if this assumption is not self-contradictory, however, it is nevertheless still possible to draw the wrong conclusion from it.

Schwartz, for example, argues that the freedom of Oedipus lies in his willing acceptance of his character. Oedipus allies himself with his destiny, and so makes it his own: "If the god is the author of Oedipus's script, Oedipus is, so to speak, the method actor who has found himself in his part. Heroic action to Sophocles, then, is not the endured part or the self-authored part, but the actively played part."[14]

Schwartz's is a version of the double motivation account. And it is not all wrong by any means. Nevertheless, the suggestion that freedom lies in accepting compulsion has a long and troublesome history, and one must be careful about such an equation. Schwartz, like so many other humanist critics, as they are called, such as Knox, seems a little overeager to find a place for freedom in the poets' account, even if freedom must be equated with the acceptance of necessity. In this regard humanist critics may be seen as reacting not merely to the poets, but to the group of critics known as religious conservatives, who sometimes seem to relish the revelation that man is but a pawn of the gods. In fact, it may well be that the most responsible act is to fight against the consequences of one's character. If, that is, one's character is bad. The issue is similar to the question of whether to love oneself. Yes, says Aristotle, but only if one is truly lovable and good (see *Nicomachean Ethics*, 1169a10–15). One may have little choice as to whether one is lovable and good but still have considerable freedom regarding how to come to terms with character. Here is where the subject resides.

The Greek view of freedom helps us think through these issues precisely because it is so naive, narcissistic, and demanding. For the Greek, to be free was to be utterly without constraint: thus the cliché, repeated so often in the tragedies, that only the tyrant is free. Or only the gods are. Such a view is neither subtle nor sophisticated. On the contrary, it is simple, straightforward, and demanding. If I cannot do anything I want, if every obstacle does not fall to my will, then I am not free. This is the ideal of freedom of the narcissist, or the five year old. Sometimes it seems to be held by the postmoderns as well. As Raymond Tallis has argued in *Not Saussure,* much of the postmodern negation of freedom represents a disappointed reaction to the failure of the Enlightenment ideal of absolute freedom, at least in reason.[15] If I cannot have it all, then I shall have nothing. These observations are, however, not intended merely as criticism, either of the Greeks or the postmoderns. On the contrary, a naive and demanding view of freedom possesses more truth than its opposite, the view that freedom is the acceptance of necessity, the willing embrace of the role that fate has chosen for one, and so forth. It is, after all, not the Greek view of freedom, but its opposite, that so frequently becomes an ideology. Perhaps we have difficulty coming to terms with the Greek view because it makes us uncomfortable, reminding us that moderns, not Greeks, tend to confuse freedom with constraint, finding the idea of not being free demeaning to human dignity. The tragic poets did not have the best and last word on the subject. But the naive simplicity of their view of freedom may be an aid to clear thinking. If we let it.

Deliberation without Choice

When we read the tragedies with these ideas in mind, two things stand out. Characters do deliberate over their actions, each recognizing that different possible courses of action stand open before him or her. We see this in Euripides' protagonists: Heracles, who at the end of the play that bears his name must decide whether to live or die (see 1280–1375); Alcestis, in the play that bears her name, must decide whether to die in her husband's place (see 280–325); so too must her husband's parents (see 675–705); and Medea, in the play that bears her name, deliberates over whether to kill her children (see 1020–1080). This introspection has led critics such as Snell and Zevedei Barbu to argue that in tragedy we see the emergence of the autonomous individual. Thus, Barbu states that "one can regard (Aeschylean) drama as full proof of the emergence within Greek civilization of the individual as free agent."[16] But though the protagonist considers other courses of action, he or she does not seem truly free to choose them. Thus, the deliberation is deceptive—it does not truly motivate a decision. Rather the protagonist recognizes that there is only one way open. The plays become even more complicated, of course, when protagonists such as Agamemnon seem glad that they have no real choices. Which should, of course, make us suspicious of whether they really do not.

André Rivier states what so many find so difficult to accept quite clearly: "Is it really inconceivable, seen from a different point of view from our own, that man should will what he has not chosen, that he may be held responsible for his actions quite independently from his intentions? (And is this not precisely the case where the ancient Greeks are concerned?)"[17] Sometimes this whole issue is reduced to one of linguistic analysis, in which it is argued that the Greeks had "no true vocabulary to cover willing." Thus, Aristotle must forge a new concept, *proairesis,* to capture what we mean today by the free power to choose, for the meaning of the term *hekon,* found in the tragedies, covers too much territory, meaning any action not made under external compulsion.[18] Such an account still renders the issue in terms too contemporary, versions of the free-will-versus-determinism formulation. The key issue for the poets lies in the distinction between external and internal constraint (*biasthesis*) or necessity, which generally corresponds to the moira-daimon distinction noted above.

Against all this Jacqueline de Romilly argues that one must make a fundamental distinction among the poets, writing that in Aeschylus the tragic action "involves forces that are superior to man; and in the face of these forces the characters of the individuals fade away and appear secondary. In Euripides, in contrast, all the attention is on the characters of the individuals."[19] Sophocles, from her perspective, would lie somewhere in the middle. The problem with this view is that it fails to grasp the similarity between external and internal necessity adequately. It would be more accurate to say that the path of tragedy from Aeschylus to Euripides is a path by which external necessity is rendered internal. When the subject acts in accordance with character, he or she is nonetheless still acting from necessity, *ex anankes*. To be sure, it is a necessity of a somewhat different order, so that the messenger who reports on Oedipus' self-blinding describes it as an evil committed of his own volition (*hekon*), not undergone despite himself ("kaka ekonia kouk akonia," Soph., *Oedipus Tyrannus*, 1230–1231). Nevertheless, as soon as the doors of the palace open and Oedipus comes onto the stage, the chorus ignores the messenger's distinction, seeing the issue strictly in terms of compulsion (see 1300–1302). As Vernant puts it, "the divine causality and the human initiative that just now appeared to be so clearly opposed to each other have now come together and, at the very heart of the decision 'chosen' by Oedipus, a subtle play of language produces a shift from the aspect of action (*drasas, autocheir*) to that of passivity (*pathea*)."[20]

Perhaps the Greeks are simply confused. Far from placing tragic character within the space between daimon and ethos, and so creating the agent, as Vernant has it, they just go back and forth between agent and victim. But perhaps their view comes as close to the truth about human action as it is possible to come. In those realms in which man is not constrained by large-scale forces, he is constrained by small-scale ones, those of his own character. Generally, however, the large-scale forces work on and through the smaller ones, making the two difficult to sort out. This is complexity, not confusion. The poets did not make precise distinctions, but they recognized them. Frequently the relationship between large- and small-scale forces is that stated by Darius in Aeschylus' *Persians*. "When a mortal himself works for his own downfall, a god comes to abet him" (742). One might just as well say the same thing about Agamemnon.

Oedipus, however, seems in the grip of even larger forces. For Oedipus one would have to change the emphasis to read, "When the gods seek a man's downfall, they create circumstances in which his character turns against him, although he may not know this for some time." The same goes for Pentheus, in Euripides' *Bacchae,* whose excessive rationalism leads to his own destruction, and for Phaedra, in Euripides' *Hippolytus*. Which formulation best fits Sophocles' Ajax seems unclear, but it must certainly be analyzed at this level. Once again, the plays show no confusion, only complexity and subtlety. What generates our confusion is the modern expectation that what stems from within, because it is of a different order of necessity from what stems without, is somehow more free, more a matter of will or choice. It may be choice, but it is not free choice, no matter how extensive the deliberation, the weighing of options. "Within" is just a different locus of necessity.

Sometimes it is argued that Medea's famous soliloquy, in which she seems to debate within herself whether to kill her children, shows the operation of choice and free will, not internal necessity (see Eur., *Medea*, 1020–1080). Perhaps, but on this issue it is easy to get confused, especially if we equate deliberation with choice, reflection upon alternative courses of action with the freedom to choose between them. The poets did not. Medea deliberates, but her actions have been decided in advance. She has already set her murderous plan in action, and she characterizes all her arguments in favor of sparing her children as arguments of weakness, which show her to be soft and hence laughable. We and she both know that *this*—not to be weak—is the concern of hers that trumps all others, and we are led to see that Medea is choosing without choice. She is reflecting on what she might have done, had she been another type of woman—that is, had her daimon been otherwise. But she is not otherwise, nor is her daimon, and she and we both know this.

My argument should be distinguished from one with which it might be confused, that of Martha Nussbaum. In *The Fragility of Goodness,* Nussbaum interprets Euripides' *Hecuba* as demonstrating that character may crumple under a harsh destiny, in this case Hecuba's loss of her husband, children, and city. Indeed, she continues in *Love's Knowledge,* the very form of tragedy, organized around a plot that concerns what happens to people under the press of events, expresses "in itself an ethical conception that was at odds with the Socratic claim (accepted by Plato in the *Republic*'s attack on tragedy) that a good person cannot be harmed by things that happen to him or her."[21] Nussbaum is not mistaken, particularly in her demonstration that much philosophy seeks to transcend such contingencies, just as it would transcend the contingency of death. These philosophies result, she demonstrates, in various philosophical versions of the rage of Creon that builds cities . . . and sometimes destroys them. My argument, however, is neither that character may crumple under destiny nor that character is destiny (see Heraclitus, Plato). Destiny is character, in the sense that we no more choose our characters than we choose other aspects of our destiny, such as the fate of our children, spouse, or nation. Only this formula truly captures the spirit of the poets.

Inconsistency or Complexity?

Even should one accept the formulation "Destiny is character," a puzzle remains. Some acts, such as Agamemnon's sacrifice of his daughter Iphigenia, seem to be regarded as especially reprehensible, which should not be the case if all action is compelled by either external or internal forces. Conversely, the Greek choruses constantly exhort prudence and self-control, practices that would seem pointless were man not free to choose. Possibly in pushing the issue this far I am demanding more logic than is appropriate, just as Edward Evans-Pritchard pushed the demands of logic too far in his study *Witchcraft, Oracles and Magic among the Azande.*[22] Like Evans-Pritchard, I may be asking for much more than we ever ask of ourselves, our own society. Nonetheless, some sense can be made from these apparent exceptions.

Agamemnon, we have seen, is too eager to combine his daimon with his moira, so to speak. He may be compelled, he may have no choice, but he should have regrets. For regrets stem not from the will but from the heart. To suffer is the least a man can do, and frequently the most, a point pursued more fully in the next chapter. On the contrary, Agamemnon, according to the chorus, "has had a change of heart that is impure, sacrilegious." He has "made himself the accomplice of a capricious destiny rather than criticize a diviner" (Aesch., *Agamemnon,* 214–218, 186–188). Just as important, he forgets his deed too easily and too quickly because he wants to forget. He may not have had a choice, but he should have suffered over his decision, holding Iphigenia in his memory as long as he lived. Perhaps he might have made recompense to her memory in some way, such as sparing the life of some loving daughter's father at Troy. Agamemnon does nothing. He simply forgets Iphigenia, which means that he does not take his responsibility seriously. Responsibility means remembering.

Here we see the danger of Schwartz's formulation, in which the self is realized by accepting its destiny. The poets recognize, as Schwartz does not, that whether acceptance is good depends on the destiny. Sometimes the self should regret the action, as Antigone does, even if this regret does not, and cannot, influence that action in any way (see Soph., *Antigone,* 890–928). The same holds for Ajax (in Soph., *Ajax,* 650–690). The regret does not make a person any less responsible for his or her actions. Let us be clear about this. Regret in the face of regrettable actions does, however, render the actor less base and venal, as in the case of Aeschylus' Orestes, who is tortured by the demand of Apollo that he avenge Agamemnon by killing his mother (see Aesch., *Libation Bearers,* 1020–1060). In Orestes' case his regret contributes to his redemption, without which it is unimaginable. This, though, is hardly the norm in the Greek plays.

Orestes' redemption does, however, emphasize an important point. The poets are deeply concerned with the inner life, the state of mind, the heart and soul, of the protagonist. What is Phaedra's state of mind, give us all the details, the chorus asks Phaedra's nurse. In turn, Phaedra answers her nurse with some fairly sophisticated distinctions, indicating that her sickness stems from within, not from actions but from thoughts (see Eur., *Hippolytus,* 265–330). The nurse responds with an equally sophisticated psychological assessment of her own, in effect distinguishing between repression and rational self-control (see 435ff). There is nothing simplistic about the psychology, no confusion of thought and deed, or of inner and outer. What is confusing to us, or rather unsettling, is that this psychological sophistication and penetration does not lead to the discovery of what we call free will—not even a little bit, deep within the interstices of character. Rather, it leads the Greeks to see how a person may deeply regret what she or he is forced to do. Or too eagerly accept destiny. Distinctions like this are central for the poets in assessing the quality of a person's character but not in assigning responsibility. Is this really a less sophisticated way of thinking about the psyche? Perhaps it is more, for the poets distinguish, as we do not (at least not quite so well), state of mind from responsibility, assimilating state of mind to a moral or qualitative assessment that remains distinct from responsibility, even though it may sometimes be a mitigating factor, as it was with Orestes. The categories are separate but connected.

What about the dozens of exhortations by the choruses in Greek tragedy to prudence, moderation, and self-control? What is the point of such exhortations if the individual does not will her or his actions? The first thing to note is that these exhortations are not generally directed toward the protagonist. Usually, however, they are generalizations about life, directed at anyone who might listen—that is, the audience. The standard view that the chorus represents the ideal spectator is helpful here, even if it is not always correct. Of course such exhortations may have an influence, but the influence is indirect. It falls not on the protagonist per se but on the culture and hence indirectly, over time, on characters. A character's daimon may not be subject to her or his individual will, but a culture may create conditions that foster a certain type of character. In this sense it may be said to influence an individual's daimon. Not, as Heraclitus would have it, because character is man's daimon (fragment 119). Rather, culture can bend people's daimons over time, even if it cannot bend that of any particular person. Aristotle's reflections on how good habits build good character are absolutely right, and any intelligent society knows this. Certainly the poets know. This is what their exhortations of prudence and moderation are concerned with: creating a culture which may bend people's daimons, in part by showing what happens to those who retain aspects of the daimon of a Homeric hero in the fifth century B.C. polis.

Sometimes the fact that actors in Greek plays wore masks is taken as metaphor for the tragic worldview, according to which the poets wished to distinguish between the inner psychic reality of the character and his external appearance, which so often misleads. But the metaphor is itself misleading. The masks did not disguise and misrepresent character. Oedipus was evidently not shown with a charming, smiling, happy face. Rather, the masks projected stereotypical character. Indeed, for this reason action becomes an even more centrally defining aspect of character. Only action tells us anything important about particular individuals. The *ekkulema* (literally, the "rolled-out thing," probably a low, wheeled platform), which brought the tragic happenings, usually in the form of dead bodies, from the inside to the outside, is often seen as metaphorically significant in the same way as masks are.[23] Through this device, the *skene*, the painted backdrop with doors, is penetrated, revealing what is truly real inside. But consider what was brought forth: not complicated reflections on the self, but the results of action. Tragic drama plays constantly with the opposition between appearance and reality, name and thing, no more so than in Euripides' *Helen*, which is concerned with this theme. So too is his *Electra*, in which an old man says "often a noble face hides filthy ways" (550). Once again, though, it is the action that is most real. We, not the poets, equate the contrast of appearance and reality with that of a man's outward appearance versus his true, inner self. The poets' concern with appearance and reality is better seen as a study of the propensity to confuse good and bad.

Responsibility and the Oikos

The concept of responsibility without freedom remains a difficult one. Why should we be held responsible for acts if we could not choose to do otherwise, may even deeply regret doing? One traditional answer, accepted even by those who believe in free will, has been that our acts are like children. They initiate a sequence of events whose consequences are unpredictable and in this sense not freely chosen. Yet, like our children, we cannot disown our acts, for they are part of us. A related answer, one with an emphasis more characteristic of the ancient Greeks, has to do with what A. W. H. Adkins calls the Greek results culture, discussed earlier. Against those who see ancient Greece as a shame rather than a guilt culture, Adkins argues that it was a culture in which only results counted.[24] Good intentions are never enough. Thus, the chorus of Furies who hound Orestes can describe his matricide as something that happened to befall him (*zumpesosin*) without in any way implying that this might lessen his responsibility—or his guilt (see Aesch., *Eumenides*, 336–337). No doubt the poets seek to soften and humanize the results culture. Orestes' good intentions count for much, whereas Phaedra falls ill because of her bad intentions not her bad acts. (Agamemnon, on the other hand, seems filled with hubris, and Clytaemestra's murder of him stems from sexual jealousy not just rage over the sacrifice of Iphigenia; by contrast, Orestes' motives seem almost pure. See Aesch., *Agamemnon*, 1446–1447; *Libation Bearers*, 270–305.) Nevertheless, there was an "objectivism" to Greek culture that influences the poets' accounts. They soften the Furies' ignorance of intentions; they do not transform it. It is particularly important to be clear about where this objectivity resides: it lies in the web of relations through which the consequences of an action are worked out. To put it simply, but not too simply, we are responsible for our actions, even though we are not free, because action is seen not from the inner-world of the actor but from the network of relations he or she participates in.

Aristotle states that tragedy is a representation neither of character nor of men but of action. "Tragedies are not performed, therefore, in order to represent character (ethos), although character is involved for the sake of the action" (*Poet.,* c6). By character Aristotle seems to mean what he means in book 2 of the *Nicomachean Ethics:* not inner depths but habit. Against habit he sets action, which means something akin to the working out of forces whose locus happens to be the psyche. The protagonist, as I have argued earlier, is akin to the carrier of these forces. For this reason, more than any other, the psychoanalytic theory of Melanie Klein illuminates the tragedies—she too views men and women in this way. Commenting on the *Poetics,* John Jones is once again impressed by the difference between Aristotle's concept of the self and our own. We fail to understand Aristotle, he says, owing to our belief in "the real self underlying, persisting through, action and suffering, and our inability to conceive the expressive vitality of the discrete and centrifugal self."[25] Certainly Jones's view is more insightful than that of Frank L. Lucas, who states that "I can only suggest that Aristotle was perhaps something of an extrovert. Constantly he stresses activity."[26]

Jones is not mistaken. Unlike many moderns, Aristotle does not hold that action stems from a solitary, inward consciousness, in which the action is somehow secondary, almost an adjective about consciousness. Nevertheless, Jones misses two points which affect how we should judge the self in Aristotle and the poets (Aristotle is not always the best guide to the poets, but on this point he is). The absence of these two qualifications leads to the implication that the Greek self is inferior. First, even though the Greek self may not have been a center of self-reflection and consciousness, it was a center of responsibility. Responsibility, I shall argue further, is actually a better measure of selfhood than self-reflection. Today many people are highly reflective and self-conscious, without being responsible. They form Christopher Lasch's "culture of narcissism." Second, Jones assumes that because we believe today that action stems from a controlling source within, then we must be correct. In fact, the achievement of Western civilization has been not so much the creation of such a controlling center as it is the creation of a myth about it. In order to make this argument I shall draw upon the work of Jacques Lacan.

The view of Aristotle and the poets is alien to our way of thinking, but there exist points of overlap. Consider, for example, the similarity between the poets' view and some older views of crime and punishment, views that may even be widely held today, although we have forgotten why. Most of Hannah Arendt's *Eichmann in Jerusalem* is concerned with Eichmann's psyche. Is he a crazed, vicious killer or the consummate bureaucrat? We may find much to argue with in Arendt's assessment of his character, but we see nothing to argue with in her assessment of why he must hang. The reason has nothing to do with the state of his psyche. Rather, he must hang in order to restore a broken web, a shattered order. Or, as Yosal Rogat, quoted approvingly by Arendt, puts it: "A great crime offends nature, so that the very earth cries out for vengeance; that evil violates a natural harmony which only retribution can restore; that a wronged collectivity owes a duty to the moral order to punish the criminal."[27] Hecuba pleads for revenge on the man who killed her son in precisely these terms: only revenge will restore a shattered and perverted order of relationships (see Eur., Hecuba, 790–805).

Here is why the actor is responsible even though he is not free. Responsibility is relational, not individual; it concerns a network of reciprocal obligations and duties that risks being shattered forever if the act itself is not made good. We look at intent, the Greek at the relationship. That most misdeeds in Greek tragedy, and certainly the most heinous misdeeds, are committed by family members against each other reinforces the point. The web of relationships that constitutes the family is the tightest and probably the most fragile, the most easily broken, of all the various connections of our lives. Nine of the thirty-two extant tragedies involve the destruction of this web in a single family: the Atreidae. The family focus heightens the pity and the fear, as I have argued. Indeed, one might well regard the family—that is, their relationships—as the real actors. Conversely, what often makes the plays of Euripides troubling is that the restoration of the web of relationships is so transparent as not to be deeply satisfying: the anxiety persists and, indeed, is deepened.

The poets' view of responsibility is familiar, concerned above all else with what we owe the network of relationships put at risk by our actions. Husbands and wives, parents and children hold each other to such a standard of responsibility all the time. What is alien is how this way of thinking seems to trump every other consideration, including intent, regret, and so forth. But the poets never connected responsibility with freedom in the first place. The issue for them is not so much, "Are there factors that mitigate responsibility, such as innocent intent?" but rather, "How should we, the audience, properly respond to the responsibility the protagonist is necessarily forced to shoulder?" With pity and compassion or with satisfaction? Not "Is it fair or just that the protagonist be held responsible for his acts?" but "How should we feel about the suffering of the protagonist as he shoulders his responsibility as he must?" is the focus of the poets. In other words, they care about the education of the proper emotions in the face of necessity, a necessity that is perhaps more subtle but no less demanding when expressed as character and hence no less an appropriate subject of pity or satisfaction.

In addition, the poets reason about justice and responsibility from the family to the polis, not vice versa. By this I mean that the model of justice and responsibility employed by the poets is not based on subsumption of particular events under universal principles like Kant's categorical imperative, even if such principles are sometimes said to exist (see Eur., *Hecuba*, 800–805). Rather, it is akin to that of the family, in which each member's contribution to the maintenance of the relationships that sustain the family is key. In fact, to see justice and responsibility in this fashion comes close to the way the women studied in Carol Gilligan's *In a Different Voice* see these concepts, as a narrative of relationships over time. In this respect too the poets do not seek to wall out the oikos: quite the contrary. Today, many moderns (or rather, postmoderns) are looking for an alternative to the dominant Western tradition. Too often they have found it in approaches that question not merely Western rationalism but the reality of emotional bonds and relationships as well, seeing them as one more instance of will and power in the name of reason and freedom. Which, of course, they often are! But not always. If the poets, who lived in a world at least as harsh and competitive as our own (an agonal culture it has been called) could draw this distinction, so can we.

Why is this view of justice and responsibility based upon relationships modeled after the family rather than universal principles so difficult for moderns to accept? One reason frequently given is that it seems to make justice itself a contingent virtue, dependent upon the quality of relationships. If trust and confidence in these relationships is destroyed, so too is the capacity for justice. In this regard it might be instructive to look briefly at the famous passage in *Hecuba,* referred to in the preceding paragraph, in which through all her travail Hecuba, once queen of Troy, now widowed slave to the Greeks, seems to affirm a universal moral order: "I am a slave, I know, and slaves are weak. But the gods are strong, and over them there stands some absolute, some moral order or principle of law more final still. Upon this moral law the world depends; through it the gods exist; by it we live, defining good and evil"(799–804).

The Greek term translated by Arrowsmith as "some moral order or principle of law more final still" is *nomos,* which might just as accurately be rendered as "convention." In fact, Martha Nussbaum states that Arrowsmith now agrees with her that "convention" would be a better translation. Thus, Hecuba's claim would be better rendered as, "We believe in the existence of gods, and make ethical distinctions (that reflect this belief)." Hecuba is more accurately seen as emphasizing the constructed rather than given character of the moral order. This, though, has not been a popular translation or interpretation. Nor has *Hecuba* been a popular tragedy in the modern era, G. Hermann (member of the first generation of classical scholars for whom Kant was a major influence) arguing in his preface to his *Euripidis Opera* that good will (Kant's "ein guter Wille") must always be made safe from "accidents of step-motherly nature," a

particularly telling phrase when one considers that family relationships constitute the real alternative to universal morality.[28]

Exceptions Are Allowed: Neoptolemus

To claim, as the poets in effect do, that most people most of the time lack
the freedom to choose among different courses of action regarding important
events does not mean that no one has any freedom any time. To make the
poets' doctrine this consistent, to render it a subjunctive universal, would be
to raise our needs for consistency and clarity above the views of the poets and
above the complexity of reality as well. Though the overwhelming majority of
the tragic protagonists seem compelled, at least one does not, Neoptolemus.

Bitten by a sacred snake, which caused a wound that refused to heal, Philoctetes has been marooned on the island of Lemnos by his shipmates, who could
not bear his suffering. After some years, Odysseus sends Neoptolemus to fetch
Philoctetes' magic bow by hook or crook. Without the bow, Troy will not be
taken. After much hesitation, Neoptolemus steals the bow only to return it: the
result, it seems, of some serious soul searching that includes his reflection upon
what it means to be the son of Achilles. Philoctetes seems to understand that
Neoptolemus is involved in a developmental odyssey, saying to him simply,
"Give it back. Be your true self (*sauto genou*) again" (Soph., *Philoctetes,* 950). As
though he had a choice to be a false self. And perhaps he did.

One of Sophocles' last plays (produced about 409 B.C.), *Philoctetes* is an unusual play, with the most modern feel of all the extant tragedies, containing
the most modern characters and the fullest character development. Nothing by
Euripides, sometimes seen as the playwright most concerned with character,
even comes close. We must, however, be careful about what we conclude from
this rarity. Nothing in *Philoctetes,* or any of the other plays, suggests that if one
person has an apparently free choice in one circumstance, then if we all just
try a little harder more of us can be free. Such a view would be strictly wishful
thinking, a defense. Nothing suggests this because lack of freedom concerns
not strength of will but the compulsion of forces. Neoptolemus is in a particularly fluid, unstructured situation, one in which the protagonists believe, at
least at first, that *how* the bow is obtained—through trickery or persuasion—
matters little to the gods. (In fact, it may have made all the difference in the
world, in which case Neoptolemus was never free to trick Philoctetes to begin
with; see, for example, 65–70, 610–622; 1410ff.) Nor was Neoptolemus' daimon, the force that compels character, yet fully formed: was he to be upright
like his father, Achilles, or tricky like Odysseus, to put the options a little too
simply? In this circumstance he may have had a real choice, but we should
not make too much of it, especially if we keep Neoptolemus' future in mind.
In the Homeric tradition Neoptolemus slaughters Priam, whom his father had

spared, before an altar in Troy. If Neoptolemus had a true moment of freedom in the course of this play, a choice as to what kind of person to be, it apparently did not last long, Sophocles seems to say with his oblique reference to Neoptolemus' future (1440–1445).[29]

THE GREEK VIEW COMPARED WITH EXISTENTIAL PSYCHOANALYSIS AND LACAN

I should now like to compare the Greek view with two extremely different psychoanalytic perspectives: existential psychoanalysis and the psychoanalytic theory of Jacques Lacan. My comparison is not structural or even strictly theoretical. The poets' view of psyche and world is often not directly comparable with that of the psychoanalysts. Rather, I shall compare conclusions. The poets assert that people are responsible for what they do without generally being free to do otherwise. For all its admirable philosophical ambition, existential psychoanalysis is an escape from this insight, a defense. Lacan's account, on the other hand, roughly corresponds with the truth of the poets. Unlike Lacan, however, the poets take reality seriously. This gives their account of psyche and world a gravity lacking in Lacan.

None of the standard definitions of tragedy work very well, not even Aristotle's. Tragedy is not generally about characters with a tragic flaw, such as hubris. Indeed, the very concept of hamartia as a tragic flaw is mistaken. Aristotle seems to have understood hamartia as simply an error in judgment (see *Poetics*, c13–14; also note 3, this chapter). Nor do tragedies always involve reversal (*peripeteia*). Euripides' *Trojan Women*, for example, just goes from bad to worse, as does his *Hecuba*. Nor are the tragedies generally about a tragic choice, in which two mutually exclusive alternatives make equally strong ethical claims. This definition, popular with Hegel and those influenced by him such as Alasdair MacIntyre (insofar as his definition of tragedy is concerned), arguably fits Sophocles' *Antigone*, possibly Aeschylus' *Libation Bearers*, and few other plays. (In Euripides' accounts, Orestes and Electra are so crazed that the idea that each faced a tragic choice becomes absurd; Sophocles' *Electra* seems capable of no choice at all.) Oedipus faced no "tragic choice," except perhaps whether to halt his investigations. If there were a single definition of tragedy, it would be something like "stories about what it is to live in a world in which people are held responsible for their acts without being free to act otherwise." Almost every tragedy concerns this issue; almost every tragedy assumes it. Existential psychoanalysis denies it, arguing that there is no human nature: man is free to be whatever he will.

For Jean-Paul Sartre, the key existentialist insight is that existence precedes essence, which means that there is no such thing as human nature. "Man is nothing else but that which he makes of himself," says Sartre, a claim that is the apotheosis of humanism, even though Sartre was to qualify his humanism markedly in later years. No single claim could be more alien to the experience of the Greek poets than Sartre's, which is not to say that their views are opposites; the relation is more complex. Consider, for example, Sartre's statement that "the existentialist does not believe in the power of passion. He will never agree that a sweeping passion is a ravaging torrent which fatally leads a man to certain acts and is therefore an excuse. He thinks that man is responsible for his passion."[30] Unlike Sartre, the Greek poets believed in the power of passion, that it could overwhelm a man no matter how noble his character. Like Sartre, however, they held that man is responsible for his passion, even when overwhelmed. A difficult distinction for many today, this forms the crux of the poets' worldview. Existential psychoanalysts, on the other hand, argue that although man is not free in every choice that he makes, he is always free in what Sartre calls his original choice (actually choices), the decision involving what kind of person to be, what kind of defenses to adopt, and how to avoid the implications of absolute freedom. Existential psychoanalysts substitute the assumption of the unity of experience for that of the dynamic unconscious— that is, they deny that man might be internally compelled by alienated aspects of his own existence.

As an example of original choice, Ludwig Binswanger, an existential psychoanalyst, refers to a woman with agoraphobia: she cannot go out alone.[31] She had constructed a worldview in which her safety depended upon everything being connected, and for various reasons this had begun to fall apart. The existential analyst would not argue that this woman was free to choose whether to go in or stay out in the midst of a panic attack. Nevertheless, she had freely, if without conscious awareness, chosen to construct the world in this fashion and thus was responsible for her condition. Therapy consists in making the patient aware of her original choice, drawing out the way she has artificially narrowed her horizon of experience. Her illness is her constricted worldview.

"Existential psychoanalysis," says Sartre, "rejects the hypothesis of the unconscious; it makes the psychic act coextensive with consciousness." In so doing it makes man whole. "The principle of this psychoanalysis is that man is a totality and not a collection."[32] The unconscious is not subject to choice and so divides man from himself. It is not a realm of freedom. To posit absolute freedom the psyche must be made one with itself, a strategy begun by Plato and central to all idealisms, as will be shown shortly. Such a view presents obvious difficulties from a psychoanalytic perspective, and existential psychoanalysts such as Binswanger and Medard Boss modify it in order better to account for cases like the woman with agoraphobia, which without something like an unconscious seem almost incomprehensible. Sartre's argument (in contrast to the reasons behind it) against the unconscious is strictly epistemological: the unconscious censor must first be conscious of what it represses in order subsequently to remove that thing from consciousness.[33] In a word, the unconscious comes about from conscious decisions. Sartre calls this act bad faith. Binswanger tries to split the difference. His patient's way of "experiencing 'world' . . . does not have to be 'conscious'; but neither must we call it 'unconscious' in the psychoanalytic sense, since it is outside the contrast of these opposites."[34]

Binswanger wants to continue to use terms like *unconscious* and *repressed* as adjectives in order to describe a type of psychic experience but avoid their use as nouns, in order to avoid reifying it. We are not always aware of all the decisions we make, especially our original choices, which almost always restrict our world in some way, making us less free than we could be. The lie without a liar this self-deception is sometimes called. Therapy brings such choices to our awareness, so that they, and we, might be more truly free. What is to be avoided at all costs is positing various hidden mechanisms "behind" our choices, such as drives. Rather, the choice is all, and the analyst tries to reconstruct the patient's attitude toward the world in terms of his or her choices. Medard Boss has a nice account of this perspective in *Psychoanalysis and Daseinanalysis*. His case studies are, however, troublesome, for in them we see awareness of the original choice leading to remarkable recoveries and beautiful lives. He omits the notion that there are tragic choices, in which anything we choose will result in pain and suffering, to ourselves or others.

In Sartre's view, consciousness is responsible for itself, nothing more and nothing less. Existential psychoanalysis grants man an absolute freedom only by isolating him from the world. Estrangement is the condition of absolute freedom, for were man seen as the poets see him, embedded in the world, participating in its nature through his passions, then the proposition that he is free would be preposterous. Isolating man in his own pristine consciousness renders him free and whole. Thus, Sartre would remove man from nature, including from passions that run through him as though they were natural forces, as well as from the network of human relationships that the poets put at the center of human existence. But at what a price. And even if man were willing to pay the price, he could not succeed. Nature (even human nature) cannot be bought off so easily.

Against this conclusion it might be argued that Sartre, like the tragic poets, takes relationships seriously. Man is not only responsible for himself, "he is responsible for all men," as Sartre puts it, because his acts fan out through a network of relationships. Like Aristotle, Sartre takes action seriously. Deep reflection upon internal conflicts and desires counts for nothing—only action matters. "There is no reality except in action. . . . [Man] is therefore nothing else than the ensemble of his acts, nothing else than his life."[35] In this regard,

Sartre does indeed stand close to the tragic poets, closer, certainly, than Lacan. Nevertheless, we must be careful not to overemphasize Sartre's continuity with the poets. Just as Sartre does not deny that there is something called the human condition that includes death, so he does not deny human relationships. Sartre is no classical idealist. He views both nature and relationships solely from the perspective of the actor, however, one in which the only constraints are those that he acknowledges and hence creates. The notion that relationships might impinge upon us, constraining our choices and freedom, is as alien to Sartre as the idea that nature might do so. In this regard his view is quite the opposite of the poets.

From the perspective of the psychoanalytic theory of Greek tragedy, existentialist psychoanalysis looks like a narcissistic (because it vastly overestimates the power of human will and choice) defense against the human condition. Central to this condition are our bodies, our passions, our fears and desires, the fears and desires of others, and the constraints of the natural world, all of which render us unfree, compelled, and less than whole. For the Greeks, however, our lack of freedom need not render us irresponsible nor make our lives meaningless. In making this point the Greek poets develop a number of distinctions that have since fallen into undeserved desuetude, such as how critically to "participate" in our own moira, or lot in life.

One finds existential psychoanalysis' narcissistic defense in a surprising place, seemingly far removed from existential psychoanalysis—the scientific model of man. As Charles Taylor argues, the ideal of the rational subject, able so to objectify the world that he comes to see himself as an objective process, one more piece of nature to calculate and control, "is a novel variant of this very old aspiration to spiritual freedom . . . to step outside the prison of the peculiarly human emotions, and to be free of the cares and the demands they make on us."[36] How could this similarity be? Because the most pressing and profound (and certainly the most humbling, for they are within us) limits to human freedom are not found in the external world but in our passions. Objectifying ourselves is a way of trying to gain control over these passions, to treat them as though they were another object of study. Perhaps this urge drives some postmoderns as well. By claiming that the subject is actually only an object of history (or of its desires, or of texts), we achieve at least some intellectual control over this reality.

What a surprise! Existential psychoanalysis and the scientific model of man turn out to have much in common, both regarding the passions as the greatest threat to human freedom. Whereas existential psychoanalysis would remove man completely from nature in order to gain his freedom, the scientific model of man would embed him in it, in order to win control over man's nature in the same way that man has gained control over so many other natural processes. Perhaps this commonality should be no surprise at all, at least not for those who have studied Max Horkheimer and Theodor Adorno's critique of the dialectic of Enlightenment.[37] It represents but another version of the inner connection they find between idealism and empiricism. Idealism seeks to transcend the constraints of this world by positing a higher one in which the rational faculties are in control and upon which this world must depend in some way, either for its existence or for our knowledge of it. Empiricism, on the other hand, seeks to overcome the constraints of this world with force. Both, however, fail to recognize that the most profound and humbling constraints lie within ourselves. Or rather, both recognize it fully and construct systems to defend against it. Those defense systems make both existential psychoanalysis and the scientific model of man variants of humanism: both see the world, including the psyche, in terms of how it might be rendered transparent to human will or reason. The poets do not share this fantasy.

There is a dry, arid, hyper-intellectual quality to Lacan's psychoanalytic writings that would seem to be just one more version of the defenses noted above. Unlike almost every other psychoanalytic writer, Lacan simply does not write about feelings and emotions—what most analysts hold to be the stuff of psychoanalysis. Nevertheless, we find in Lacan an account of the self which in important respects comes close to the truth grasped by the poets: that people are responsible but not free. I shall go right to that account, bypassing Lacan's fascination and play with language that so many have found so interesting but which I regard as a distraction from the main issue.[38] We are convinced, says Lacan, "that our researches justify the epigram of the philosopher who said that speech was given to man to hide his thoughts; our view is that the essential function of the ego is [a] very nearly systematic refusal to recognize reality."[39] What is this reality? That people are not subjects but the objects of their desires. Prime among these desires is not sex or love but to be free and in control of their lives and selves. This desire is destined to be eternally frustrated by all our other desires.

For Lacan, the ego, understood as that entity which exercises control over one's desires and one's world, is itself the symptom, the disease. "The ego is structured exactly like a symptom. Interior to the subject, it is only a privileged symptom. It is the human symptom par excellence, it is the mental malady of man."[40] David Hume stated that whenever he looked inside himself, there was no self to be found. Lacan might put it like so: "If I am honest with myself, every time I think that I find myself, I realize that I have found only one more defense, one more symptom, one more layer of rationalization protecting me from the truth: that I am an object of my desires that does not exist, never has, and never will."

In one respect, Lacan simply takes the Freudian revolution further. Rather than being masters of ourselves, we are generally dominated by our passions and fears—that is, by the unconscious. Freud appears to have believed that a few exceptional individuals might transcend this way of life, a possibility expressed in his famous characterization of the successful outcome of analysis as "Wo es war, soll ich werden," usually translated as "Where id was, there ego shall be." Lacan, arguing that Freud has generally been misinterpreted on this point, states that one could better read Freud's intent this way: "There where it [id] was just now, there where it was for a while, between an extinction that is still glowing and a birth that is retarded, 'I' can come into being and disappear from what I say."[41] By this he seems to mean that we become authentic to the degree that we abandon the illusory attempt at control, the attempt, bound to fail, to be more than the desiring, lacking subject. Or as Louis Sass puts it, the point is not that the ego should replace the id, but that the ego should come to exist in the realm of the id. "That is, it should shed the illusion of integral, controlled selfhood and dissolve into those associative chains normally repressed into the unconscious."[42]

Expressed in the language of the poets, each of us achieves authenticity to the degree that we accept our moira and our daimon. We need not accept them with the fervor of Agamemnon, but we must recognize that they are ourselves. They define what it is to be a self. The belief in a "real self underlying, persisting through, action and suffering," as John Jones puts it in contrasting the modern view with that of the poets, is one more defense of the ego against the desiring subject. That is, it is a defense against the experience of being acted upon by our passions rather than being the center who controls them. In particular, it is a defense against the disappointment of desire—the desire to be the image in the mirror: coherent, clearly bounded, and in control. The defense may be as old as Plato and sanctified by the Enlightenment, but this makes it no less a defense. It just makes it more difficult to recognize as such.

Two Important Qualifications Regarding the Relationship
between the Poets and Lacan
My argument is not that the poets are Lacanians, or that Lacan is a Greek poet in disguise. Their accounts are incommensurable. Nevertheless, if the passions are *our* gods, as I have argued, then Lacan's view seems to come close to the truth of the poets: that we are the carriers of our passions, their locus, but not their agents. They control us more than we control them. Man may, as the "ode to man" in *Antigone* suggests, conquer every external constraint upon his freedom but death. This though would not make him free, for the sources of constraint lie within. Or rather, they travel through us like a cosmic ray, a power in the universe against which we can never shield ourselves, just as we cannot shield ourselves against a god.

It is, of course, common to argue that the Greek gods are best seen as unconscious forces such as fears and desires. Indeed, some have argued that this is Euripides' position. Usually, however, this reformulation of the reality of the gods serves as a prelude to the conclusion that if we recognize their origins within, then we can achieve a level of control over our passions that the Greeks never achieved. Once they are located within, then our passions may be reasoned with. It is this conclusion that I am rejecting as a defense, an illusion, a rationalization, which is why I think that Lacan is correct.

Nevertheless, Lacan seems mistaken, or at least misled, in two fundamental respects, both of which may be illuminated by the perspective of the poets. The result of both these qualifications is to render Lacan's critique of humanism less antihuman: the pretensions of the ego are dissolved but not the relationships with others that make us human. First, there seems to be a heroic element in accepting one's destiny with courage and responsibility that belies Lacan's claim that the subject does not exist. Sophocles' Oedipus may claim three times at Colonus that he is innocent, but this is not why he is taken to the bosom of the gods (whether they be sky or earth gods). The gods care not one whit for innocence. He is rewarded because he has lived his moira and daimon with grace and dignity, neither embracing them to escape himself, nor fighting them for the same reason. The situation of Euripides' Heracles is similar. In the end he appears noble and attractive because he accepts full responsibility for acts done under the compulsion of Madness. That his madness was actually the result of his own violent nature makes no difference: his nature was his daimon. Consequently, the key question is not "Could or should he have done otherwise?" but "With how much courage, grace, and nobility does he accept his responsibility?"

Lacan is no tragic hero, although Stuart Schneiderman subtitles his book about him *The Death of an Intellectual Hero,* perhaps without exaggeration.[43] But Lacan greatly resembles a man who is, Oedipus. Like Oedipus, Lacan pushes the question of identity as far as he possibly can. And what does he find at the end of the road? He discovers himself to be "enigmatic, without consistency, without any domain of his own or any fixed point of attachment, with no defined essence."[44] These are Vernant's words, used to characterize what Oedipus learns about his own identity, but they may be applied to Lacan's conclusions as well. Perhaps the riddle of Oedipus' final resting place reflects this: not even in death is his identity clear. Upon finding what he believes is the answer to the riddle of his identity, Oedipus mutilates himself. Lacan does not go so far, but even Lacan's answer requires a certain self-mutilation, in which one abandons the ideal of the self as free, rational, autonomous, and in control. Yet there remains a nobility to this act, just as there was to Oedipus'. Not merely because the self-inflicted destruction of a fantasy of an ideal self takes courage, but because that destruction is focused and limited: an ideal of the self as rational and in control is shattered but not the responsibility that goes with it.

One might, however, say something quite different about Oedipus. Or rather, say much the same thing in ways that lead to a conclusion even less congenial, albeit not fundamentally different. Oedipus' search is not for himself at all, but for *jouissance,* that supposedly untranslatable Lacanian term that connotes not sexual pleasure alone but a pleasure so primitive and profound that it involves the loss of self, boundaries, and control, more akin to the pleasures of the Bacchae. Lacan argues that this pleasure can never be achieved, at least not by any subject who seeks to remain within the symbolic order and thus participate via language in relationships with others. Otherwise expressed, men too are castrated in the sense that they must also give up "the phallus, symbolizing unmediated, full *jouissance,*" in order to enter the symbolic order. Seen from this perspective, Oedipus pursues not the truth of himself but jouissance. Where he thought he would find himself, he finds only ever more primitive desires, which culminate in the desire for a reunion with mother so primordial that it combines loss of identity with sexual pleasure: that is, jouissance. Most men only fantasize about such events. Oedipus lived them, and the price is, of course, his exile from the community of others, which Lacan (quite aridly) conceptualizes in terms of language. The price is also castration, as symbolized by Oedipus' blinding, not only in the Freudian sense of accepting the authority of the father but also in the Lacanian sense of accepting the lack in being that is the self. "The ultimate Lacanian goal is for the subject 'to assume his/her castration.' "[45] But this too may be noble. It certainly requires courage and responsibility.

Lacan's second mistake, and this is really the mistake of many moderns, is to assume implicitly that because the subject is not as real as he thinks he is then nothing else is as real as it seems to be either. Note the affinity between this way of thinking and what Freud calls the narcissism of primitive thought, in which the reality of everything else is measured by the reality of me: how real I feel myself to be. If upon reflection I do not experience myself as fully real, then nothing else is fully real either, expect perhaps the language with which I reflect upon myself. In approaching the world in this fashion, Lacan ignores or downplays the reality of society: the network of relationships which to the poets is so real that they frequently reify it, treating it as given by nature. That reification surely reflects a limit of the poets' perspective, perhaps its most profound limit. Nevertheless, this limit should not be allowed to obscure the opposite tendency in Lacan, his desire to treat the individual, and even language, separate from the relationships that make a family, society, polis, culture, and nation.

There are complexities to Lacan's view of the real that it will not pay to get into here. Suffice to say that although Lacan respects reality, particularly as expressed in the experiences of jouissance and death, he holds that we can never gain direct access to it. Only language is truly accessible. Of course we can never gain direct access, unmediated presence as it is sometimes called, to anything. These epistemological and ontological considerations are no reason to ignore the reality, in the everyday sense of the term, of human relationships. Putting them at the center, as the poets do, helps to overcome some of the isolation of the subject who desires his selfhood most of all, as well as some of his desperation. For if the subject is not free and in control, indeed, if the subject is not one with itself, he or she is still part of a meaningful order, a network of relationships, participating in a larger world. Addressing Electra's loneliness (in Sophocles' account), Jones suggests that it was perhaps not as unbearable as it would be for most moderns, for we lack "the containing *oikos* to vivify Electra's dry scheme of family relations, and to counterbalance the faint personal self with the strength of collective consciousness."[46] Though such an interpretation risks condescension toward the Greek self, in this case it seems accurate.

Indeed, only from this perspective does the value of responsibility truly make sense. One takes responsibility not only out of some existential act of courage, but because the consequences of one's acts are real, and they are real because they rebound through a network of others. The reality of this network gives responsibility its weight and hence gives meaning to our lives, including the real, if limited, sense of agency that stems from taking responsibility. In this regard the poets are the first object relations theorists. Commenting on Jean Racine's *Phèdre* (1677), his version of Euripides' *Hippolytus,* critics have argued that even though Phèdre is in fact impelled by her desire for Hippolyte, and hence not free, she feels shame, thus acting "as if" she were responsible. This "as if" thinking elevates her to tragic greatness. Insightful in some respects, this remains a modern interpretation. For the tragic poets there is no "as if" about it. People like Phèdre simply *are* responsible, because what they do has objective consequences in the world. To argue that she possesses tragic greatness because she acts as if she were responsible misses the point insofar as it implies the corollary "but she knows, and so do we, that she really is not." She really is.

Different in most respects, both existential psychoanalysts and Lacanians pay little attention to the reality of relationships with others, except as these relationships represent projections of our own desires. Conversely, if one pays attention to these relationships, as the poets do, then the concept of responsibility without freedom loses some of its terror. Responsibility ties us to others (even in death, as I argued in the last chapter) and so may be a source of comfort in the face of the lack in the subject that Lacan uncovers as the ground of unfreedom. Conversely, responsibility without freedom most frightens us when we feel so unconnected and apart from others that our only relationship with them is as an instrument, a means, in which we become responsible for what they would have us do. The reality of community can do much to assuage this anxiety, by giving gravity to our acts, causing them to matter in the world, and in this way linking the acceptance of responsibility to a sense of self as a creative, responsible agent who is not merely absurd.

"Logon Didou Sauto"

The poets' view of the self is not, it is apparent, identical with that of Lacan, even if they reach similar conclusions about its freedom. Nevertheless, there is a Lacanian element in the poets' account of the psyche, particularly in the way the protagonists are such active projectors, projecting their psyches into other people and things and then finding them there, what psychoanalysts call projective identification, a phenomenon that Lacan sees arising in the mirror stage of development ("le stade du miroir"), in which the child seeks himself in the image in the mirror.[47] He will, suggests Lacan, spend his whole life doing this, seeking to be desired by others as part of themselves, so that he may realize himself in their desire for him—a confusing series of multiple projections and reintrojections, that seem to put the psyche itself up for sale. Jones sees a related phenomenon in the tragedies. "We may venture the general observation that the boundaries of the self in Greek and especially Aeschylean tragedy are more fluid than we allow."[48] As evidence he mentions Electra's strange assumption that the lock of hair she has just found is her brother's because it is just like her own, as well as the way in which Orestes treats his dead father's robe as though it were Agamemnon himself (see Libation Bearers, 164–204; 980–1015). He might have also mentioned Electra's assumption that because some footprints match hers exactly, they must belong to her brother (in Libation Bearers, 175, 210). Jones concludes that in Greek tragedy "not only are objects psyche-drenched but human subjects objectify, externalise themselves—at first sight very strangely. . . . This picture of the individual's emotional life (which would not have surprised Aristotle) strikes quaint and cold to us who are strangers, almost, to the multiple self, and who take an inward concentration . . . for selfhood's principle."[49]

I warned earlier that such a perspective on the ancient Greek risks condescension, and now we see why. Not because it is wrong, for it is absolutely right. But it assumes that the modern self has transcended this tendency. In fact, if Lacan and Klein are correct, the Greeks were simply less repressed, more open and less self-conscious, about what we all do unconsciously: we live much of our lives as though we were living in the minds of others. The Greek poets wrote when humankind was young. Perhaps this too is part of the meaning of this cliché. When humankind was young it was not fundamentally different from the way it is now, but it was less self-conscious, which makes the operations of its psyche easier to see, being more out in the open, so to speak. This is why the tragedies are such great psychological studies: they concern the play of passions free of the self. The question, of course, is whether an increase in self-consciousness leads to an increase in self-control and the freedom that goes with it—that is, the genuine freedom that would stem from bringing the passions under the reign of the psyche. Certainly the history of modern warfare, the estimated one hundred million killed in this century alone does not support this thesis. Nor are the novels of such contemporary authors as Philip Roth, and Donald Barthelme, in which the protagonists' great insight into their own characters neither allows nor motivates them to change their conduct.

Dignity and agency, I have argued with the help of the poets, depend not on human freedom but upon human responsibility, which takes our actions seriously by connecting them to a world of others, and so making our acts count. In taking responsibility we take ourselves seriously as human beings in the world. Too much is made today of the power of self-reflection, be it the linguistically mediated self-reflection found in the earlier work of Jürgen Habermas that is supposed to lead to truth or the self-knowledge (*gnothi sauton*: "know thyself") that has been at the center of philosophy since Socrates. Not self-knowledge, but the willingness to answer for oneself and one's deeds, matters, what might be called "logon didou sauto" (self-answerability), after a term used in the law courts and audit of magistrates. With this as one's motto all the genuine achievements of the Western philosophical perspective on man are retained, without the hubris and self-deception that so often go with that view. Under logon didou sauto, man remains an agent in the world, as well as a locus of value, not because he possesses free will but because he is willing to act as though what he does makes a difference, as it surely does. It is this perspective that is key to the poets' humane antihumanism.

A sympathetic reader might respond that even if the poets are more right than wrong, why not regard the story of increasing freedom and rational self-control as a magnificent myth or a noble lie: an ideal to which people may aspire and in doing so fall less short than if they did not try at all? The answer has been given by Sophocles, in his study of what happens to the ideals expressed in the "ode to man," by the Frankfurt school in its critique of instrumental reason, and by Freud. To treat the desires as one more piece of unconquered, recalcitrant nature leads to rebellion, rage, and revenge, against nature and man. That is, it leads to the rage, violence, and pursuit of death studied in chapters 3 and 4.

HUMANE ANTIHUMANISM AND THE MEANING OF
RESPONSIBILITY WITHOUT FREEDOM TODAY

In his later work, Michel Foucault seems to soften his antihumanism a bit, arguing that human freedom may be achieved in thought, which is "what allows one to step back. . . . Thought is freedom in relation to what one does," the freedom to take acts as objects of reflection.[50] Alexander Nehamas makes a similar argument about humanism. Humanism does not require that humans be autonomous, free and self-constituting, but only that "we are able to distance ourselves from any specific situation in which we happen to be. . . . All that we need in order not to be defined by one role is our ability to occupy another role."[51] This, though, does not seem quite right, and not only because it risks identifying the contemporary fragmentation of roles and identities with the realization of man's *humanitas*. Nor is it wrong simply because the ability to reflect on our acts does not necessarily imply the capacity to act otherwise, which was the point of my Medea example, what I called deliberation without choice. Rather, Foucault and Nehamas are not quite right because what we do with the distance matters. Responsibility does indeed require distance, in order that we might see the effects of our acts on others, and over time. But distance is not enough. We act humanely only when this distance eventuates in taking responsibility. Responsibility implies distant nearness: the distance that allows us to grasp the effects of our acts on others; and the nearness that allows us to see these consequences as virtual extensions or expressions of ourselves. The subtle combination of distance and nearness is lacking in the revised humanism of the later Foucault and of Nehamas.

It is also, I believe, lacking in Derrida and Jean-François Lyotard, though the influence of Emmanuel Levinas on postmodern concepts of freedom and responsibility makes this a difficult judgment. In *Difficult Freedom* Levinas argues that we ought to constrain our freedom in the name of responsibility. Freedom is "a miraculous centre of radiance," from which one should take delight; it is not actually necessary to "radiate" in order to do so.[52] From a much darker perspective this seems to be Derrida's position as well, at least in the interview " 'Eating Well.' " There the position is not so much that the subject is not free, but that he should not be. A free subject is carnivorous, rapacious, greedy, devouring, and all the rest, as Auschwitz conclusively proved, a view shared by Lyotard.[53] Best, Derrida seems to say, to deconstruct the subject, to use language as Christians have used the notion of humility before an omnipotent God, in order to take this subject apart, much as Zeus bisected the arrogant human race in order to weaken it in Aristophanes' account of the origins of love (see Plato, *Symposium,* 189c–193e). In this vein Derrida adopts Levinas' view of the subject as willing hostage, one who delivers himself over to the other, making himself so open and vulnerable to the other that he can no longer dominate the other, even if he wishes.[54] Lyotard as usual puts it more austerely, stating simply that "the splitting of the self would, at least, have the finality of destroying its presumptuousness."[55] Although such a view has similarities to that of the tragic poets, one must be careful not to ignore the difference. Like the tragic poets, Derrida and Levinas both place responsibility over freedom. Like the poets, neither sees a need to connect these concepts.

Nevertheless, there is a sharp difference between their view and that of the poets, one highlighted by Derrida's use of Levinas. Derrida clearly holds that the sovereign constituting subject is a myth, but he also recognizes that it is not merely a myth. Men and women who believe that myth try to put it into practice and end up in no end of trouble—the point, I have argued, of the "ode to man" in *Antigone*. If, however, men and women could be convinced that they are really fragmented objects of experience, subjects only in relationship to another who comes first, then much pain, sorrow, suffering, and evil could be avoided. The deconstruction of the subject is, in other words, a rhetorical strategy and in this sense similar to Levinas's attempt to persuade men and women to hold themselves hostage to the other. Here, Derrida finds more freedom and choice in the human situation than do the tragic poets: he allows the freedom to respond to a rhetorical strategy designed to convince the subject that he is not one. Else why bother wondering *Who Comes after the Subject* (the title of a recent collection on the topic) in the first place?

The tragic poets did not attribute to man even such limited freedom. They did not assume that he might change his character. On the contrary, they assumed that character is univocal, fixed and identifiable, though of course they did not use these contemporary terms of abuse. Nor did they assume that man could or would abandon his hubristic attempt to impress and impose himself upon the world, but only that he might be shown the vainness of certain ways of doing so. Hence men are unlikely to be convinced to subordinate themselves to the other. Self-abnegation is part of the Judeo-Christian tradition, even when it is carried out in the medium of language. It is not, however, part of the classical tradition, which is why not even Plato argued that man should be just for the sake of the other. Rather, man should be just for the sake of his own psyche, the theme of the *Republic*. Not self-denial but an understanding of the self's connection to others in a network of responsible relationships is the strategy of the poets, the way they would humanize a fundamentally inhuman world. Both poets and postmoderns conclude that man is responsible without being free. For the poets, however, man must learn to come to terms with this brute fact as best he can, which means in the company of fellow humans. For the postmoderns, responsibility without freedom is yet another myth of the subject, albeit one less destructive to civilization than that of the sovereign subject. This is a difference worth learning from.

Responsibility without freedom is most terrifying when we feel so unconnected and apart from others that the only conceivable relationship with them is as an instrument, a means, in which we become responsible for what they would have us do. It is this that postmoderns would overcome with their veneration of the other, the subordination of the subject to the other. The tragic poets, on the other hand, would overcome this same fear by embedding men and women more deeply in responsible relationships with others, a strategy that requires not the subordination of the subject to the other but their mutual connection. Such connections can do much to assuage the fear of being a mere instrument (or Levinas' hostage, actually a terrifying prospect) to the other. Such connections also make it less likely that the inhumanity within each of us will lead us to regard the other as a mere instrument or means. Responsible connections do this by giving gravity to our acts, causing them to matter in the world, in this way linking the acceptance of responsibility to others with a sense of self as a creative, responsible agent who is not merely absurd. Foucault states that if we are still to talk of the subject, it must be one "stripped of its creative role," and analyzed strictly as an effect.[56] Such a conclusion misunderstands creativity, in effect equating it with rational autonomy. In this way it overlooks how taking responsibility, as well as demanding it from others, is a self-constituting act: a way of asserting the earnest reality of ourselves, and others, by taking our acts seriously. This is the view of the subject held unintrospectively by the tragic poets. That they take it for granted makes it hard for us to recognize it. But this view forms the assumed but unacknowledged background to their dramas.

Pity and the Foundations of Civilization

CHAPTER 6

> The supreme tragic emotion, to judge from the surviving tragedies, is
> *eleos* or *oiktos*. Both words are generally translated into English as pity.
> —W. B. Stanford, *Greek Tragedy and the Emotions*

In this chapter I shall consider the social and political implications of
the psychoanalytic theory of Greek tragedy, a project begun in the conclusion of the last chapter. As I stated in chapter 1, in order to "enlarge"
contemporary psychoanalysis by means of the tragedies, I must show
that psychoanalysis can address the fundamental questions of civilization, questions that until now only the psychoanalytic theory of Freud
has seriously addressed.

There is a school of political thought that holds that the history of
modern political philosophy beginning with Machiavelli is one of de-
cline. Whereas the ancients, Plato and Aristotle, held that reason might
come to know man's place in the cosmos and order his world accordingly, moderns are satisfied with far less: a commodious and peaceful
social order. How this order might best be achieved is, of course, a subject of debate among them. In *The Passions and the Interests,* Albert O.
Hirschman argues that while moderns disagree on much, a surprising
number hold that the solution to the riddle of civilization is to transform
passionate desires into interests so as to replace the love of pleasure,
domination, and honor with the love of gain. Such a solution became
attractive, in part, because moderns were no longer convinced that reason, the standard of Plato and Aristotle, constituted an adequate bulwark
against passion and desire.

Hirschman recounts a number of steps in the transformation of passion
into interest that need not be recapitulated here. Most striking are the
alternatives that such a strategy replaces. On the one hand is the rational
repression of passion and desire, the method, it was argued in chapter 3,
shared by Plato and Freud: self-control as the harsh control of one part
of the self by another part. But on the other it also replaces the strategy
of setting passion against passion: the insight that "one set of passions,
hitherto known variously as greed, avarice, or love of lucre, could be
usefully employed to oppose and bridle such other passions as ambition,
lust for power, or sexual lust."[1]

Of the possibilities considered by Hirschman, however, one is distinctly missing. He ignores the notion that society might be ordered by setting powerful *civilizing* passions, passions that reflect a genuine concern for others such as love and pity, against the uncivilized passions like ambition, lust for power, greed, envy, or unbridled sexual desire. It seems such an obvious solution: to set love, care, and concern for others against the passions that lead us to exploit others. Yet this solution finds almost no place in classical or modern thought, seemingly regarded as even more utopian than the classical ideal, the rational control of desire.

There is, however, a tradition in which this obvious solution, as I have called it, is central: that of Greek tragedy. It must be teased out, however, for the tragedies are not texts in political theory but works of art. The solution of the tragic poets to the riddle of civilization is pity, though it is not pity as moderns understand it. Nor is it identical with Christian pity, which is why we will derive no benefit from drawing figures such as Saint Augustine into the fray. Before characterizing this solution, however, let me consider Hirschman's study of the passions and interests in a little more detail. Of course doing so will lead me to take some of Hirschman's generalizations about political thought in the early modern era out of context. But his insights should prove fruitful to this argument, so I hope my readers will forgive my liberties and turn to Hirschman himself for larger contexts that are irrelevant to my discussion.

PASSIONS AND INTERESTS

By the seventeenth century, says Hirschman, it was widely held that moralizing philosophy and religious precept could no longer be trusted to restrain the destructive passions. Although repression and coercion suggested themselves as alternatives, the instability of such solutions was widely recognized. Harnessing the destructive passions, transforming them in some way so that they might serve society, became the modal strategy. Harnessing the passions might mean several different things, however. It might even characterize Plato's methods: harnessing *thumos* (which may in this context be rendered as "a sense of honor") to *nous* (reason), and so create a powerful bulwark against desire is one Platonic strategy (found in the *Republic*); another involves combining eros with the good and beautiful, so that man desires only them (see *Symposium, Phaedrus*). In the modern era, however, this strategy quickly came to mean the principle of countervailing passion: to set ambition against ambition, avarice against avarice, and so forth, as the authors of the *Federalist* (1787–1788) put it.[2]

Perhaps the most compelling and fascinating aspect of Hirschman's argument is the wide range of theorists he shows to have embraced the principle of countervailing passion. Francis Bacon ("to set affection against affection and to master one by another"), Baruch Spinoza ("an affect cannot be restrained nor removed unless by an opposed and stronger affect"), David Hume (to restrain the "love of pleasure" by the "love of gain"), and of course Thomas Hobbes, who set fear against desire, are exemplary. Important, and commented upon only infrequently by Hirschman, is that none of these theorists proposed setting what might be called the civilizing passions, such as love and pity, against the uncivilized ones. Rather, their programs called for placing one uncivilized passion against another. Against this conclusion it might be argued that the fear upon which Hobbes relies, for example, to say nothing of the love of comfort and commodious living, other favorite Hobbesian passions, are themselves civilizing, insofar as they promote civilization. But *any* passion becomes civilizing if only society is clever enough to turn it back against its unruly possessor: the strategy of countervailing passion. By *civilizing passions* I mean those passions that are originally and primarily (but not exclusively) concerned with the welfare of others, such as pity, compassion, and some types of love. That society might be based upon such passions is, I believe, a stranger and more alien notion than at first appears, which is perhaps why there is a tendency to assimilate it to more familiar notions, such as regarding a passion as civilized if civilization can somehow exploit it.

These authors have not ignored love and pity as bulwarks of civilization because they are generally regarded as too weak or ineffective to counter uncivilized passions. On the contrary, love, and even pity, are recognized to be sufficiently powerful to impel men and women to virtually anything, including the sacrifice of their lives. Thus, David Johnston interprets Hobbes's *Leviathan* as rhetoric designed to convince men of the improbable proposition that fear of death really is their paramount concern, trumping all others. Only then will they be effectively subject to the sovereign, who may inflict death.[3] Emotions like love and pity are not too weak to civilize society but too strong, too unpredictable, too difficult to bring under civilization's sway. The sheer immediacy and intensity of the passions, even the civilizing ones, gets us into trouble. For this reason Immanuel Kant (not one of the authors examined by Hirschman) distrusts love and compassion in all their guises, for they cannot be commanded. On the contrary, their "object may determine the will by means of inclination," for Kant a most troublesome outcome. The love that is commanded in the Scriptures, says Kant, "is beneficence from duty . . . [and it] is practical love, not *pathological* love; it resides in the will, and not in . . . feeling, in principles of action and not in melting compassion; and it alone can be commanded."[4] Compassion is "pathological" because it attaches us to particular persons, leading us to do something because of our feelings toward the person rather than because we have chosen the action for its own sake by an act of will. Compassion is dangerous precisely because it cannot be "commanded."

Hume doubts man's ability to command even his civilized passions. He draws a distinction "betwixt a calm and a weak passion; between a violent and a strong one," concluding that society need not risk unleashing the most powerful civilizing passions, such as love and compassion, in order to counteract the most powerful uncivilized ones.[5] Rather, certain calm passions are actually more powerful than their apparently violent and turbulent counterparts. In particular, the rational pursuit of wealth is a calm passion that is nonetheless powerful enough to triumph over uncivilized passions like lust.

Here is the path from passion to interest. Originally understood in the late sixteenth century in terms of what Bishop Butler calls "reasonable self-love," that is, the rational pursuit of all aspects of human fulfillment, almost a classical ideal, interest soon came to be defined in strictly economic terms.[6] Clearer about the character of this transformation than its sources, Hirschman's study, particularly of Hume, supports the conclusion that fear of the uncontrolled nature of the civilizing passions as much as fear of the uncivilized ones led to the solution of interest. Otherwise expressed, love, pity, and compassion are not only powerful enough to control greed, lust, ambition, and desire, but they are so powerful that they themselves become the problem. To set the civilizing passions against the uncivilized ones invites disaster, even should the civilizing passions prove more powerful. Better to channel uncivilized passions into the activity of acquisition and so render them sacred, almost a calling. This is the strategy of interest. Inherent in this strategy, and seemingly inseparable from it suggests Hirschman, is the idealization of interest. Disruptive, uncivilized passions are somehow rendered calm and beneficent when transmuted into the pursuit of economic interest. I shall return to this point in the conclusion.

Now, however, it will be useful to look at the tragic poets, who pursued a strategy for civilization represented neither by Hirschman's philosophers nor by the ancients, Plato and Aristotle. The poets unleashed pity and compassion as a civilizing force, but in such a way as to educate these powerful passions, to make them less dangerous. In a word, tragedy is *paideia* in pity (the cultivation of pity, its *bildung*), an insight dimly grasped by Aristotle in his definition of tragedy as the "katharsis of pity and fear" (*Poet.*, c6).

PITY IN GREEK TRAGEDY

Recall how Plato sought to solve the most important social problem faced by the Athenian polis, the problem of how to civilize Homeric *arete,* the agonistic, individual struggle for excellence at no matter what cost to society. (The similarity between this problem and that of the passionate pursuit of glory addressed by the protagonists of Hirschman's book should not be overlooked.) Plato's solution, as A. W. H. Adkins has argued, was to redefine the meaning of nobility, so as to make the standard of arete *sophrosune,* self-control and prudence.[7] Radical in key respects, Plato's approach remains bound to the Homeric tradition insofar as it continues to interpret excellence in individualistic terms: as a contest in self-control. Only this time it is a contest with oneself.

The tragic poets' strategy for civilization is different from Plato's, by which I do not mean opposed to. One sees it most clearly in Sophocles' *Ajax*. When in a fit of madness Ajax kills sheep instead of the leaders of his own army, his intended target, his humiliation is complete, and he must kill himself to salvage whatever personal honor he can, regardless of the effect of his death on his wife and child. A selfish man who even at the moment of his death regrets only that he failed to kill the Greek generals, Ajax nonetheless appears an attractive character in important respects. He is forthright, courageous, and without guile, willing to die for the principles for which he lived.

But even though Ajax is admirable in many respects, he cannot exist in the polis: he would destroy it, or the polis must destroy him. Odysseus represents the virtues of the polis. Not, in Sophocles' account, because Odysseus is the better talker but because he can feel pity and compassion, emotions quite absent from the heroic Ajax (see 1355). In a word, Sophocles sees pity as an aspect of arete, just as Plato regards sophrosune to be part of it. As H. D. F. Kitto puts it, "Pity, generosity, gratitude for what has been well done, forbearance towards injuries: these are what Odysseus urges in the final scene too, thinking here also, as he says, of himself, as well as of Ajax."[8] These values civilize the polis. *Ajax,* a play that spans the distance between the archaic world and that of the fifth century B.C. polis, is about precisely this. So too are most of the extant tragedies, not just those of Sophocles, although he is the poet most concerned with pity. As Bennett Simon says about Euripides' *Heracles:* "A new notion of heroism is defined in the *Heracles,* a heroism that incorporates rather than disowns the suffering and enduring that are the lot of the old, the child, and the woman."[9]

From this perspective, civilization stems neither from control of uncivilized passions by reason nor from rechanneling of uncivilized passions into less harmful pursuits but rather from the mobilization of the civilizing emotions, centered on pity. To be led by such emotions is real heroism. In a typically Greek remark, Oedipus locates his greatness in his ability to bear enormous pain, more pain than any other man could bear (see *Oedipus Tyrannus,* 1415). His remark reflects the influence of the heroic ethic on tragedy, but it remains a version of the heroic ethic, a contest in agony. Civilizing this ethic, the tragic poets seem to say, is a measure of a man's greatness, and that of the polis, in terms of pain sharing, not just pain bearing. Sophocles shows us that it is not Oedipus' ability to bear more pain than another but his willingness to share the pain of the citizens of Thebes and grant it priority over his own that marks the true measure of his greatness (see *Oedipus Tyrannus*, 59–64, 93–94). With this principle all three tragic poets agree, so that in *Heracles* (for example at 1234–1236), Euripides portrays King Theseus as the symbolic embodiment of the sound polis not merely because he is brave and steadfast, although of course these virtues are important. In Theseus is embodied the entire constellation of virtues centered upon pity, such as compassion, generosity, decency, and love of humanity (*philanthropia*).

When I refer to *pity*, I mean this constellation of emotions. For, as Jean-Jacques Rousseau asks in his *Second Discourse*, what are generosity, clemency, and humanity but pity (*pitié*) applied to the weak, the guilty, and the species in general?[10] Pity is the paradigmatic civilizing passion. I have not found it useful to distinguish among such closely related terms as *pity*, *mercy*, and *compassion*, all of which, the *Oxford English Dictionary* relates, have their French and English origins in Latin-based Christian thought. *Pity*, for example, stems from the Latin *pietas*, "piety," as does Rousseau's *pitié*. One reason I have not found such distinctions useful is that mine is a rhetoric of the passions, which are often not as amenable to fine distinctions as the terms that signify them. Even more important, the Greek concept of pity is pre-Christian. It focuses on the felt connection to the suffering of others rather than the disposition to mercy and compassion. The Christian disposition stems from the Greek connection and I am most concerned with the origin and quality of that disposition itself.

Jean-Pierre Vernant argues, as noted in chapter 2, that Greek tragedy confronts heroic values and ancient religious representations with the new modes of thought that characterize the advent of law within the city-state.[11] This is certainly part of the story. Another part, which I have chosen to emphasize in this chapter, would put the definition of tragedy a little differently. Tragedy is born when men become convinced that they can act more nobly than the gods, not because they can compete with them, but because humans can offer what the gods never can: pity and compassion. Tragedy is born when men begin to redefine nobility (which is of course Adkins' point as well). Where Plato would make sophrosune the measure of nobility, the tragic poets would make pity and compassion its standard. So Amphitryon, father of Heracles, says to Zeus, "I, mere man, am nobler [have more arete] than you, great god" (Eur., *Heracles*, 342). This is not mere hubris talking, but fact: Amphitryon is capable of depths of pity and compassion that Zeus can hardly imagine.

This does not, of course, equip man to compete with the gods—that would be hubris indeed, the hubris of Ajax. Rather, it allows men to think of the polis as a place where they may offer each other support, pity and compassion in the face of the depredations of the gods and the harshness of life in general. J. Peter Euben's comments on the puzzling resolution of Aeschylus' *Oresteia* trilogy captures this ideal well. "The *Oresteia* does not end suffering but collectivizes it through the medium of dramatic performance."[12] To collectivize suffering is, I shall argue, a key dimension of pity, what humans can do for each other that the gods cannot. Tragedy not only describes this shared suffering, it *is* this shared suffering, suggests Euben. Such an interpretation gives new meaning to the insight that tragedy is a civic celebration, "an occasion to say something about the city . . . and essentially a festival of the democratic polis," as Simon Goldhill puts it.[13] From the perspective of pity, Greek tragedy celebrates the willingness and ability of the citizens of Athens to share each other's pain. It is to this aspect of Athenian greatness that Thucydides' Pericles refers when he states that "since a state can support individuals in their suffering, but no one person by himself can bear the load that rests upon the state, is it not right for us all to rally to her defence?" (*History*, 2.60). Like the tragic poets, Pericles transforms pain-sharing into an act of nobility.

Virtually every extant tragedy contains calls for and expressions of pity. *Eleos* and *oiktos*, the words we translate as "pity," both seem to stem from inarticulate cries of grief, commonly rendered as *eleleu* and *oi*, and are among the most common terms in Greek tragedy, far more common than words frequently seen as central to the tragic vision like *arete* or *hubris*. Aristotle defines tragedy in terms of its ability to evoke pity (he always uses the term *eleos*, which seems to be the slightly less emphatic of the two) and fear (*phobos*). Pausanias (1.17.1) states that there was an Altar of Pity at Athens, though it may have been Hellenistic. Pity was obviously a central emotion to the Greeks, as W. B. Stanford argues in his *Greek Tragedy and the Emotions*. What Winnington-Ingram says about Sophocles applies, with only slightly lesser force, to Aeschylus and Euripides as well: "That pity was for Sophocles a supreme value need hardly be argued. Pity inspires every work of his that has come down to us—pity and *suggnome*, that capacity to enter into the feelings of another which made possible every aspect of his dramatic creation."[14]

Founding Myths of Pity: *Philoctetes*, or
Pity in the State of Nature
I propose to read Sophocles' *Philoctetes* as an account of pity in the state of nature. Unlike modern state-of-nature theorists, Sophocles does not assume that man was originally asocial. In this sense my comparison is limited. On the other hand, Sophocles does assume that in suffering, at least, we are all rendered potentially asocial: isolated and alone. Pity brings us back into the community of others. Because of the difference between ancients and moderns regarding human sociability, it might be argued that it is misleading to equate Philoctetes' isolation on a deserted island with a state of nature. My key argument for the comparison (and it is that, not an identity) is that the setting of Sophocles' play serves the same function as the state of nature in modern

theory: to reveal aspects of human nature (such a dangerous term these days!) so basic that society ignores them only at its peril.

After much hesitation, Neoptolemus steals Philoctetes' bow, but, overcome with remorse, he gives it back. The question of justice never enters into the matter on either side. In presenting his desire to keep the bow, Philoctetes appeals neither to justice nor to the norm of reciprocity. Rather, he says simply, "take pity on me" (*su m'eleeson,* 501). In deciding to return the bow, Neoptolemus refers not to justice but to his ability to feel Philoctetes' pain. "A kind of compassion, a terrible compassion, has come upon me for him. I have felt it for him all the time" (965). As has been frequently pointed out, for example by Edmund Wilson in his essay "The Wound and the Bow," the location of this play on a deserted island is significant, making the play a metaphor for civilization itself.[15] There the isolated and wounded Philoctetes struggles with the wily and instrumental Odysseus (so different from the Odysseus in Sophocles' *Ajax*) for the soul of the young Neoptolemus, who is filled with compassion for Philoctetes but remains vulnerable to the persuasions of his commander, as well as to his own greedy desire to possess Philoctetes' bow (see 658–670). Which side of man is to prevail? The play suggests that whereas pity is a profound and powerful emotion, the harshness of our circumstances, as well as the intensity of our desires and fears, may lead us to cut ourselves off from those who suffer. Aristotle argues similarly, as will be shown shortly.

"You are not bad yourself," says Philoctetes to Neoptolemus. "By bad men's teaching you came to practice your foul lesson" (972). Recall in this regard the father of Neoptolemus: Achilles, the original prepolitical man, raised not in civilized society by corruptible humans but in natural purity by the half-human centaur Chiron. The question in the play becomes whether Neoptolemus will be able to return to his own true nature. "Be your true self (*sautou genou*) again," pleads Philoctetes (950). But is Neoptolemus already too corrupted? Like almost all accounts of the state of nature, *Philoctetes* shows how civilization might be built on the basis of what one finds in nature, in this case the conflict between pity, greed, and glory. What is pity in this context? Here it is Neoptolemus' ability to stay connected to Philoctetes' suffering and not render him merely outcast, scapegoat, or other. Conversely, what Philoctetes asks of Neoptolemus is not to be cured by him but simply to remain emotionally connected to him and so to humanity. "The sickness in me seeks to have you beside me," says Philoctetes simply (675).

What if this were the foundation of civilization: not justice but the ability to stay connected to others and so sympathetically to share their emotions, ease their isolation, and alleviate their alienation from humanity? Easy enough in joy, sorrow makes such sharing even more important. This, I argue, is the poets' answer to the riddle of civilization. If their answer is different from that given by most philosophers in the Western tradition, however, it is no less fragile than theirs, as Neoptolemus' future exploits suggest.[16] Though fragile, pity may nonetheless be strengthened through an education in pity. This is the task of tragedy.

Prometheus' Gift of Pity

Aeschylus' *Prometheus Bound* may be read as a founding myth of pity in addition to being a founding myth of blood ritual, civilization, and man's relationship to death. Even more than *Philoctetes, Prometheus Bound* concerns a prepolitical state in which the building blocks of society are being laid. Like *Philoctetes, Prometheus Bound* is exceptionally located, all other extant tragedies (with the exception of Euripides' satyr play *The Cyclops*) taking place within established society, if not within the polis, then among barbarians who generally turn out to be about as civilized, or uncivilized, as the Greeks themselves (see Aesch., *Persians*; Eur.: *Iphigenia in Tauris; Helen*).

Earlier I suggested that Prometheus' gift of unseeing hope, rather than his gift of technology constituted his greatest gift, allowing people a chance to construct a meaning for their lives relieved of the imminent pressure of death. Now it is time to consider a further possibility. Not unseeing hope, but himself, his own suffering that teaches us pity, represents Prometheus' finest gift. For this offering makes decent civilization possible. "I gave to mortal man a precedence over myself in pity," Prometheus says (240). By this he suggests that he gave man the example of his own suffering, so that man might learn pity. "Yes, to my friends I am a spectacle of pity" (248). Indeed, Prometheus suffers so much that the whole earth comes to pity him.

> The wave cries out as it breaks into surf;
> the depth cries out, lamenting you; the dark
> Hades, the hollow underneath the world,
> suddenly groans below; the springs of sacred flowing rivers all lament
> the pain and pity of your suffering,

says the chorus (430–435). Through his suffering pity is born, evoked as though Prometheus were its suffering midwife. Like justice for Plato, what is most important for the poets, pity, cannot be reduced to a techne, the broad sense of technology that I described earlier.

Unlike Prometheus' other gifts, pity doesn't *do* anything. It connects us to others and so allows us to be human rather than "like swarming ants in holes in the ground," as men and women were before Prometheus' sacrifice (450). Thus, the chorus (although they are not human, the daughters of Oceanus act and react as humans would be expected to) vows at the end of the play that they will suffer with Prometheus, even if doing so achieves nothing, at least in the short run (see 1065). In this way they will express their solidarity with him against the tyranny of Zeus. Here it seems pity becomes a virtual political principle (see 400). If we guide our lives by the constellation of emotions centered upon pity, as Theseus (see Soph. *Oedipus at Colonus,* Eur. *Heracles*) does, then no one could become a despot, nor tolerate tyranny.

Prometheus is made easier to identify with because of an almost schizoid quality (an aspect of his personality in which different emotional states are not well integrated, appearing almost as though they were held by separate selves), that makes him at one moment manlike and at another, godlike. At one point he stops in the midst of bemoaning his suffering and agony and says, "Wait, what am I saying? / I know how it all turns out: no unforeseen heartbreaks for me" (100–101, Scully and Herington translation; see too 185–189). It is as though he suddenly remembers that he is a god, who knows, if he cannot change, the future. Prometheus, say the translators of the Oxford edition, "appears to be deliberately represented as an unstable compound of mortal sufferer and immortal prophet."[17] I suspect that any god with whose sufferings men are expected to identify must have this quality. Christians, for example, can readily identify with the sufferings of Jesus but not with those of God, who also apparently suffers (see *Genesis,* 6:6–7), though in a way that is humanly incomprehensible.

Prometheus does not suffer alone. The last half of the play (beginning at line 560) primarily concerns Io, who suffers horribly from the sting of the gadfly inflicted on her by Hera, who does not want her to stand still long enough for Zeus to make love to her again. Io wants to know whether there is something that can ease her pain or at least when the pain will end. Her situation reflects that of humanity after Prometheus took away man's knowledge of when his suffering would end—that is, knowledge of the hour of his death. In its place Prometheus put hope. But in the face of intense suffering not even hope is enough. In a world of suffering we need the pity of others, understood as their willingness to share our pain and so ease our isolation, as the daughters of Oceanus do for Prometheus (see 1065). Io, human rather than divine, pious victim (a priestess of Hera, she was punished for being raped by Zeus) rather than bold benefactor, becomes in this regard even an easier object of pity than Prometheus. Prometheus, like Theseus, is the distant benefactor who teaches pity. Io is our counterpart, the suffering human for whom we should have the pity that Prometheus teaches. Io makes the story complete.

The Tragedies as the Cultivation of Pity
Tragedy is *paideia* in pity, an untranslatable term, as Werner Jaeger points out, but perhaps best rendered in this context as an upbringing in the civilizing emotions centered on pity.[18] Pity may be natural, but it is not therefore auto-

matic. It is easy to feel pity. What is difficult, and requires education, is to feel pity toward the right person to the right extent at the right time for the right reason in the right way. Not everyone can do this. Hence to do it well is a rare, laudable, and fine achievement. This sounds like Aristotle (see *Nicomachean Ethics*, 1109a25–30) because the idea is similar: pity may be natural, but it requires education and proper guidance so that it may be properly channeled. In part the education of pity concerns removing barriers to it. Or as Orestes puts it in Euripides' *Electra*, "Uneducated men are pitiless, but we who are educated pity much. And we pay a high price for being intelligent. Wisdom hurts" (295).

Like Orestes, Aristotle recognizes in his *Rhetoric* (see 2.1378a–1385b) that pity is much more likely to be evoked in some people and circumstances than in others. Eleos is less likely to affect people who are themselves in desperate circumstances, as is Iphigenia, who states, "Unhappiness, O friends, can harden us toward sorrow harsher than our own" (Eur., *Iphigenia in Tauris*, 352–353). Similarly, pity is not to be expected from those in a mood of arrogant self-confidence. It is also less likely to be effective in those who are angry, rash, afraid, or shocked. Finally, those filled with spiteful envy (*phthonos*) at the prosperity of others are unlikely to feel pity. Those most likely to feel it are more experienced in living, less bold, more sensible, and weaker than powerful, heroic, and pitiless figures like Ajax. Aristotle points out that people most likely to feel pity include "those who have children, and parents, and wives; for these are part of them, and are such as to suffer . . . evils" (*Rhet.*, 2.1385b). From this perspective, the poets' frequent call, generally through the chorus, for temperance and sophrosune takes on a new meaning. These virtues are not only valuable in themselves, they create the conditions in which pity can operate. They are a call to clear the mind of rash emotions, the better to feel the civilizing ones, above all pity. Pity both reflects and is the cause of the connections to others that sustain community.

The Katharsis of Pity and Fear

As is well known, Aristotle defines tragedy in terms of its ability to evoke the *katharsis* of pity and fear (see *Poetics*, c6). Much ink has been spent on this definition, in large measure because Aristotle cryptically promises more detail elsewhere (in *Politics*, bk. 8, c7), but if he ever wrote that other work, it has been lost. Interpreting *katharsis* as a type of *elenchos* (a form of controlled dialogue, like a Socratic dialogue) and paideia, Stephen Salkever argues that Aristotelian katharsis involves introducing order into disorderly souls and so reducing the lust for power and glory.[19] In defining *katharsis* as he does, Salkever steps outside the usual debates over the term, which concern whether it is best seen as a type of ritual purification and cleansing or as emotional and intellectual clarification. Although Salkever's use of the term is unusual, it finds support in Plato's *Sophist* (see 231b), which characterizes the process of paideia through elenchos rather than admonition as the cathartic art (*kathartike*).

In the democratic polis, suggests Aristotle, the fundamental flaw is *pleonexia* (greed) especially as it takes the form of *kerdos*: "love of gain." (Unlike the moderns studied by Hirschman, the ancients almost never idealize interest.) Laws can help to contain such greed, but they are insufficient. Education aimed at the passions is also necessary. This is the task of tragedy. Average citizens (the people most capable of feeling pity) learn the value of self-restraint through the pity and fear aroused by the fearsome fates of those who grasp for too much. They learn, that is, to fear that the same thing might happen to them. The pity they feel for others is in the end self-pity, as in the *Iliad,* where the captive women in Achilles' tent join in the lamentations over the body of Patroclus. But, Homer adds, "It was a pretext, for each was bewailing her own personal sorrows" (19.302).

The strength of Salkever's piece is twofold. First, it recognizes that there is nothing mysterious about katharsis. It is not an enigmatic psychological principle, but an education in basic truths necessary to live in civilized society. Second, Salkever grasps that this education is primarily emotional, directed not so much at imparting principles of behavior as at emotional attitudes, an education of the passions. Nevertheless, I disagree with Salkever. To me, katharsis is valuable not so much because it teaches fearful self-restraint, but because it helps create a calm space within which pity may flourish. Whereas Salkever's Aristotle runs pity-and-fear together as though they were one, the poets recognize that too much fear is a barrier to pity. For the poets, what Aristotle calls the katharsis of pity and fear might better be rendered as the katharsis of fear, so that pity might find its proper place.

My argument is not that Salkever gets Aristotle wrong. Rather Aristotle gets the tragic poets wrong, rendering their account overly individualistic and self-centered, in which the experience of watching dramas about the destruction of people who lack self-control teaches us to fear the consequences of this lack in ourselves. When a lot of individuals, one by one, learn this lesson in fear and so fear the same thing, then the polis will act in a self-controlled way, believes Aristotle. Salkever subtitles his study, "Aristotle's Response to Plato." Plato would, of course, drive the poets from the polis (or censor them), whereas Aristotle argues that the tragic poets play an important role in educating the emotions. True enough, but whereas Aristotle and Plato disagree on the educational contribution of the poets, both agree on what is to be taught: the rational self-control of individuals (or at least of the political leadership). To be sure, Aristotle understands man to be a political animal in a way that most moderns do not. Nevertheless, we should not let Aristotle's famous definition of man as *zoon politikon* obscure his point: the moral virtues are all self-regarding. People practice temperance and generosity because of the effect of these virtues on their own psyches, not for the sake of others.

Pity Hurts

The view of the tragic poets differs from that of Aristotle but not radically. We pity neither for the sake of others nor for ourselves. In pity this distinction is itself dissolved. We pity because we are connected to others—their pain becomes our own. Seen in this light, it may be somewhat misleading to translate *eleos* and *oiktos* as "pity." "Compassionate grief" would be a better translation, suggests Stanford, for in *eleos* and *oiktos*,

> there is no question here of the pitier being separate from another's agony. You respond to it in the depths of your being, as a harp-string responds by sympathetic resonance to a note from another source. . . . The same depth of physical feeling is expressed in the Greek versions of the Bible by a verb that indicates a sensation in one's entrails (*splanchnizo*), and in the phrase in I John 3, 17, translated in the Authorised Version as "bowels of compassion."[20]

Whereas today we generally hold that to be an object of pity demeans us the Greek wants to be such an object. Now we are in a position to understand why. Although it is easy and painless simply to "pity" others, to feel sorry for them, it is difficult to identify with their pain so closely that it becomes our own, so that we feel it in our bowels. Who wants or needs more pain? "I haven't got time for the pain, I haven't got room for the pain," goes a popular song, subsequently perverted into a jingle to sell an analgesic. For this reason we generally stand back, offering objective solutions and the like. Kant's labeling "melting compassion" pathological serves a similar function, insulating us from others' pain as well as from our own, which might be awakened by participating in another's suffering. In Aristotle's account of self-centered pity in the *Poetics*, the fear (*phobos*) of pity-and-fear serves to create a protective distance, so that we focus upon the pain we might feel were we in the position of the other, rather than remain connected to the immediate reality of another's pain.

In *The Violence of Pity in Euripides'* Medea, Pietro Pucci holds to a more stringent view than either Aristotle or Salkever, arguing that for Euripides at least, we pity others in order to identify our own suffering with theirs, so that we can externalize our own suffering in them and gain control of it there. Pity is violent because it represents the imposition of our own suffering on others via a process of projective identification (though Pucci does not use such psychological terms), in which we force suffering parts of ourselves into others the better to contain them. Although Pucci's interpretation has its place (it helps to explain Medea's pity for the children whom she is soon to murder), it hardly seems a complete explanation of pity in the Greek tragedies. Only by assuming, as Pucci does, that writing is itself a violent imposition ("Internal and external violence begin in the very act of writing, for they are inscribed in the general structure of the sign"[21]), can we argue that the pity written about in the tragedies is always an act of violence. Pucci seems to confuse writing with what is being written about, although he might argue that this distinction is itself naive.

If we focus on what the protagonists of Greek tragedy do, we see that they spend a lot of time participating in others' suffering, mourning with them over their pain and so joining in it. As Neoptolemus says to Philoctetes, "I have been in pain for you: I have been in sorrow for your pain" (Soph., *Philoctetes*, 805). He does not say "you have been in suffering for my pain," though of course Pucci's argument is more subtle than this. Often pain sharing is the task of the chorus, and we see this no more clearly than in Sophocles' *Electra* (at 135 and *passim*), where the chorus of women of Mycenae seeks to become one with the protagonist's suffering. The chorus in Aeschylus' *Prometheus* (at 1065 and *passim*) seeks to do the same, as do the choruses in *Philoctetes*, Euripides' *Trojan Women* (see 198–210 and *passim*), and a number of other plays. As is so often the case, the chorus represents not so much the ideal observer as the ideal pain sharer. In Sophocles' *Ajax*, the chorus of Salaminian sailors demands to play this role: "How at the start did the catastrophe swoop down. Tell us: we share the pain of it" (282–283).

Why is sharing pain so important? Why does it help? Pain and suffering isolate us, as Elaine Scarry emphasizes in *The Body in Pain*, her study of physical pain. This is the reason Philoctetes says that "the sickness in me seeks to have you beside me" (675)—he wishes to escape his isolation. Similarly, it is why Prometheus asks the chorus if it has come "to howl feeling with me" (305–306, Scully and Herington translation). Emotional pain similarly cuts us off. Pain and suffering, then, threaten to fragment our sense of who we are, by threatening our sense of connection to the world. It is no accident that Philoctetes' terrible suffering results in his isolation on a deserted island. Isolation is both the cause and result of suffering, and it offers as well a psychologically acute metaphor for the experience of pain, physical and psychic. In *The Vision of Tragedy*, Richard Sewall sees the tragic vision rooted in humanity's terror at finding itself alone and isolated in a meaningless world.[22] Similarly, much modern art is devoted to this, representing what it is to live in an inhumane world, filled with unfeeling objects. Through pity, the willingness to share another's pain if only for a few moments to help him rejoin the human world, humans express their solidarity in a world that was not made for humans, and certainly not for human happiness. This is often all we can do, say the tragic poets. It is surely the most distinctively human thing, what humans can offer that the gods cannot, and perhaps the only way we are superior to the gods.

The gods do not pity, nor can they share human pain, for they lack *suggnome,* the capacity to identify intuitively with another's experience, a term Nussbaum translates as "fellow-thought-and-feeling." Hyllus, son of Heracles (who has been horribly burned to death by a poisoned robe given to him by his wife Deianira), puts it this way in instructing the servants in how to handle his father: "Take him up, servants, showing your great fellow-thought-and-feeling (*suggnomosune*) with me concerning these events, and knowing the great lack-of-thought-and-feeling (*agnomosune*) of the gods concerning the events that have taken place—they who, having engendered us and calling themselves our fathers have overseen these sufferings" (Soph., *Women of Trachis,* 1265–1270).[23] In this regard it is interesting to compare the pity of the choruses with the pity of Theseus, which is more detached. Theseus, mythical king of Athens, is almost a god, virtually a male version of Athene, whose benevolence is similarly detached. He is benevolently humane, *philanthropos*; but genuine pity remains the province of humans.

In this regard the pity of the Greek tragedies differs from Christian pity as well. Prometheus is not really a progenitor of Christ. To be sure, the biblical concept of pity resembles that of the tragic poets. The catalogue of basic human emotions is not, after all, infinite. God's pity, like his mercy and compassion, stems from God's ability to share man's feelings and agonies, a capacity enhanced by the mediation of Jesus, the embodiment of pity (see, for example, Psalms 69:20, 72:13, 102:13, 103:13; Isaiah 63:9; Hosea, 1:6; and Jonah, 4:11; as well as Matthew, 20:30–34; First Corinthians, 15:19; and James, 5:11). For the tragic poets, on the other hand, only humans can feel pity. An implication of this difference is that for the tragic poets pity frequently cannot *do* anything: it neither heals the lame, nor restores sight to the blind, though it may well provide refuge, as Theseus does for Oedipus. Rather, tragic pity establishes a connection to others, as though to say "no matter how great your sorrow, I shall not let you fall out of the world." Tragic pity is based upon the acceptance of necessity and doom, whereas the Christian quest for transcendence may lead us to downplay earthly suffering.

How Does Pity Work?

If the connection formed through pity does not heal pain and suffering, how does it work? If it does not do anything, what does it offer? The psychoanalyst James Grotstein writes in *Splitting and Projective Identification* that what men and women want most is to be "relieved of the burden of unknown, unknowable feelings by being able to express them, literally as well as figuratively into the flesh," so that the other person may come to know and share them. He calls this the need to be shriven: to confess one's pain and so receive absolution, in the sense, I believe, of participating in a communion of pain sharers. This is similar to how Euben defines tragedy, as the collectivization of suffering. The problem is that this need to share suffering is not always and automatically expressed through acts of pity. Acts of violence, which forcibly impose one's pain on another, stem from the same need. Pucci is not all wrong; he just equates a not uncommon perversion of pity with its essential character. Or as Grotstein puts it, "the sadist and the murderer desire to see the look of agony on their victim's face so as to be sure that the murderer's own tortured experience can be transmitted through the network of projective identification to the victim whose agonized face completes the communication—'over and out!'"[24] Blood ritual is, I have suggested, a version of this logic. The confrontation of tragedy with blood ritual, and more generally with the fear of death, rage, and confusion behind it, is an attempt to limit the violence that these experiences threaten to evoke by providing an opportunity to share one's pain vicariously with others and so be shriven. This experience, what Aristotle calls the katharsis of pity and fear, offers an alternative not only to blood ritual but to the crazed agonal culture that encourages men to deal with their pain by inflicting it on others.

Seen from this perspective, the stories of the tragedies are *themselves* a type of sacrifice, in the sense that they, like the ritual scapegoat, encourage the observers to project their agony into the tragedy and experience it there. However, rather than pretend that the observer's agony is movable, as it were— virtually a physical object that can be located in another and destroyed there— the tragedies recognize that suffering cannot be moved but only understood. In giving the observer's suffering a name, a character, and above all a story, tragedy helps him to tell the tale of his own agony by giving him its script. All sorrows can be borne if you put them into a story or tell a story about them.

Many of the structural and formal conventions of Greek tragedy, such as its use of familiar stories (myths) removed from everyday life, its protagonists whose inner lives are suppressed for the sake of the story, its masks, its stylized and formal language, and so forth, encourage this projective identification. A space of distant-nearness is created in which the audience may find its own feelings and experience them there, without being overwhelmed by details. This explanation of how tragedy works possesses the additional advantage of explaining the deep and puzzling connection between tragedy and sacrifice, ultimately the human sacrifice that the Greeks excitedly feared lay somewhere in the prehistory of the festival of Dionysus. Tragedy is the sacrifice of human suffering, in which the protagonists suffer horribly and generally die so that those watching might experience the communion of pain and so be shriven. An implication of this interpretation, addressed in chapter 7, is that, *pace* Klein, the content of the story, not the beautiful tragic form, provides the key to the reparative power of tragic art.

PITY AND CIVILIZATION

Not merely the classical philosophers, but the tragic poets too, recommend rational self-control, understood by *phronesis* and *sophrosune*. What is especially characteristic of the poets, however, is their equation of rational self-control with the injunction to think mortal thoughts ("ta thneta phronein"). This constitutes the mark of wisdom for the poets. What is it to think mortal thoughts? To know the condition of man: that he is born in pain and is fated soon to die, while experiencing much pain along the way. Xerxes, watching his Persian army cross the Hellespont to invade Greece, pities the shortness of man's life, that so many will soon die. No, King, responds Artabanus, his uncle, "weep rather for this, that brief as life is there never yet was or will be a man who does not wish more than once to die rather than to live" (Herodotus, *Histories*, 7.46). To think thus is to think human thoughts, as does the drunken Heracles in Euripides' *Alcestis*. Do you know what it is to be a man? he asks. Do you know what the human condition is really about? We all have to die. In the face of this fact, wine is a comfort. So too is love. Most important, however, "mortal man must be mortal-minded" (798).

What are the implications of this insight? Heracles, no intellectual, concludes that one should party hearty. To this should be added that to know one's place as a mortal being is to know that one lives in a world of suffering, ironic recoil, enormous waste of potential, and death, all of which is made bearable only by the compassion of fellow sufferers. It is just this that the gods cannot offer, for they do not suffer as men do. As Arrowsmith puts it, "the man who 'knows himself' always knows one thing—his mortality. It is because he knows he is doomed that he will, in theory, act compassionately toward other men no less doomed than he."[25] Thus, Odysseus can pity the corpse of Ajax because he recognizes that "I too shall come to that necessity" (Soph., *Ajax*, 1365). This same way of thinking leads Philoctetes to state:

> Take pity on me.
> Look how men live, always precariously
> balanced between good and bad fortune.
> (Soph., *Philoctetes*, 501–503)

Only when we appreciate—indeed, embrace—mortal life are we likely to feel pity. Why? Is it because when bad things happen to others, we fear that they will happen to us, and so we pity them as we would really pity ourselves? This is part of the story, the part emphasized by Aristotle. The other part is that in thinking mortal thoughts we understand that detaching ourselves from the pain of others will not save us. It will only make a painful life even more so, by depriving us of the human consolations available to those who do not shrink from confronting the pain and suffering of human existence.

The consolations of pity do more than make life easier to bear. They make decent civilization itself possible. As postmodern interpreters of human nature (though they do not call it that) such as Lacan have done so much to emphasize, a good deal of the aggression and other craziness present in the world represents an acting out of the pain and terror that stems from the isolation of human existence. We behave as if we could overcome our own pain and mortality by inflicting pain and death on others. This is what the heroic ethic, the agonal culture, ultimately offers: a constant struggle for excellence as an alternative to confronting personal weakness and mortality. It may well be what much of the politics among, and within, nations also concerns. Certainly this is the thesis of Hans J. Morgenthau, who argues in "Love and Power" that the quest for power, whether individual or national, is an attempt to remedy "the awareness of insufficiency born of loneliness and which only love can give. . . . The power relationship is, then, in the last analysis, a frustrated relationship of love. Those who must use and suffer power would rather be united in love. Master and subject are at the bottom of their souls lovers who have gone astray." [26] I have written not of love, but pity; the idea, however, is similar. Pity is not merely consolation for man's isolation and pain. It is the recipe for civilization. The connections of pity help to contain the aggressive acting out by which men, women, and nations would otherwise seek to overcome their pain. It will be recalled that I ended chapter 5 with similar conclusions. Even in an unfree world, empathic connections with others, which this chapter defines in terms of suggnome (translated by Nussbaum as "fellow-thought-and-feeling"), are the alternative to the instrumentalization of the other, as well as of the self.

Not merely the acts of individuals and nations, but much of Western philosophy, beginning with Plato, may be interpreted in terms of the attempt to escape the isolation and pain of human existence. For Plato, as for the tragic poets, self knowledge and the wisdom that goes with it involve knowing one's place in the scheme of things. For Plato, however, this scheme includes what he calls the Ideas. Through knowledge of these ideas, one escapes the human condition, to consort with them forever. The goal of reason is to aid in this escape and so give the philosopher a choice not available to the ordinary man: to live in the human world, or in another, one in which it is unnecessary to think human thoughts. For the tragic poets, on the other hand, there is no choice, the goal of reason being to keep us from thinking such hubristic thoughts. Hubris, of course, gets men and women into trouble, but the poets are concerned with something more. Only by thinking human thoughts do men and women create in themselves the conditions under which pity and the civilizing emotions may flourish.

Prime among these conditions is the experience of oneself as connected to others who suffer similarly. This too is the education of pity. Education for pity, it might be called, the education of men and women in the human condition, in which pity finds its central place. From this perspective, the problem with Plato's account of civilization is not so much that he relies too much on rational self-control. Rather, by so relying, Plato would isolate men from each other, especially from each other's pain. In this way, Plato quells the spring of the civilizing emotions at its source in human connectedness. A similar danger comes when social peace is based upon the idealization of interest.

Aristotle stands closer to the poets on this issue, though their views are not identical. Aristotle appreciates that tragedy involves learning to whom one is really connected, as well as recognizing the value of connection. Aristotle's famous definition of tragedy in terms of discovery or recognition (*anagnorisis*) refers not merely to the actual recognition of another, but it also implies recognition of a connection, a relationship where none was understood previously (see *Poetics,* c11). Recognition represents emotional rather than strictly intellectual knowledge, like Oedipus' discovery of who he is only through his recognition of whom he is really connected to, a recognition so powerful it nearly kills him. As Diskin Clay puts it, "the kind of learning peculiar to tragedy was the recognition of blood ties."[27] Referring to Aeschylus' *Agamemnon,* in which Agamemnon sacrifices his daughter Iphigenia so that his expedition might sail to Troy, Nussbaum draws out further implications of this insight. "Agamemnon *knows that* Iphigenia is his child all through, if by this we mean that he has the correct beliefs, can answer many questions about her truly, etc. But because in his emotions, his imagination and his behavior he does not acknowledge the tie, we want to join the Chorus in saying that his state is less one of knowledge than one of delusion. He doesn't *really know* that she is his daughter. A piece of true understanding is missing."[28]

True understanding comes through the experience of connectedness to others, especially in their suffering, but only to those who think human thoughts and so remain open to the experience of connection. What Agamemnon fails to understand is a type of knowledge that stems from acknowledging the connectedness of human beings: parents to children, husbands to wives, and so forth. It is not the type of knowledge that can be put in the form of propositions. Through the experience of connectedness comes no rational, propositional wisdom, but, rather, through the experience of connectedness comes a wisdom about relationships, about how people come to participate psychologically in one another's lives. We know something because we feel something about others, we make a living connection. This wisdom defines civilization, telling us (or rather, showing us in a way that is deeper than words) why decent social order demands mutual care and concern. Only by acknowledging our connections to others can we live a fully human life, a central dimension of which involves confronting the pain of all human existence. To this wisdom Creon comes too late. At the conclusion of Sophocles' *Antigone,* Creon's political power remains, and so does his gold. But his life is destroyed. The connections that gave it meaning are gone; his son and wife have both been driven to suicide by his tyranny. "So wisdom comes to the old" the chorus concludes (1353). Without these connections not even the tyrant's life is worth living.

Pity, the Paranoid-Schizoid Position, and Melanie Klein

I want to say that the pity written of by the poets corresponds to what Klein calls reparation, so that in making pity the foundation of civilization the poets in effect recognize the limits of paranoid-schizoid solutions like the one embodied in blood ritual, substituting solutions that integrate love and hate. Klein considers such solutions the hallmark of emotional maturity. In fact, something like this appears to be the case, but it is not quite so neat. Many tragic protagonists express great hatred and great pity in virtually the same breath, as Oedipus does in Sophocles' *Oedipus at Colonus,* where his care and concern for his daughters matches his hatred of his sons (see 1365ff). Similarly, Philoctetes can call for pity and revenge at the same time (see Soph., *Philoctetes,* 1070), as can Prometheus (see Aesch., *Prometheus Bound,* 188–195), a particularly schizoid character, I argued earlier. From a strictly Kleinian perspective, these characters remain within the paranoid-schizoid position, in which care and concern for some is purchased only by directing anger and rage at others. This is the psychology of blood ritual as well.

Whereas many protagonists may be characterized in such a fashion, it would be a mistake to conclude that the poets endorsed or accepted this psychology. On the contrary, most admired by all three poets are people who are in a position to take revenge, have legitimate reasons for it, but refrain, or persuade others to refrain, from doing so. Most admirable of all in this regard is Odysseus in Sophocles' *Ajax,* who takes pity on the corpse of the man who would have tortured and killed him. In Aeschylus' *Eumenides,* Athene seeks to put a halt to the cycle of revenge-killing, even as she recognizes that the Furies make a legitimate claim. Theseus, both in Sophocles' *Oedipus at Colonus* and in Euripides' *Heracles,* represents a similar principle. Conversely, many gods in the tragedies exact horrible revenge when their honor is impugned—one more sign of their inferiority to humans in the civilizing passions. Indeed, almost all the poets' critique of blood ritual and much of their critique of the Greek way of death represents an argument against revenge. It does not serve life by displacing hatred and fear safely away from the self and those we love (the point of the paranoid-schizoid defense), nor does it allow us to gain control over death. Revenge only perpetuates the violence and fear of death that we seek to defend ourselves against. It is a defense that, acted out (as most tragic psychology was), not only does not work but makes matters worse.

Does this make the poets Kleinians? Insofar as Klein and the tragic poets share an insight into the dangers of revenge, the power of pity, and the origins of civilization in the civilizing emotions rather than in rational repression, the answer is yes, although one might just as well call Klein a tragic poet as the tragic poets Kleinians. Nevertheless, they do differ, and their difference is highlighted by Klein's interpretation of Aeschylus' *Oresteia* noted in chapter 2 that overlooks most of the ambiguous, paradoxical aspects of the resolution of the *Eumenides*. The poets seek to confront the power of the uncivilized emotions with the strength of the civilizing ones, but they offer no sense that the two are ever truly integrated or harmonized. Even Aeschylus cannot allow this. Peaceful coexistence under the dominance of the civilizing emotions represents the ideal but the balance remains precarious. Klein grasps this with her comments on the closeness of the vote in favor of Orestes, but such recognition is not always captured in her work.[29] In this sense, at least, the poets share Plato's view that psychic life contains constant mental conflict. Whereas Plato would set reason against desire, however, the poets set civilized desires against uncivilized ones.

In chapter 5 I argued that Lacan's account of the psyche has much to recommend it, coming close to the poets' conclusions. Where Lacan goes wrong is in ignoring the connections that stimulate the civilizing emotions. While it would be too much to argue that the poets reconcile Klein and Lacan completely, they do in one respect. For the poets' account of the psyche combines the permanently unintegrated aspects of the Lacanian psyche with the appreciation of the role of human connectedness that marks Klein as the founder of object relations theory. I believe the poets come closer to the truth than either Lacan or Klein does alone. Some, but not all, of Klein's discussion of emotional integration under the influence of the civilizing emotions can be viewed in much the same way that Lacan views the ego: as a defense against the experience of the unintegrated subject. The psychoanalytic theory of Greek tragedy lends support to this conclusion.

TALKING PASSION

Why does the poets' solution to the riddle of civilization seem so distant today, so improbable and far-fetched? In part the answer must surely be that it does not fit in the Great Tradition of political philosophy. The poets' solution is comprehensible neither in terms of classical confidence in reason nor of modern distrust of reason in favor of interest. In addition, the poets pit virtue, not vice, against vice. Their solution thus falls outside the usual story, into that dangerous netherworld of passions not easily commanded or harnessed. Nor is it reflected in the work of the man who shadows the Western tradition, Rousseau. Elsewhere I have argued what can only be asserted here. What Rousseau calls pitié is indeed comparable to the eleos and oiktos of the tragic poets, but Rousseau turns to pity in order to avoid positing the principle of sociability: that morality and civilized society stem from the felt connections of men and women.[30] Such an approach is not only internally contradictory, but it has little to do with that of the tragic poets.

There is, however, another reason that the poets' solution seems so alien today—more alien, one suspects, than it would have seemed to those early moderns who sought to set one passion against another. To conceptualize social harmony in terms of a balance of power among the passions is to think in terms of the catalogue of the passions, their dynamics, the way they divide the self against the self. Such an approach, I have argued, fails fully to appreciate and cultivate the civilizing passions. Nonetheless, it respects all the passions: their power, their integrity, their manifold complexity, as well as their irreducible presence in almost every aspect of life. To substitute interest for passions loses this respect, particularly when interest is subsequently idealized as a calm, gentle, sociable, and humane activity, as Hirschman shows it to have been.[31] Are greed and the lust for power and domination somehow rendered pure and beneficent when pursued as an economic interest? Or, as Dr. Johnson puts it, are "there . . . few ways in which a man can be more innocently employed than in getting money"?[32] In fact, commerce, money-making, and acquisitiveness may lead to hell on earth, especially when they create two classes of people: those who have acquired much and those who have acquired almost nothing.

Hirschman pays less attention to the way in which the pursuit of interest also distorts the passions of those who have succeeded, though he notes in closing that it is no accident that capitalism is accused of stunting peoples' development, crippling the "full human personality." Nor is this a mere side effect, an unintended consequence. Rather, it was the philosophers' point all along: to cripple the passions by perverting them into interests makes man safe for society.[33] The term *perverting* is mine, not Hirschman's, and I use it intentionally. A perversion is the substitution of a part for the whole, as when a foot fetishist substitutes a fascination with one part of the body for an interest in the whole.[34] The pursuit of economic interest, insofar as it takes the place of the desire for glory, sexual conquest, the domination of others, and the like (and of course this *is* the assumption; this is the whole point!) is similarly perverted, the substitution of the part for the whole. It does not work, of course, a key sign of this being that acquisition, like a perversion, never truly satisfies, which is why one keeps coming back for more and more, be it money or feet. Not only that, but one forgets the rhetoric, as it were, of genuine fulfillment: the place in a good life of sexual lust, the desire for power, glory, and control over others. Such things have their place, as do pity and compassion. What does the perversion of the passions look like today? It looks like what Christopher Lasch calls the culture of narcissism. It looks like those Yuppies and others who find their souls in their expensive commodities. It looks like the commercialization of every aspect of culture.

This perversion of passion (the condensation of passions into interest) characterizes not only many contemporary lives but much academic discourse as well. Interest becomes king, the task of public policy (and even sometimes political theory) being seen as that of protecting diverse but actually remarkably similar—and boring—interests. My criticism overlaps with the concerns of certain classical theorists and others who question the value relativism implicit in regarding interests as given, but it is not identical. Rather, I wish to restore the dialogue of passions, first perhaps within the academy. In the absence of such a dialogue, there can be no discussion of a policy for pity or a regime based upon compassion. Consider, for example, how many academic treatises are written on interests: essays on national and self-interest, critiques of the claim of liberal pluralism to protect diverse interests (which nonetheless assume that interests are real and important), theories of an ideal society designed to guarantee that individuals will be able to protect their own self-interest, and theories of politics that purport to explain everything in terms of interests. Conversely, consider how few articles are written with titles like "Foreign Policy as a Defense against Loneliness," "Lust as a Motive in the Pursuit of Political Power," or "The Acquisition of Wealth as Means to the Pleasures of Domination." Morgenthau's "Love and Power" is exceptional. In part because few write on such topics, few seem to argue for the proper role of pity and compassion in public life. The condensation of the passions into interests squeezes out both the civilizing and uncivilizing passions and has for some time.

One would have hoped that the postmodern focus on desire (for example, Lacan's discussion of *désir,* an insatiable quest for fulfillment) would have contributed to a renewed dialogue of the passions, and perhaps it eventually will. Currently, however, postmodernists are so arcane and abstruse, and conduct their discussions at such a high level of abstraction, that few others can understand enough to join in. We are left with the situation not unlike that characterized by Robert Bellah and others in *Habits of the Heart,* in which neither social science nor popular culture possesses the conceptual resources with which to explain or understand the most immediate, intense, and profound experiences of our lives. We recognize neither the passions that lead us to exploit others, nor how they come into conflict with the passions that lead us to love and care for others.[35] People still have these passions, of course, but it becomes ever more difficult to educate them as the tragic poets sought to educate pity. Greek tragedy is valuable not only because it contains a rhetoric of passion, but also because this rhetoric is not isolated, not a text lifted out of life, but a part of life, a story about life's meaning in terms of the play of the passions. Anyone who has had the pleasure of teaching Greek tragedy to undergraduates will know what I mean.

Conclusion: *Oikto Mathos*

CHAPTER 7

As if every passion didn't have its own quantum of reason.
—Nietzsche, *Gay Science*

An antihumanism that leaves room for humans, such as I have tried to outline, need not be based on what I have called the civilizing passions. But they help. Although humans may be sorely tempted to find an order amenable to reason behind the events and circumstances of their lives (that the world is organized according to principles in accord with human reason is, as stated in chapter 1, a key principle of humanism), it is more difficult to find pity and compassion for the fate of human beings behind these events. But many manage, as the millions who believe in a just and merciful God reveal. In fact, such belief is likely to devolve into confusion, denial, and the mystifications of theodicy when confronted with catastrophic events like the Lisbon Earthquake of 1755, which killed thirty to forty thousand innocents. One response was that of Voltaire, who published *Candide* four years later. Not merely a pessimistic ridiculing of Panglossian optimism, the work concludes with Candide remarking that "we must cultivate our garden." The conclusion of the tragic poets is not dissimilar, though the garden is a collective one: the human community that collectivizes suffering.

Support without shelter, holding without containment, connection without transcendence: these are what men and women can realistically expect to offer each other in the face of a hostile world. It is through pity, and the identification pity is based on, that humans can offer these things. Generally, pity remains all that humans can give, for they are not powerful enough to shelter each other from the caprice of the gods or a hostile fundamental reality, or at least not for long. To offer these things at all, however, is to give what is most distinctly human and so to make this world a little more human.

THE POETICS OF PSYCHOANALYSIS

In the previous chapter I argued that katharsis should be seen not as the goal or end of tragedy but rather as a means: a way of removing emotional obstacles to pity and the civilizing emotions. The katharsis of fear, so that pity might find its place. Yet there is another respect in which katharsis is usefully seen as an end, as long as we bear in mind that the poets are not only therapists to the polis but artists. As artists, their concern is to tell the truth, not heal the polis nor even the psyche. But we should not offer this argument as if truth and therapy were two different things, an assumption that the poets do not hold. Consider again, for a moment, the most famous and perhaps the most perfect of all Greek tragedies, Sophocles' *Oedipus Tyrannus*. The play concerns pollution, *miasma* (or, sometimes, *mysos,* 137). Not only is Thebes suffering from pollution at the opening of the play, but pollution constitutes the background as well, for Oedipus became king by solving the riddle of the sphinx, so saving Thebes from an earlier pollution. The therapy necessary to save Thebes from pollution is *katharsis,* understood strictly as clarifying the truth, whether the truth is the solution to the riddle of the sphinx or of Oedipus' own history. From this perspective there is no difference between therapy and truth. The best therapy, the only genuine therapy, is truth. Conversely, the reason that blood ritual makes bad therapy (therapy that does not work), is that it is built on a lie that splits the self.

Drawing upon her rich discussion of the etymological origins of the term *katharsis* in words used to refer to clarity and lack of obstruction, Nussbaum argues that it is best translated as "clarification." The function of tragedy is to accomplish through pity and fear a "clarification (or illumination) concerning experiences of the pitiable and fearful kind."[1] This is my argument too. By *clarification* I mean truth, however, a definition compatible with the view of truth (*aletheia,* "an uncovering") central to the pre-Socratic philosophers, as Heidegger reminds us in his essay, "*Aletheia:* Heraclitus, Fragment B 16."[2] Understood as aletheia, truth is the uncovering of that which is already present, allowing the thing to appear as it is. Sometimes it is argued that the poets and psychoanalysts both employ katharsis to purge the self of disruptive emotions that can create conflict and anxiety. This gets the emphasis wrong. Both poets and psychoanalysts are concerned with katharsis, but ideally it is katharsis aimed at removing obstacles to the emergence of truth rather than at purgation.

In fact, there is a way to bring these two definitions of *katharsis* together, though I would not want to argue that this is what Aristotle intends (on the other hand, Aristotle's reference to katharsis is so cryptic that it is difficult to know what he means). The problem with katharsis as purgation is that it is too easily evoked by cheap sentimentality, soap operas, love stories, "happy" endings, and the like. Such cathartic experiences remain true to the emotions—it is no emotional lie to cry at a cheap love story, or to feel fear and pity when reading a Stephen King novel (indeed, it is hard to know what would constitute an emotional lie in this regard: if I feel sad and cry, then I feel sad and cry). But such experiences are untrue to life. Life has few happy endings, and even the purest love is mixed with greed, envy, and hatred. If we look at the world with open eyes what is most striking is the enormous waste of potential: young lives cut down by illness, hatred, neglect, and violence; older lives compromised by fear, greed, cynicism, and quiet desperation.

Great tragic art is defined by its ability to evoke the katharsis of emotional experience in the face of what is most truly tragic. In doing this, tragedy clarifies (katharsis) for us what is most genuinely fearful and pitiable by inviting us to experience these emotions (katharsis) in the face of truly fearful and pitiable events. Only when these two senses of katharsis are one can there be great tragic art. Clarification without emotional experience brings intellectual understanding, philosophy not art. Emotional experience without clarification may be art, but it is at best melodrama. Great tragic art evokes emotional experience, particularly pity and fear, regarding only those experiences that are truly pitiable and fearful. Great tragic art, in other words, makes a value judgment about the emotions, precisely what Aristotle was up to in book 2 of his *Nicomachean Ethics*. So should we.

I have been concerned with truth, insofar as man may know it, about the five questions around which this book is organized. To these questions any psychoanalytic account that aspires to be a worldview must be subordinated, which means in practice that I must draw upon a number of theories. This risks too extreme an eclecticism, a mixing of incommensurables. For this reason I have used Greek tragedy as a framework, not only because it poses the most profound questions, but because it provides a narrative structure—an account of the meaning of human experience within which the various psychoanalytic theories find a place. My account of Greek tragedy is intended to hold, in Winnicott's sense, this eclectic combination of theories. Only those who value theoretical elegance above all else or those who are still searching for a single theory that explains everything should find this *methodologically* problematic. Anyone may disagree with my conclusions, of course, but that is a different—and far more interesting—matter.

Implications for Psychoanalytic Therapy

Although a poetically framed account of psychoanalysis may have much to tell us about psychoanalytic theory, there is no guarantee that it has anything to say about psychoanalytic therapy. The gulf between theory and therapy is deep and wide in any case, and it is by no means obvious that the implications of the poets' account can stretch this far. (Indeed, it is by no means obvious that many more familiar psychoanalytic theories stretch this far!) Different psychoanalytic theories have similar therapeutic implications, similar theories have different therapeutic implications, and—most important—the actual therapeutic practice of analysts often departs sharply from their theories in any case. This last point is revealed by accounts of the patients of famous analysts, who have told us of Freud's familiarity with his analysands (asking after their families, loaning them money, writing them long letters, and so forth) and Klein's great warmth with the children whose play she interpreted, for example.[3] It is also revealed by talking with analysts, who in my experience rarely stick to a particular theory. They use different theories with different patients, as well as different theories with the same patient at different times, if, in fact, they employ any theory at all, rather than relying on their own intuition coupled with an eclectic mix of theory and experience.

An approach to psychoanalysis based upon the worldview of the poets would couple pity with the demand that individuals be responsible for themselves and for their decisions, especially for what the existential analysts call original choices. By *pity* I mean what the poets mean: joining in another's suffering, sharing in it, so as to relieve the sufferer's isolation. This helps overcome alienation and hopelessness by holding, in Winnicott's sense, the suffering individual within a network of human relationships and so saying to her that however intense her pain, she will not be allowed to fall out of a world of others. Nussbaum's translation of *suggnome* as "fellow-thought-and-feeling" captures this sense of being held in a relationship. Conversely, psychoanalytic theories that emphasize analytic objectivity and detachment often function as defenses against pain sharing, even though many analysts who hold such theories do not use them in this way.

Heinz Kohut, probably the most influential analyst in the United States today (his self psychology, as it is called, has been labeled the "new orthodoxy"), argues that a psychoanalytic cure is brought about by "transmuting internalization," during which the analysand slowly comes to internalize the empathic response of the analyst, so that this response becomes part of the analysand's own psyche. It is as though we build and cure our psyches by borrowing, via empathy, the psyches of others.[4] Although Kohut's terminology is unique, his basic idea is shared by most of the British School of object relations, made up of Winnicott, W. R. B. Fairbairn, and Harry Guntrip, among many others. They see the psyche as originally weak and incoherent, depending for its coherence upon the support of others, first of all mother. This is what holding is originally about. Gradually, however, the child is able to internalize this support as part of him- or herself, and so act autonomously.

Holding may be part of the story, but the perspective of the poets reveals another dimension. We realize our full potential as human beings—we think human thoughts well—by taking responsibility for ourselves. We cannot, finally, take or borrow this from others in the psychoanalytic transference, although we may learn from examples set by them. Pity and empathy set the stage for this lesson, in part by teaching us that responsibility need not result in isolation and death. But empathy cannot teach this lesson or substitute for it. The contribution of therapeutic empathy, pain sharing, and holding is rather to reassure the analysand that he or she lives in a human world, with others enough like him- or herself that the pain involved in coming to take the self seriously (as a responsible agent) becomes bearable, for it may be shared with others. Responsibility cannot be shared, but its pain can be.

From a psychoanalytic perspective it is especially important that individuals be responsible for what the existential analysts call our original, world-narrowing choice of what kind of person to be and what kind of defenses to adopt. On this point the existential analysts are absolutely right, even if, as I argued in chapter 5, this original choice was a Hobson's choice: that is no choice at all, for it was either to narrow one's world or go insane. For some people, taking responsibility for this choice may allow them to make others. The determinism of the poets need not be the last word on the subject. For others, probably most, taking responsibility may mean learning to live with unchosen choices.

Consider, for example, the situation of Julia Flyte in Evelyn Waugh's *Brideshead Revisited*. She made her original choice, albeit not a fully conscious one and certainly not a mature and reflective one, to believe the tenets of her Catholic religion. Her religion is not part of an archaic, split-off set of beliefs held in a part of herself that is not truly herself. On the contrary, it is central to herself, the same self that feels enormous guilt over her affair with Charles Ryder. She dislikes the central role of judgment, heaven, hell, and the catechism play in her experience of herself. But, unlike many people today she does not suffer the illusion that she can change herself as she might change her hair color. Rather, she says simply, "it becomes part of oneself, if they give it one early enough." In these circumstances, all that an analyst could and should do would be to lead her to understand her original choice better, so that she might behave responsibly in light of it. Her religion is her moira and her daimon. She cannot believe otherwise, or do otherwise, except at the cost of crippling anxiety and guilt. She is more free, perhaps than Philoctetes, who is finally compelled by Heracles to accept necessity, abandon the familiar comfort of his illness and isolation, and go to Troy, where he is healed and becomes a hero. But Julia's is a freedom that we should not make too much of (even by those desperate to find in our lot a tiny portion of self-determination): she can either behave responsibly in light of her original choice or be driven insane by anxiety and guilt. In the end, after she knows that she must leave Charles, she sends a priest to see her dying father, saying, "I take full responsibility for whatever happens."[5] Here is how the psychoanalytic theory implicit in Greek tragedy works its cure.

From the perspective of original choice, the analyst would resemble Lacan more than Kohut or Winnicott, though it is really the capacity of the analyst to be both at once that is crucial. Unlike the British School, Lacan does not consider it the task of the analyst to supply the missing empathy and responsiveness that the analysand failed to get from his or her parents. Rather, Lacan sees the analyst as akin to the tough father, who in effect says to the analysand: "Grow up. You cannot overcome your lack in being, and if you spend your entire life trying to be the master of yourself you will live an inauthentic, miserable, symptom-plagued existence. If, however, you learn to accept your lack of self-mastery, you can experience a certain authenticity, and occasionally a certain joy. Your desires need not tear you apart, and you can learn to 'organize [your] menu.' To do this, however, you must recognize that you do not really exist as a subject, but are 'in the position of the dead.'"[6]

Lacan holds that analysis may cure some dramatic symptoms of emotional distress, such as psychosis, which irrupt through holes in the symbolic order, as he puts it. Analysis may also help us lead more authentic existences, but only in the sense that it teaches the disingenuousness of the strategies by which we avoid confronting our lack: wild self-assertion, the frantic pursuit of pleasure, perpetual immersion in relationships, and so forth. One is reminded here of Freud's statement that a successful cure will consist of transforming the analysand's hysterical misery into ordinary, human unhappiness. One is reminded too of an aspect of Klein's work that, although it has been rightly criticized, is not without its virtues. Particularly in her early works, Klein tends to ignore actual responses of parents. Not the failure of parental empathy, as Kohut would have it, but the analysand's own aggression, greed, and hatred, to Klein are inevitably the underlying cause of the analysand's problems. As with Lacan, such a view ignores the reality of relationships. (One biographer implies that Klein's view defended her against recognizing her own contribution to her strained relationships with her children.) Still, there is much to be said for a psychoanalytic perspective that places responsibility for negative emotions and experiences directly on the shoulders of the analysand.

All the qualifications imposed by the poets' worldview upon Lacan discussed in chapter 5 apply in the present therapeutic context as well. The reality of relationships, as well as of responsible agency that makes us aware of the reality of our acts as they affect others, makes Lacan's conclusion—that one can exist authentically only in the position of the dead—false. Nevertheless, Lacan makes an important point. Authenticity is not a matter of discovering the true, hidden self. Nor is it a matter of self-mastery, self-control, or even self-knowledge, all of which are likely to be little more than self-defense. Authenticity requires thinking human thoughts ("ta thneta phronein"), which means recognizing that most actions are performed under constraint, under the necessity of desire—most of all, perhaps, under the unfulfillable desire to be whole and free. One may live responsibly in the face of this fact only by recognizing it. Rather than saying with Lacan that authenticity involves living in the position of the dead, we should say that authenticity means living responsibly under the yoke of necessity.

I suspect that many analysts combine the therapeutic approaches of the British School and Lacan, blending pity and empathy with the demand that the analysand take responsibility for his or her choices. What the mix looks like will vary considerably, of course, from analyst to analyst and from patient to patient. In fact, I expect there is an intimate connection between the world-view of the tragic poets and the practice of therapy, for both concern how to live a distinctly human life well. The disconnection more often comes between the poets' worldview and psychoanalytic *theory*, for the theory too often fails to address the fundamental realities with which the poets are concerned adequately, such fundamentals as the pressure of necessity, the pain of human existence (including the pain of not being master of oneself), pain sharing as the ultimate human gift, and the need to spend most of life coming to terms with death.

Perhaps no single psychoanalytic theory could embrace all these concerns. Until it does, those who see psychoanalysis as more than a therapeutic technique or structural model of the mind will have to pick and choose from among its theories in order to construct an account adequate to the richness of the poets' worldview. Against this conclusion it might be argued that any such conjunction or combination of theories must lack the narrative unity of the poets' worldview, which provides a coherent account of the world and man's place in it. Alasdair MacIntyre in *After Virtue,* for example, contrasts the coherence of the poets' worldview with the incoherence of our own. Although MacIntyre's argument is not all wrong, it idealizes the unity of the poets' vision, which was both filled with and a confrontation of confusion and incoherence. Psychoanalysts such as Klein, Lifton, and Lacan (the last of whom MacIntyre turns to in order to make sense of the failures of liberalism[7]) make sense of significant portions of the world, in ways that do not automatically render what remains outside an incoherent and threatening other. Is this not enough to start with— and to work with?

PHOBO MATHOS, PATHEI MATHOS, OIKTO MATHOS

Drawing upon Aristotle's *Rhetoric,* as well as on the tragic poets, I have argued that reason is best conceived as creating a calm and quiet space in oneself, free of constant fear, envy, and the like, so that pity and other civilizing emotions may emerge. Seen from this perspective, the problem addressed in chapter 6 with transforming passion into interest is that this transformation creates not a quiet space but a space filled with greedy desire for more goods. In fact, the reality of the civilizing process to which the poets refer is more complex than simply creating a quiet space in which pity may emerge. A temperate mind that thinks human thoughts, which is what the poets mean by *reason,* creates the conditions under which pity may emerge. In turn, pity becomes our teacher. *Pathei mathos*: "through suffering comes wisdom" (see, for example, Aesch., *Agamemnon,* 177, 250, and throughout the tragedies; it is a proverbial expression). What pity, understood as pain sharing, allows is learning from the suffering of others, not just from our own, by sympathetically participating in it. If wisdom comes from suffering, few of us will suffer enough to become truly wise. Our lives are too limited; or perhaps the sheer immediacy of our suffering blots out its lessons, at least in the short run, else we could not bear to go on living. There is, however, more than enough suffering in the world to make us all wise, if we would but open ourselves to it.

What does suffering teach? Too often, as I argued in chapter 6, the lessons of suffering are reduced to Aristotle's formulation that our fear of suffering as others have makes us wise, understood as keeping us on the straight and narrow. This is Salkever's argument, as well, and it might be expressed with the motto *phobo mathos,* "the wisdom that comes from fear." Pathei mathos is different, more like this: I see another suffering over the loss of her child. Though I have no children, and do not expect to have any, by opening myself to her suffering I gain some insight into what her pain must be like and what the connection between mother and child must be like. I do not, of course, come to experience this loss as the mother does. My life goes on, whereas hers will be sunk in grief for years. Nevertheless, through this experience I learn something important about pain, motherhood, grief, and loss that, I think, makes me a better person, certainly a wiser one.

But how could I know what a mother's grief is like? Because I have my own grief, my own losses. Through an act of sympathetic participation in another's sorrow I bring my own grief into contact with another's, so that my understanding of her loss is illuminated by my grief—which does not mean that I am "really" mourning over my own grief. Rather, I combine my latent grief with my ability sympathetically to share her sorrow, as well as other aspects of her life such as the meaning of her child in it, and so create out of these an emotional picture of what it is to lose a child. The result is not merely increased concern for the suffering of others, but a deeper connection between me and my own grief. *Pathei mathos* might well be considered the motto of Klein as well: through suffering I bring split-off and disowned aspects of the self into contact with my conscious self. By connecting with and mobilizing these aspects, I become more whole, and hence more capable of having wisdom about the whole world. By whole, I do not mean that I am free, autonomous, and in control, the ideals of ego autonomy criticized in chapter 5. I mean that I make connections between previously unconnected emotions, in order to become better connected to others' emotions, particularly their sorrow. For now their sorrow no longer threatens to drown me in my own. These are the understandings that the poets seek to teach with their tragedies. *Oikto mathos,* it might be called: "through pity comes wisdom."

For Charles Segal the suffering that brings wisdom is the "wound which the otherness of the world makes as it impinges upon us," by which he means "the dimensions of life that our structures cannot encompass."[8] My language is different, stressing not the wound of otherness but the emotional wholeness that helps us know the whole world by allowing us to connect with a wider and potentially more threatening range of emotional reactions to it. In a word, emotional wholeness means having available the full range of human passions in their most cultivated form (as tragedy seeks to cultivate pity) as our guide to what to feel and how to act. This will not make us free, at least not in the sense that this term is used from Plato to Kant and beyond: able to subject our desires to reason. On the contrary, our properly cultivated desires will guide us—or drag us along. But emotional wholeness can contribute to our willingness to accept responsibility. We are most likely to deny responsibility for our actions when we can feel no connection between who we are, what emotions we experience, and what we do. My perspective resembles Aristotle's view of the development of moral virtue in the *Nicomachean Ethics,* with two key differences. First, my perspective—drawn from the poets—stresses the other-regarding virtues (and for other-regarding reasons), not the self-regarding virtues, as Aristotle does. That is, I take the object related character of human experience seriously. Second, the poets and I better appreciate the sheer intensity of the uncivilized passions, and we know that only equally intense civilizing passions can overcome them.

Segal's language differs from mine, but our views are complementary. All along I have stressed the confusion and disorder confronted by the poets, what Segal calls the "fragility and artificiality of those structures" that hold the world together. Only if we mistakenly assume that confusion and disorder may alone know confusion and disorder does Segal's argument contradict mine. Today there is much talk of otherness and difference, and these are certainly important categories, even if they are frequently dealt with at a level of abstraction appropriate only to the most arcane metaphysical debates. But to know otherness and difference and to appreciate it (in people, cultures, or ideas) requires a measure of personal wholeness, as well as a vision of the world that possesses wholeness. Earlier I made a related claim about Lacan. His willingness and ability to confront lack in being implies fullness of being, albeit not the fullness associated with the Freudian ego or ideals of autonomous selfhood. Rather, it is the fullness that stems from taking responsibility in the absence of freedom and being willing to stay connected with the suffering of others: the wholeness of oikto mathos.

Here is the irony of otherness, difference, and openness to lack of structure: it cannot be grasped in the absence of wholeness and structure. I do not mean by this that traditional ways of thinking about these attributes are therefore just fine. As J. Peter Euben points out, Euripides' *Orestes* challenges many of the traditional polarities found in Greek thought, such as the difference between male and female.

> From one point of view the confounding of male and female, like the con-
> founding of other oppositions (such as slave and free, Barbarian and Greek,
> inside and outside) is a liberating negation of the putative "naturalness" of
> Athenian categories and a demystifying of Aeschylean reciprocity between
> the sexes, which some regard as sustaining patriarchy. . . . Still, on balance,
> [Euripides'] emphasis seems to be on the confusion of moral roles and the
> loss of identity such "liberation" portends, rather than the opportunities for
> reconstitution it provides.[9]

To appreciate another's difference I must have some sense of my sameness as a person over time, otherwise I just melt into the difference, which means either that the two of us become the same, or I obliterate the other, in order not to disappear. What happens in the absence of wholeness and structure is not openness to otherness and difference but confusion, reversal, and the rigidifi-cation of paranoid-schizoid structures of thought that organize the world into Manichaean dualities. The poets knew this in a way in which many postmod-erns, including Lacan, do not, which is why we cannot ally them. What the poets did not know is how to create structures that hold without crushing, and distinctions that differentiate without reifying. But they had the right idea. These ordering principles must stem from the civilizing emotions, which support an intellectual and emotional order far less rigid than the paranoid-schizoid order that stems from the uncivilized emotions.

Throughout this book I have downplayed the way in which the form of tragedy promises an order and reconciliation denied by its content, in large measure because this insight has been used as an excuse not to confront the full extent of the confusion and reversal found in the tragedies. Nevertheless, the general point implicit in the form-content dialectic is valid. To grasp the rich-ness, freedom, and value in the particulars that remain when old structures are dissolved requires a new kind of structure, not merely a mimicry of the chaos and confusion that arises when structures fail. It is interesting in this regard to read modern translations of the tragedies into colloquial English, such as

Ezra Pound's translation with Rudd Fleming of Sophocles' *Electra*. Contrast the
Loeb Classical Library translation by F. Storr with Pound's of lines 516–518.
Clytaemestra is speaking to Electra.

> So once again I find thee here at large,
> For he who kept thee close and so restrained
> Thy scandalous tongue, Aegisthus, is away.
> (Loeb)

> Out here again making trouble, might have known it
> now Aegisthus' not here,
> he keeps you from making dirt on the family doorstep.
> (Pound)

For all its cleverness, the Pound translation (and it is that, not a mere version
or adaptation) fails. The play falls utterly flat, chaos and confusion being all
that remain. The colloquial language isolates the characters from the formal
and mythological context of the tragedies, a context which says, in effect, that
the protagonists are part of a larger order and structure, something universal.

Hanna Segal, a Kleinian analyst with a deep interest in aesthetics, argues that
beautiful form promises an order denied by the content: "Without . . . formal
harmony the depression of the audience would be aroused but not resolved.
There can be no aesthetic pleasure without perfect form."[10] Her argument,
however, runs the risk of promising only mock reparation. The highest goal is
not to resolve the depression of the audience (katharsis as purgation) but to
achieve emotional clarification. Seen from this perspective, beautiful form uni-
versalizes the lessons of tragedy while distancing us from them a bit, through
the aura created by the form. In universalizing these lessons (for example, that
Electra's destructive bitterness, desire, and jealousy is not unique; it is a potential within us all), beautiful form actually makes them more distressing while
at the same time protecting us from them by creating a separation between
the characters and ourselves. Electra may be part of us all, but the form puts
her at a distance. Perhaps this is what Rilke means when he says that "Beauty
is nothing but the beginning of terror that we are still just able to bear." As I
earlier said, though far less eloquently, beautiful form is the sugarcoating on
the pill, enticing us to swallow it before we know how bad it truly tastes.

If my argument in chapter 6 regarding how pity works is correct, it is not
the beautiful form of the tragedies but the content of the stories that brings
relief, allowing members of the audience to identify with the suffering of the
protagonists and so give their own suffering a name. All sorrows can be borne
if you put them into a story. Even someone else's story helps—as long as I
can identify with it. Form is, of course, important. If the form becomes too

fragmented, as it does in Euripides' *Orestes,* for example, then the content can no longer hold the suffering by telling a meaningful story about it, for the content too loses its coherence. In fact, the form-content distinction is at this level meaningless, recalling Nietzsche's similarly problematic distinction between Apollonian and Dionysian aspects of tragedy. One advantage of my view is that it is less likely to risk mock reparation, always a danger in the Segal-Kleinian account. What we learn from tragedy is not that suffering can be redeemed, or that beauty, order, and wholeness can be restored. Often this is impossible. What we learn is that suffering can be made bearable, by reducing its potential to fragment the suffering self. Conversely, it is not suffering but the threat to the integrity of the self posed by seemingly unbearable suffering that leads the sufferer to inflict his suffering on others.

WHY ARE THE POETS SO SMART?

The poets recognize that the ideal of the autonomous self is part of a vain attempt to escape from the real self, especially from the way in which passions and desires transfix a person as if they were weapons of the gods. It is from this perspective that we should view the "ode to man" in Sophocles' *Antigone.* The problem with all that man makes, his technology and culture (including, I would emphasize, philosophies of transcendence, such as Plato's and Kant's), is that these marvelous achievements mislead him into thinking that he can transcend the human condition itself, so that one day even death might fall before his cleverness—or his piety. In fact, Prometheus had the right idea: take from man the knowledge of the hour of his death, so that he can use his cleverness to make sense of the meaning of his brief life. He can make connections between his life and his death. Technology and culture have a role to play here as long as they are understood properly. They do not represent doomed attempts to transcend human connections but are themselves connections to this world, tying us more closely to it. Through them, even in death some connections remain, connections that reflect our investment in the world.

Here is the real significance of the embeddedness of the tragedies in the polis. Unlike Plato, who would transcend the polis, or even Thucydides, who takes a stand outside any particular polis (albeit not outside history or human nature), the poets write from within the polis. The tragedies were written for civic festivals and judged by citizens (a point frequently commented upon by those eager to show the relevance of tragedy to political theory), subjecting myth to the standards of the polis, as Vernant points out. This, though, should not cause us to think of the poets as more political or civic-minded than they in fact were. They did not set out to write about the polis. They wrote of human connectedness in hate and love, and the polis is where this connectedness took place in the fifth century B.C. In fact, the poets generally project the connections of the polis back into the family relationships of the archaic, heroic era, in order to capture an important truth: every political connection, both civilizing and uncivilized, has its origin and foundation in the prepolitical connections of the family.

Those who would analyze the tragedies as political theory would do well to recognize this truth. Behind the connections of politics lie the connections of families. The civilization of the one depends upon its ability not to exclude the connections of the oikos but to cultivate the civilizing connections born there and extend them to the polis. Often the Greeks are admired by political theorists because of the purity of their public life. Arendt's *Human Condition* epitomizes such polis envy. Once again, however, the poets frame the issue quite differently, showing this insight to be misleading. Public spheres cannot be separated from the private, polis from oikos. There are only two choices. Either the uncivilized emotions that stem from the connections of private life will dominate the polis, or the civilizing emotions that stem from these same connections will. We make the former more likely to the degree that we pretend we do not have to make this choice.

Although the poets are theorists of emotional connectedness, that connectedness provides little emotional shelter. Indeed, the most striking aspect of the poets' tragic vision is the way it juxtaposes connectedness, the network of relationships that gives gravity to our acts and succor to our lives, with exposure. This juxtaposition remains alien to modern thought, but this same juxtaposition makes the poets so smart, for it enables them to capture what it means to live a distinctly human life. A human life is connected to others in love and hate while at the same time terribly exposed to contingency, from which all our connections cannot protect us. We must face this too. Which does not mean that we should devalue our connections. On the contrary, this is the problem that runs from Plato to Lacan and beyond: the risk that we shall devalue our worldly connections because they cannot free us from contingency (which includes the lack in being of which Lacan writes). The expectation, often unstated, that our relationships should do this leads to inhumane antihumanism: if all our human connections cannot help us avoid contingency and become one with ourselves, then the hell with them, we say. The poets, on the other hand, know that those who think human thoughts well will accept their exposure without devaluing their relationships. This is the lesson of the poets. It constitutes their humane antihumanism, which should be sharply distinguished from the mere antihumanism of some postmoderns.

In order to see this more clearly, it may be useful to conclude by briefly comparing modern drama with the Greek tragedies. Arguing that modern drama begins with Ibsen's *Brand*, Arthur Ganz sees the plays of Oscar Wilde, Jean Giraudoux, Luigi Pirandello, Tennessee Williams, Arthur Miller, and Harold

Pinter as romances, in the special sense that they concern the attempt to dis-
cover, or carve out, a realm in which the self may realize its true self. To be
sure, most modern drama represents the failure of this attempt, but this makes
the quest no less central, only more poignant. What constitutes self-realization
differs for each playwright, of course. For Williams, it is a return to the lost
innocence of the natural self, in which sexuality is equated with the vitality of
natural life (see, for example, *A Streetcar Named Desire*). For Ibsen it involves
the quest for a higher, nobler life, which requires the rejection of the comforts
of this one (as in *Brand*). Sometimes, as in the work of Arthur Miller, the quest
for the true self involves a search for lost innocence, on the assumption that the
true self has been corrupted by society (look at what happens in *All My Sons*).
And sometimes, as with Oscar Wilde, it involves the search for an aesthetically perfect life as an alternative to both Philistinism and Victorian morality
(such as in *The Importance of Being Earnest*). But all these playwrights make the
romantic ideal of self-realization through transcendence central, even if the
ideal is rarely achieved.

Not only, says Ganz, are modern dramatists concerned with self-realization,
especially its failure. They also wish to construct a realm in which the self can
be free to be itself. Sometimes this construction is negative, as it were. It does
not exist, but only in it could the self be real. Consider how Ganz characterizes
Pinter in this regard: "Yet so pressed are Pinter's characters by the overweening
demands of the self that they can only escape by withdrawing to some room—
a world where they will be sheltered."[11] For the Greek poets there is no shelter,
not even in the negative sense of there being a nonexistent place in which the
self could be real. On the contrary, the self is constantly exposed, open, and
vulnerable. The image of Prometheus staked out on a rock for ten thousand
years is exemplary. So too is the image of Pentheus, who climbs high up in a
tree to spy on the Maenads, only to be utterly exposed to them (see Eur., *Bacchae*, 1075). Charles Segal characterizes the Sophoclean hero as "more exposed
than other men to the extremes of" existence.[12] Consider in this regard Oedipus, who believed that he was sheltered from contingency by reason, yet was
always exposed to fate. This is finally symbolized by his blinding, which results
in his never knowing when he is exposed to others—thus making manifest
what had been true all along. For the Greek poets there are no hiding places,
no "realms of the self" (the title of Ganz's book), in which the self, free from
the pressures of the world, may commune with itself. I am tempted to say that
only in death is the individual no longer exposed, but the great Greek concern
with the vulnerability of the exposed dead body reveals that there is no refuge
here either.

The self remains exposed because what moves it, its passions, are not located
in it but pass through it, carrying the self with them as if they were natural forces. What Kitto says about Euripides fits all three poets. "Character is

wanted by Euripides only as a vehicle for the passion of which it consists."[13] It is important, however, to be clear about the implications of this. As noted in chapter 5, Vernant, Jones, and others conclude that the Greek self is shifting and feeble, as evidenced by its inability to master the subjunctive ("If I were in another situation, which of course I am not, then I would . . ."). I would put the emphasis differently. The Greek self is not master of the subjunctive because it is not free. There is no reason to imagine yourself in different circumstances if you cannot alter the circumstances.

Consider Medea's soliloquy noted in chapter 5, in which she imagines how she might have behaved had she been another type of person. This is the subjunctive speaking. But because she and we know that she is not another type of person, and hence that she has no choice in her present situation, her mode of thinking does not get a big workout, so to speak. The Greek self was quite capable of reflecting upon itself—that is, upon the sources of its compulsion at the hands of its daimon and moira. Because reflection did not change anything, its object, the inner self, was not equated with the true self. The quest for the inner self has been historically bound from Plato on to the quest for freedom from contingency and compulsion. When one does not assume (and the poets do not) that man can ever be free, the inner self becomes a less compelling presence. But if the inner self becomes less important, the self's connectedness in relationships with others becomes more so. So too does the sense of responsibility that this brings. I have argued that these are quite enough for a sound psychoanalytic theory, one which takes seriously the two-sided character of man's exposure to worldly contingency and to his own passions. Or perhaps these are really the same. On this point it seems appropriate to let Freud have the next to last word.

> And now, I think, the meaning of the evolution of civilization is no longer obscure to us. It must present the struggle between Eros and Death, between the instinct of life and the instinct of destruction, as it works itself out in the human species. This struggle is what all life essentially consists of, and the evolution of civilization may therefore be simply described as the struggle for life of the human species. And it is this battle of the giants that our nurse-maids try to appease with their lullaby about Heaven.[14]

What I have written of is how life and death may themselves become confused and what it takes to sort them out: responsibility and pity. This is as true of psychoanalytic therapy as it is of civilization itself.

How can one live as a tragic hero today? Christopher Lasch's recent *True and Only Heaven: Progress and Its Critics* contains some interesting suggestions, particularly his emphasis on the acceptance of limits, though regrettably he does not turn to the tragic poets. I would argue that to live as a tragic hero means to accept one's status as victim of circumstance without becoming merely a victim. It is common, I understand, for analysands to assert repeatedly their enraged refusal to be victimized by parents, spouses, bosses, or others. The popular media is filled with heroes whose sole virtue seems to be their angry refusal to be victims, even at the risk of victimizing others. Certainly the passivity and vulnerability associated with being a victim horrified the Greeks, Medea being a prime example.

In fact, we are all victims of circumstance: of the parents who bore us; of our primitive conflicts and desires; of the society, culture, and era into which we are born; of the fears of our political leaders, as well as those of other countries; of the greed of plutocrats; of the desires of loved ones; of the anger of our neighbor and the rage of the man who assaults us; of the drunk who crashes into us; of the state of medical and scientific knowledge; of the boss who resents our creativity; of large-scale systems and bureaucracies that care nothing for individuals; and on and on. We are, of course, also victims of our bodies, our limits, especially our mortality. We are, in other words, constantly and perpetually exposed to fate. We are all exposed—some more than others.

To take the lessons of the tragic poets seriously requires understanding that there is no escape from contingency, not even in victimizing others. Rather, we must learn to live well as victims, which means with courage, dignity, and above all with responsibility. If we can do this well then we may properly care for others without expecting them to shelter us from our fate. This is what it means to live a human life in an inhospitable world. Perhaps in the end this is why Admetus, who allows his wife to die in his place, gets off lightly in Euripides' *Alcestis*. As the world's most hospitable guest-host, Admetus learns what humans can and cannot offer each other: hospitality, but not shelter. Or rather, we can give each other shelter for a little while, before we must meet our lives, and our deaths, alone.

The Epic Self and Psychoanalytic
Theory of Greek Tragedy

Homer having made the gods into men, man learned to know himself.
—M. I. Finley, *The World of Odysseus*

Implicit in my argument has been what to many must be a troubling assumption: that the philosophy of Plato, as well as that of moderns such as Sartre, represents progress not toward autonomous selfhood but in the construction of defenses against the insight of the poets that the self is responsible but not free. Often, as noted in chapter 1, the history of the self is written as beginning with the epic poets, whose self consisted of a paratactic aggregate of loosely connected parts. The tragedies represent the "discovery of mind," to use Bruno Snell's famous phrase. For many the rational, autonomous self finds its full realization in Plato: a self so in control of its own desires that it chooses its own daimon (see *Republic,* 617d–e). My focus in this book has been on the second stage of this history, the tragic poets' discovery of mind, which might more accurately be called the creation of the fully responsible self. If my argument is correct, the psychology of Greek tragedy has implications not only for the modern psyche but for how moderns interpret the psyche as it is portrayed in the *Iliad* and *Odyssey* as well.

From the perspective of object relations theory, particularly as enriched by the insights of Lacan, the self is best seen in terms of the quality of its relationships and connections. From this perspective we should not be too impressed when Odysseus talks to his internal organs ("Patience, my heart!") as though they were multiple selves. Especially since Odysseus is quite capable of engaging in monologues that involve no organ talk at all (see, for example, *Odyssey,* 20.60–80, or 17.220–230). Yet this organ talk is often taken as a key piece of evidence that the epic self is schizoid (though this term is not used)—a not-very-well-integrated collection of parts. Psyche and soma are not yet differentiated, so that the emotions are characterized almost strictly in terms of their bodily location: *thumos, menos, kardia, phren/phrenes.*[1] To be sure, the self of the epics is remarkably embodied, so much so that even by the fifth century B.C. psyche and soma remain closely bound. Nevertheless, we should not conclude more from this fact than is warranted. The true measure of the self is neither its ability to transcend the body (Plato's *nous,* Kant's "ego as it is in itself"), nor to take itself as an object of reflection, both of which may evince only an illusory self-control. Nor is rational autonomy a good measure, for the reasons already mentioned. The best measure is the self's ability to establish whole object relationships and maintain object constancy. As noted in chapter 1, whole object relations refer to the ability to avoid splitting the other into all good and all bad part objects. Object constancy refers to the ability to hold the other in the mind during the other's absence rather than indiscriminately connecting with whatever object happens to be present.

Seen from this perspective, Odysseus of the *Odyssey* possesses a fully developed self, as does Penelope. More important, one may read the *Odyssey* as a journey of self-development, in which Odysseus rejects the regressive charms of part-object relationships with Circe, Calypso, and the sirens, overcoming his own paranoid-schizoid anxieties, as reflected in his experiences with Scylla and Charybdis. Odysseus reestablishes his relationship with his wife, Penelope, and with his house, a relationship that is characterized by wholeness and constancy. Both are symbolized by the marriage bed Odysseus had built many years earlier out of an olive tree still rooted in the ground. Unsure whether the man who confronts her after twenty years' separation is truly her husband, Penelope tells Odysseus she will have their bed moved to the hall. Only when Odysseus asserts that it cannot be moved is she convinced that he is her husband. Then there are no doubts; they are as bound to each other in love and duty as the day he left home. There is, to be sure, a blending together in Odysseus's mind of his wife, house, and kingdom as though all three were a single object that is for us a little strange. I do not assert that Odysseus thinks the same way we do but that both he and Penelope participate in whole-object relationships and have a tremendous capacity for object constancy, the most important signs of a developed self. Whatever differences there are between the world of Odysseus and our own, they are not captured by characterizing the Homeric self as a paratactic aggregate.

Bennett Simon makes a related point in *Mind and Madness in Ancient Greece* and *Tragic Drama and the Family*. Though Homeric man may have many parts, they are generally not in conflict. On the contrary, his parts are generally well integrated and act in harmony. Furthermore, Homeric man is in many respects less conflicted than his tragic counterpart. For example, the fearful, enraged, deeply ambivalent attitude toward wives and marriage found in the tragedies is largely absent in the epics, even though the image of woman as dangerous enchanter is certainly present especially in the *Odyssey*.[2] I suspect that this reflects the fact that the world of Odysseus was characterized by a good deal of culturally sanctioned splitting and projection. Perhaps too it represents a literary convention. My argument is not that the world of Odysseus was a bastion of mental health, however, but only that we should be careful about drawing psychological conclusions about the epic protagonists from the textual and literary studies of Claus, Snell and others, who reveal what is to us a rather strange emotional vocabulary. The heroes of the *Odyssey*, in particular, are real people with real relationships—frequently sustained, close, and intimate ones. One sees many more part-object relationships in contemporary novels by Philip Roth, Donald Barthelme, Erica Jong, or Paul Theroux than in the *Odyssey*.

What about the *Iliad*? It can hardly be denied that the *Iliad* is filled with part-object relationships, organ talk, and characters who are often little more than stereotypes. I agree, and cast my lot with the separatists, who hold that the *Odyssey* was composed a generation later than the *Iliad*. The self of the *Iliad* comes closer to the paratactic aggregate so often assumed to characterize both epics. Nevertheless, much can be explained, as the unitarians emphasize, by the different contexts of the two works. For the characters in the *Iliad* are terrified of physical mutilation, penetration, fragmentation, and death. Reading the epic I am struck by the hundreds of accounts in which the body of a warrior is penetrated and mutilated, as when the son of Phyleus struck his opponent "with the sharp spear behind the head at the tendon, and straight on through the teeth and under the tongue cut the bronze blade, and he dropped in the dust gripping in his teeth the cold bronze" (5.70–80). Difficult enough for any man or woman to confront, the constant threat of mutilation must be especially terrifying for those whose self-concept is so corporeal. We should not, however, congratulate ourselves on having transcended the body ego. In *Wartime* Paul Fussell points out that there is no such thing as getting used to combat, particularly to the encounter with the mutilated bodies of the wounded, dying, and dead. Anyone who remains in combat long enough will break down, "long enough" being defined by military psychiatrists during World War II as being between 200 and 240 days of consecutive combat.[3]

The Trojan War lasted ten years. Its wartime context, the constant threat of mutilation and dismemberment and the constant confrontation with it, accounts for the portrayal of the self in the *Iliad*: a self involved for the most part only in part-object relationships with others, who are seen almost strictly in terms of their role as enemy or ally. Such part-object relationships are characteristic of regression to the paranoid-schizoid position. But perhaps *regression* is not quite the right word. For the heroes of the *Iliad,* persecutors really were trying to kill, dismember, and mutilate them! Under these circumstances, the self may be expected to employ its most primitive defenses. What we should not do is assume that the self of the Greek warrior after almost ten years of combat defines the Greek self as such. Context counts. This interpretation is supported by the fact that the gods in the *Iliad* (quite unlike the gods in the tragedies) are generally more multidimensional than the humans, capable of caring for their favorite humans in ways that approach a whole-object relationship (see, for an example, 1.360–365). Unlike humans, the gods do not fear dismemberment and death. Some gods are also capable of object constancy, not always their strong suit. Consider, for example, the constant affection of Thetis, a sea-nymph, for her son, Achilles (see 6.342–475). As a result, the epic heroes, although not always trusting of the gods, are not confused by them either, as Achilles' account of the caprice of Zeus reveals (at 24.525–550). Zeus administers a lottery, unfair, perhaps, but not confusing. The confusion comes later, as pointed out in chapter 2.

This interpretation is supported by the larger structure of the epic, which, like the *Odyssey,* may be read as an account of self-development. Achilles withdraws from combat in a narcissistic rage, as a result of Agamemnon's seizure of his concubine. In so doing, Achilles contributes to the death of his beloved Patroclus, with whom he has had a lifelong relationship so close that Achilles will have their ashes mixed together after Achilles' death. Returning to battle in rage and grief, Achilles slaughters the killer of Patroclus, Hector, whose corpse he then disgraces. But the *Iliad* ends with Priam, Hector's father, appealing to Achilles to release Hector's body for funeral. Achilles assents, in part because Priam's love and grief for his son "stirred in Achilles a passion of grieving for his own father" (24.507–508). Shortly before this encounter, Achilles had conducted the funeral games in honor of his slain friend, games in which the wholeness, smoothness, and vitality of the competing bodies stand in stark contrast to the scenes of dismemberment amid bloody battle. It is as though the diminished fear of death and dismemberment for Achilles and his army (the funeral games were part of a break in the fighting), coupled with his ability to mourn for Patroclus, not just rage against his killer, finally allows Achilles to share the pain of Priam and so govern his conduct by the principle of pity.

The series of projections, introjections, and identifications that leads to this outcome is complicated. At one point, Patroclus comes to Achilles in a dream, directing Achilles as to how he must be buried. In this way Achilles is finally able to mourn Patroclus because he can internalize him as a whole object: the image in the dream so complete that it tells Achilles how to mourn the loss of itself. One might analyze other themes that emerge late in the poem in a similar fashion, as when Achilles battles the pristine river, which all of a sudden begins to disgorge dead bodies: the source of goodness is itself being contaminated by Achilles' bloody violence: "For the loveliness of my waters is crammed with corpses. . . . I am congested with the dead men you kill so brutally," says the river to Achilles (21.215–225). But the place to pursue these themes is not here. Suffice it to say that the *Iliad* may be read as the journey of the heroic self from narcissistic rage to a new level of emotional wholeness, in which mourning leads to the internalization of a whole object and with it pity for the enemy. Once again, all this is likely to be missed if the self is conceptualized and valued strictly in terms of its autonomous splendor. That is just as true whether this splendor is measured by excellence in rational autonomy or by excellence in battle.

In throwing everything else into question, the tragedies problematize the self as well. Indeed, one reason the self of the epics is not clear to us is that it is so perfectly integrated with its culture, as the psychoanalyst Joel Kovel convincingly argues.[4] Only as the culture becomes less coherent does the self begin to stand out from its background. In many respects this is good, for it creates an opportunity to redefine the self by redefining its pertinent connections. As social critics the poets do precisely this, extending the bonds of pity (one of the connections by which the self is defined) to new classes, such as those who lack nobility, like those ignoble characters to whom Euripides was frequently accused of granting significant roles. This is moral progress. It is part of what it means to claim that tragedy subjects myth to the standards of the democratic polis. But it is not development of a more rational, autonomous, or reflective self, even as this inclusion involves reflection upon society and hence upon the selves who inhabit it. On the contrary, the self of the tragic poets is in some ways less coherent and in control than the epic self.

One can see this in the ways the gods influence the self in both genres. In the *Iliad* and *Odyssey,* gods generally intervene as physical presences, jerking warriors' hair, throwing rocks, breaking chin straps, misdirecting spears, and so forth. When they penetrate the psyche it is generally to enthuse (*entheos*) a warrior. In the tragedies, on the other hand, the intervention of the gods is more abstract and profound—they inflict madness, hubris, and self-destructive desire. This requires that the gods dip more deeply into the psyche. There are exceptions to this generalization (Agamemnon in the *Iliad,* for example, who says a god put wild *ate* in his understanding), but the more the gods act like psychic, rather than physical forces, the more they must penetrate and dominate the psyche to do so. The result is that the gods more deeply and thoroughly transfix the tragic self than the epic self. What Zeus says at the beginning of the *Odyssey* applies to that poem better than to most of the tragedies: "What a lamentable thing it is that men should blame the gods and regard *us* as the source of their troubles, when it is their own wickedness that brings them sufferings worse than any which Destiny allots them" (1.32–36). In the tragedies, as we have seen, men are not generally the source of their own troubles, at least not quite in the sense Zeus seems to have in mind. They are just responsible for them.

Seen from this perspective, the tragedies do contain a more sophisticated psychology than the epics, even if the basic elements of that psychology are already present in the epics. What advances tragic psychology, however, has nothing to do with its discovery of mind—that is, its creation of an autonomous self. Quite the contrary; tragic psychology appears more sophisticated precisely because it captures the fact that men are driven, compelled, and rendered unfree by forces operating internally as well as externally. The tragedies show man as even less free, autonomous, and in control than in the epics, for the forces that render him thus operate within the self: not on the self, as in the epics, but through it.

This seems such an obvious point it is a wonder that it is so often neglected. Yet the reason is apparent. Its neglect stems from a perspective that views Greek tragedy as a way station on the road to the Platonic account of the psyche, that sees the tragic poets internalizing the psychic forces that the epic poets naively render as external. Internalization supposedly opens the door for Plato, who on this basis creates the autonomous, rational psyche. If, however, one distinguishes internalization, responsibility, and control, then Plato is not part of this trajectory but tangential to it. Internalization increases responsibility. It may also enrich our capacity for pity, for responsibility requires recognition that our acts make a difference to others because we are all bound in a network of relationships. Internalization cannot make us autonomous or free. Not internalization, but a splitting of psyche and soma, of ego from the self as Lacan puts it, is necessary for that. In that way, the Platonic psyche represents progress in defense rather than progress in freedom.

Notes

Chapter 1 Introduction

1. R. P. Winnington-Ingram, *Sophocles*, p. 8; John Jones, *Aristotle and Greek Tragedy*, p. 8.
2. George Devereux, *Dreams in Greek Tragedy*, p. 11.
3. Philip Slater, *Glory of Hera*, pp. 337–396.
4. Ibid., pp. 349–351.
5. Sigmund Freud, *Totem and Taboo, Standard Edition*, 13:155–156.
6. Heinz Kohut, "On Courage," pp. 37–38; Kohut, "Remarks about the Formation of the Self," pp. 753–754.
7. Erik Erikson, "On the Generational Cycle."
8. Bennett Simon, *Tragic Drama and the Family*, p. 261. Simon discusses Kohut and Erikson along these lines. On Simon's brief psychoanalysis of Euripides, see pp. 98–103. The concept of an artist "holding" something for the culture implies that in the artist's work will be enacted the modal conflicts of his culture, as well as, perhaps, new solutions. My chapters 3 and 4, particularly, rely on this idea. Although they are related, this use of the term "holding" should not be confused with that of D. W. Winnicott, discussed in chapter 4.
9. Jean-Pierre Vernant, in Jean-Pierre Vernant and Pierre Vidal-Naquet, *Myth and Tragedy*, p. 87. In this coauthored book, each chapter is written by a single author.
10. Peter Winch, "Understanding a Primitive Society," pp. 106–107.
11. Ibid., p. 107.
12. Artemidorus, *Interpretation of Dreams*, I, p.45.
13. Michel Foucault, *Care of the Self*, p. 26. Foucault does note exceptions, in which sex is the signified, in note 1 to chapter 3, p. 242.
14. Vernant, in Vernant and Vidal-Naquet, *Myth and Tragedy*, pp. 110–111; see Herodotus, *Histories*, VI, 107.
15. Freud, *Interpretation of Dreams, Standard Edition*, 4:1–95; Devereux, *Dreams in Greek Tragedy*, pp. xxvi–xxix.
16. Charles Segal, "Greek Tragedy and Society," *Greek Tragedy and Political Theory*, ed. J. Peter Euben, p. 45.
17. Vernant, in Vernant and Vidal-Naquet, *Myth and Tragedy*, pp. 23–28.
18. Charles Segal, *Tragedy and Civilization*, p. 15.
19. See E. R. Dodds, *The Greeks and the Irrational*.
20. As an example of this forgetting see Segal, "Greek Tragedy and Society," *Greek Tragedy and Political Theory*, ed. Euben, p. 75.
21. Segal, *Tragedy and Civilization*, p. 53.
22. Unless otherwise noted, quotations from the tragedies are drawn from *The Complete Greek Tragedies*, edited by David Grene and Richmond Lattimore. 9 volumes (Chicago: University of Chicago Press, 1953–1959): *Aeschylus I: Oresteia* (*Agamemnon, The Libation Bearers, The Eumenides*), trans. Richmond Lattimore, © 1953 by the University of Chicago (*Agamemnon* © 1947 by Richmond Lattimore); *Aeschylus II: The Suppliant Maidens, The Persians*, trans. S. G. Benardete, *Seven against Thebes, Prometheus Bound*, trans. David Grene, © 1956 by the University of Chicago (*Prometheus Bound*

© 1942 by the University of Chicago); *Euripides I: Alcestis*, trans. Richmond Lattimore, *The Medea*, trans. Rex Warner, *The Heracleidae*, trans. Ralph Gladstone, *Hippolytus*, trans. David Grene, © 1955 by the University of Chicago (*Hippolytus*, © 1942 by the University of Chicago); *Euripides II: The Cyclops, Heracles*, trans. William Arrowsmith, *Iphigenia in Tauris*, trans. Witter Bynner, *Helen*, trans. Richmond Lattimore, © 1952, 1956 by the University of Chicago; *Euripides III: Hecuba*, trans. William Arrowsmith, *Andromache*, trans. John Frederick Nims, *The Trojan Women*, trans. Richmond Lattimore, *Ion*, trans. Ronald Frederick Willetts, © 1958 by the University of Chicago (*The Trojan Women* © 1947 by the Dial Press); *Euripides IV: Rhesus*, trans. Richmond Lattimore, *The Suppliant Women*, trans. Frank Jones, *Orestes*, trans. William Arrowsmith, *Iphigenia in Aulis*, trans. Charles R. Walker, © 1958 by the University of Chicago; *Euripides V: Electra*, trans. Emily Townsend Vermeule, *The Phoenician Women*, trans. Elizabeth Wyckoff, *The Bacchae*, trans. William Arrowsmith, © 1959 by the University of Chicago; *Sophocles I: Oedipus the King*, trans. David Grene, *Oedipus at Colonus*, trans. Robert Fitzgerald, *Antigone*, trans. Elizabeth Wyckoff, © 1954 by the University of Chicago (*Oedipus the King* © 1942 by the University of Chicago; *Oedipus at Colonus* © 1941 by Harcourt, Brace & Co.; *Antigone* © 1954 by the University of Chicago); *Sophocles II: Ajax*, trans. John Moore, *The Women of Trachis*, trans. Michael Jameson, *Electra, Philoctetes*, trans. David Grene, © 1957 by the University of Chicago. Used by permission. Lines given in the text refer to the lines in this series, which roughly correspond to the Greek text. Greek phrases in the text are from the Loeb Classical Library Greek-English editions from Harvard University Press.

23. Alford, *Melanie Klein and Critical Social Theory*, chapter 2.
24. Freud, "Splitting of the Ego in the Process of Defense," *Standard Edition*, 23:271–278.
25. Donald Meltzer, *Kleinian Development*, pt. 2, p. 64.
26. Robert Jay Lifton, *Nazi Doctors*, pp. 430–433.
27. Melanie Klein, "Mourning and Its Relation to Manic-Depressive States," *Writings*, 1:344–369.
28. Freud, "Thoughts for the Times on War and Death," *Standard Edition*, 14:289.
29. Evelyn Waugh, *Brideshead Revisited*, p. 331.
30. Thomas Ogden, *Projective Identification*, pp. 1–2.
31. Lifton, *Broken Connection*, pp. 13, 115.
32. Otto Rank, quoted in Lifton, *Broken Connection*, p. 56.
33. Lifton, *Broken Connection*, p. 117.
34. Ibid., p. 64.
35. Jean Baudrillard, *L'échange symbolique et la mort*, p. 195, quoted and translated by Douglas Kellner, *Jean Baudrillard*, p. 103.
36. Kellner, *Jean Baudrillard*, p. 103.
37. Jacques Lacan, "Mirror Stage as Formative of the Function of the I," pp. 1–7.
38. John Jones, *Aristotle and Greek Tragedy*, p. 278.
39. Ibid., p. 197.
40. Alford, "Psychoanalysis and Social Theory," pp. 1–25, contains a discussion of what I call generic object-relations theory: assumptions so basic that they are shared by all object relations theorists. Because my account in the present book is quite brief, the reader may wish to turn to this piece for further elaboration.
41. Harry Guntrip, *Psychoanalytic Theory, Therapy, and the Self*, p. 58.
42. E. Victor Wolfenstein, "Eating Psychoanalytic Marxism."
43. Alexander Nehamas, "The Rescue of Humanism," p. 28.

44. Martin Heidegger, *Discourse on Thinking* ("Conversations on a Country Path"), pp. 88–89. Here Heidegger uses the term "that-which regions" (*Gegnet*) in place of Being, but the idea is virtually identical. For Heidegger's views on the early Greeks, I draw on the four essays collected in his *Early Greek Thinking*, "Anaximander Fragment," "*Logos*," "*Moira*," and "*Aletheia*." Heidegger's *Brief Über den Humanismus* and *Holzwege* were also consulted, as was his "What Is Metaphysics?" in *Existence and Being*. Useful were Marjorie Grene, "Heidegger," and Robert Henri Cousineau, *Humanism and Ethics*.

45. Stephen K. White, *Political Theory and Postmodernism*, pp. 34–35, from which I draw heavily in this paragraph.

46. J. Peter Euben, *Tragedy of Political Theory*, p. 90.

47. Luc Ferry and Alain Renaut, *Heidegger and Modernity*, p. 105.

48. Ibid., p. 95.

49. Michel Foucault, "Truth and Power," p. 117. Sonia Kruks, in *Situation and Human Existence*, notes the problem of translating *constituent*, which may be rendered either as "constituent" or "constituting," depending on the context (p. 191, n. 11).

50. Jacques Lacan, *Le Séminaire*, 1:22, my translation; Pierre Bourdieu and Jean-Claude Passeron, "Sociology and Philosophy in France since 1945"; Jean-François Lyotard, *Differend*; Kruks, *Situation and Human Existence*, pp. 181–183.

51. Vincent Descombes, "Apropos of the 'Critique of the Subject,'" *Who Comes after the Subject?* ed. Eduardo Cadava, Peter Connor, and Jean-Luc Nancy, pp. 123–124.

52. Derrida, "'Eating Well,' or the Calculation of the Subject," *Who Comes after the Subject?* ed. Cadava, Connor, and Nancy, pp. 96–119.

53. Sylviane Agacinski, "Another Experience of the Question," *Who Comes after the Subject?* ed. Cadava, Connor, and Nancy, p. 21.

54. Lyotard, *Differend*, p. xiii.

Chapter 2 Greek Tragedy and the Dionysian Crisis

1. Gilbert Murray, quoted in R. P. Winnington-Ingram, *Studies in Aeschylus*, p. 8.

2. E. R. Dodds, *Greeks and the Irrational*, p. 32.

3. Ibid.

4. Isocrates, V. 117.

5. During their confrontation with Clytaemestra, the chorus cries "Woe, woe, it is on account of Zeus, who is responsible for all, doer of all" (*Agamemnon*, 1485ff). The doubts are being resolved but not in Zeus's favor.

6. R. P. Winnington-Ingram, *Studies in Aeschylus*, pp. 158, 160.

7. D. J. Conacher, in *Aeschylus' Oresteia*, reviews the semantic complexity of the parodos, as well as the entry of Clytaemestra, pp. 76–101.

8. Winnington-Ingram, *Studies in Aeschylus*, p. 166. See too p. 149.

9. Ibid., p. 172.

10. Melanie Klein, "Some Reflections on 'The Oresteia,'" in *Writings*, 3:298.

11. Kate Millett, *Sexual Politics*, and Anne Lebeck, Oresteia, quoted in Simon Goldhill, *Reading Greek Tragedy*, pp. 53–54.

12. Hugh Lloyd-Jones, quoted by D. J. Conacher, *Aeschylus' Oresteia*, p. 168. Several points in this paragraph stem from Conacher.

13. Bennett Simon, *Tragic Drama and the Family*, p. 263 and chap. 2.

14. The Oxford translation of *Prometheus Bound,* by James Scully and C. John Herington, contains an appendix with a translation of all the Aeschylean fragments. Especially relevant are the ones they number 11–13. The original Greek and Latin texts are contained in H. J. Mette, *Die Fragmente der Tragödien des Aischylos.* On the question of whether Aeschylus is the author of the *Prometheus Bound* (there is more evidence than one might expect that he is not), see below, chap. 4, n. 31.

15. Dodds, *Greeks and the Irrational,* p. 49.

16. Winnington-Ingram, *Sophocles,* p. 19.

17. Ibid., p. 49.

18. H. D. F. Kitto, *Greek Tragedy,* pp. 145–150.

19. Laius, Oedipus' father, abducted and sodomized Pelops' illegitimate son. Since Pelops was Laius' guest-host at the time, this was an especially heinous crime, and Pelops, together with Zeus and Hera, condemned Laius to be murdered by his son, who would then replace him in his wife's bed.

20. C. M. Bowra, *Sophoclean Tragedy,* p. 349.

21. Winnington-Ingram, *Sophocles,* p. 275.

22. C. K. Williams and Gregory Dickerson, introduction to their translation of *Women of Trachis,* p. 13. Theirs is a marvelous translation; my criticism applies only to this interpretation.

23. J. Peter Euben, "Political Corruption in Euripides' *Orestes,*" *Greek Tragedy and Political Theory,* ed. J. Peter Euben, 235.

24. Charles Segal, *Interpreting Greek Tragedy,* p. 258.

25. Cedric Whitman, *Euripides and the Full Circle of Myth,* p. 60.

26. Winnington-Ingram, *Studies in Aeschylus,* p. 207.

27. Gunther Zuntz, quoted by John Frederick Nims in *Complete Greek Tragedies: Euripides III,* ed. David Grene and Richmond Lattimore, p. 71.

28. Cedric Whitman, in *Euripides and the Full Circle of Myth,* pp. 69–103, traces in fascinating detail the imagery by which badness and purity interpenetrate in the play, beginning with Apollo's rape of Creusa.

29. Winnington-Ingram, *Euripides and Dionysus,* p. 80.

30. Euben, *Tragedy of Political Theory,* p. 160.

31. Translation from Winnington-Ingram, *Euripides and Dionysus.* I follow Winnington-Ingram in this and the next paragraph.

32. See Heinz Kohut, "Thoughts on Narcissism and Narcissistic Rage."

33. Whitman, *Euripides and the Full Circle of Myth,* p. 99.

34. J. Peter Euben, in "Political Corruption in Euripides' *Orestes,*" *Greek Tragedy and Political Theory,* ed. Euben, quotes Froma Zeitlin as holding this view, p. 243.

35. Jean-Pierre Vernant, in Jean-Pierre Vernant and Pierre Vidal-Naquet, *Myth and Tragedy,* p. 33. In this coauthored book, each chapter is written by a single author.

36. Ibid., p. 26.

37. A. W. H. Adkins, *Merit and Responsibility,* and *Moral Values and Political Behavior in Ancient Greece.*

38. Segal, *Interpreting Greek Tragedy,* pp. 101–102.

39. George Steiner, *Antigones,* pp. 175–176.

40. Martha Nussbaum, *Fragility of Goodness,* p. 75.

41. See Segal, *Interpreting Greek Tragedy,* p. 147.

42. Ibid., pp. 159–160.

43. Kitto, *Greek Tragedy*, p. 229.

44. Jean Bethke Elshtain, *Public Man, Private Woman*. This theme is pursued by Elshtain and several other authors, particularly Susan Moller Okin, in "Philosopher Queens and Private Wives," *Family in Political Thought*, ed. Elshtain.

45. Sigmund Freud, *Civilization and Its Discontents*, p. 56.

46. Walter Kaufmann, introduction to his translation of Friedrich Nietzsche, *Birth of Tragedy*, in *Basic Writings of Nietzsche*, p. 9.

47. Paul Shorey and A. C. Person, quoted in Segal, *Tragedy and Civilization*, p. viii.

48. Nietzsche, *Birth of Tragedy*, p. 17.

49. Ibid., p. 60.

50. Theodor Adorno, *Prisms*, p. 34.

51. Herbert Marcuse, *Aesthetic Dimension*, p. 66.

52. Ranier Maria Rilke, *Duineser Elegien*, first elegy, translation mine.

53. Nietzsche, *Birth of Tragedy*, pp. 83–84.

54. William Arrowsmith, notes to his translation of *Alcestis*, p. 109.

55. Alford, *Melanie Klein and Critical Social Theory*, pp. 50–56.

Chapter 3 Failure of Blood Ritual in the Tragedies

1. Mary Douglas, *Purity and Danger*; Victor Turner, *Ritual Process*.

2. Walter Burkert, *Greek Religion*, p. 59, and p. 369, n.31.

3. Ibid., pp. 55–60, 80–82.

4. William Arrowsmith, notes to his translation of *Alcestis*, p. 101.

5. Burkert, *Greek Religion*, p. 58.

6. E. R. Dodds, *Greeks and the Irrational*, pp. 28–63.

7. A. W. H. Adkins, *Merit and Responsibility*, pp. 48–60.

8. Melanie Klein, "Some Reflections on 'The Oresteia,'" in *Writings*, 3:291–298; Klein, "Notes on Some Schizoid Mechanisms," in *Writings*, 3:1–24.

9. René Girard, *Violence and the Sacred*, p. 36.

10. Sigmund Freud, "The Antithetical Meaning of Primal Words," *Standard Edition*, 11:153–163.

11. Victor Turner, *Ritual Process*, p. 185.

12. Mary Douglas, *Purity and Danger*, p. 126.

13. Ibid., pp. 138–139.

14. I elaborate this point in my *Melanie Klein and Critical Social Theory*, pp. 83–87.

15. Girard, *Violence and the Sacred*, pp. 39–44.

16. Janine Chasseguet-Smirgel, *Ego Ideal*, pp. 10–25.

17. Robert Jay Lifton, *Nazi Doctors*, p. 482.

18. One critic has argued that this line (1234) refers not to the relationship of Heracles and Theseus, but to Heracles and his children. I cannot see this reading at all (Heracles' children are dead, and the line occurs in the midst of a long exchange between Heracles and Theseus) but it would not change my basic point.

19. Klein, "Early Stages of the Oedipus Complex," *Writings*, 1:186–198.

20. Richmond Lattimore, introduction to his translation of *Helen, Complete Greek Tragedies*, ed. David Grene and Richmond Lattimore, pp. 261–262.

21. Segal, *Tragedy and Civilization*, p. 7.

22. Freud, *Civilization and Its Discontents*, pp. 78–79.

23. Alford, *Narcissism*, chap. 3; Alford, *The Self in Social Theory*, chaps. 3–4.

24. Burness E. Moore and Bernard D. Fine, eds., *Psychoanalytic Terms and Concepts*, entry under "Ego," pp. 58–59.

Chapter 4 Tragic Discontinuity of Life and Death

 1. Some philologists argue that Alcestis does not speak because *Alcestis* was written for only two actors. See Cedric Whitman, *Euripides and the Full Circle of Myth*, p. 112. It does not matter. All that matters from a dramatic point of view is that Euripides calls attention to her silence.

 2. Richmond Lattimore, introduction to his translation of *Alcestis, Complete Greek Tragedies*, ed. David Grene and Richmond Lattimore, p. 3.

 3. William Arrowsmith, introduction to his translation of *Alcestis*, p. 12.

 4. Richard Emil Braun, notes to his translation of Sophocles' *Antigone*, p. 86. Actually, the chorus talks of how love twists the just, not how it straightens the unjust. Love causes strife, but does not heal it (see 780–805). This is part of Greek traditional thinking about eros, that it is more troublemaker than healer. See Hesiod, *Theogony*, 115–125.

 5. George Steiner, *Antigones*, devotes considerable attention to Hölderlin's account of *Antigone;* see pp. 66–106.

 6. Sigmund Freud, "Mourning and Melancholia," *Standard Edition*, 14:243–260; Melanie Klein, "Mourning and Its Relation to Manic-Depressive States," *Writings*, 1:344–369.

 7. Otto Rank, quoted in Robert Jay Lifton, *Broken Connection*, p. 180.

 8. Peter Winch, "Understanding a Primitive Society"; Freud, "Thoughts for the Times on War and Death," *Standard Edition*, 14:289.

 9. Dylan Thomas, "Do Not Go Gentle into That Good Night," *Collected Poems of Dylan Thomas*, p. 128, quoted by Lifton in *Broken Connection*, pp. 108-109.

10. Eugène Ionesco, quoted by Lifton, *Broken Connection*, p. 70.

11. Robert Jay Lifton, *Broken Connection*, p. 153.

12. Lifton, *Broken Connection*, p. 139.

13. Klein, "A Contribution to the Psychogenesis of Manic-Depressive States," *Writings*, 1:275.

14. H. D. F. Kitto, *Greek Tragedy*, p. 144.

15. Lifton, *Nazi Doctors*, p. 449.

16. Norman O. Brown, *Life Against Death*; Herbert Marcuse, *Eros and Civilization*, chap. 4.

17. Bennett Simon, *Tragic Drama and the Family*, p. 57.

18. Gustave Glotz, *Greek City*, pp. 107, 258. On this point see also Joel Kovel, "Mind and State in Ancient Greece," in his *Radical Spirit*, pp. 208–225.

19. David Claus, *Toward the Soul*, p. 13; see also pp. 107–109, 153–155.

20. Lifton, *Broken Connection*, pp. 18–35.

21. Robert Garland, *Greek Way of Death*, p. 123; see also p. 59.

22. Hannah Arendt, *Human Condition*, pp. 7–21, and throughout.

23. Quoted in Walter Burkert, *Greek Religion*, p. 293. I draw my account of the mysteries primarily from Garland.

24. A. W. Gomme, *Population of Athens*, pp. 67–70. See too A. H. M. Jones, *Athenian Democracy*, pp. 82–83.

25. William Arrowsmith, introduction to his translation of *Alcestis*, pp. 21–22.

26. Freud, *Civilization and Its Discontents*, p. 12.

27. D. W. Winnicott, *Maturational Processes and the Facilitating Environment*, pp. 60, 44–48, 113; Winnicott, *Holding and Interpretation*, pp. 16–18.

28. Burkert, *Greek Religion*, p. 192; Garland, *Greek Way of Death*, pp. 21–37.

29. *New English Bible*, Oxford Study Edition.

30. Lifton, *Broken Connection*, p. 95.

31. There is more doubt than one might expect over whether *Prometheus Bound* is actually by Aeschylus, but its authorship does not affect my argument. R. P. Winnington-Ingram, *Studies in Aeschylus*, pp. 175–176, reviews the evidence, concluding "to treat it as without question Aeschylean is no longer sensible."

32. Marcuse, *Eros and Civilization*, p. 161.

33. Paul Bowles, *Sheltering Sky*, p. 248.

34. Max Weber, *Protestant Ethic and the Spirit of Capitalism*, p. 182; Karl Löwith, *Max Weber and Karl Marx*, pp. 57–60.

35. Marcuse, *Eros and Civilization*, p. 231.

36. Ibid., pp. 234–235.

37. Garland, *Greek Way of Death*, p. 29.

Chapter 5 Responsibility without Freedom

1. Jean-Pierre Vernant, in Jean-Pierre Vernant and Pierre Vidal-Naquet, *Myth and Tragedy in Ancient Greece*, p. 83. In this coauthored book, each chapter is written by a single author. Charles Segal, *Tragedy and Civilization*, p. 41, makes a similar point.

2. John Jones, *Aristotle and Greek Tragedy*, pp. 278, 197.

3. Originally *hamartia* meant "wide-shot," as in missing the target. Used by the Greeks to cover everything from a mistake to what another era would call sin, the context in which it is used by Aristotle (see *Poetics*, c13, 1453a10–16), makes clear that he meant a mistake or blunder: an action not maliciously undertaken that proves harmful because too little is known about it. Thus, for example, Aristotle can say that it is due to some error (hamartia) that both Oedipus and Thyestes fall: Oedipus because he did not know his real parents, Thyestes because he unknowingly ate the flesh of his children. It is, evidently, a Renaissance invention that gives to hamartia the sense of a moral correlation between guilt and disaster, what has come to be called poetic justice. On this see J. M. Bremer, *Hamartia*, especially pp. 195–197. These considerations are, of course, relevant to the relation between freedom and responsibility. Hamartia implies a restriction on freedom imposed by ignorance that does not result in a mitigation of responsibility.

4. E. R. Dodds, *Greeks and the Irrational*, pp. 1–18.

5. Charles Krauthammer, *Washington Post*, May 11, 1990, p. A27. Also the source of the Marion Barry quote.

6. R. P. Winnington-Ingram, *Sophocles*, pp. 175–178.

7. Joel Schwartz, "Human Action and Political Action in *Oedipus Tyrannos*," *Greek Tragedy and Political Theory*, ed. Euben, p. 202, and pp. 200–204 generally. I am following Schwartz on the Greek.

8. Dodds, *The Greeks and the Irrational*, p. 186.

9. Winnington-Ingram, *Sophocles*, p. 177.

10. Vernant and Vidal-Naquet, *Myth and Tragedy in Ancient Greece*, pp. 53, 71–73.

11. Bernard Knox, *Oedipus at Thebes*, p. 5.

12. William Chase Greene, *Moira*, p. 138.

13. Winnington-Ingram, *Sophocles*, pp. 177–178.

14. Schwartz, "Human Action and Political Action in *Oedipus Tyrannos*," *Greek Tragedy and Political Theory*, ed. Euben, pp. 203–204.

15. Raymond Tallis, *Not Saussure.*

16. Zevedei Barbu, quoted in Vernant and Vidal-Naquet, *Myth and Tragedy in Ancient Greece*, p. 52.

17. André Rivier, quoted in Vernant and Vidal-Naquet, *Myth and Tragedy in Ancient Greece*, p. 53.

18. Vernant and Vidal-Naquet, *Myth and Tragedy in Ancient Greece*, pp. 46–60.

19. Jacqueline de Romilly, quoted in Vernant and Vidal-Naquet, *Myth and Tragedy in Ancient Greece*, p. 71.

20. Vernant, in Vernant and Vidal-Naquet, *Myth and Tragedy in Ancient Greece*, p. 79.

21. Martha Nussbaum, *Fragility of Goodness*, pp. 395–421; Nussbaum, *Love's Knowledge*, p. 43.

22. Peter Winch makes this point about Evans-Pritchard in his "Understanding a Primitive Society," pp. 308–314.

23. See Ruth Padel, "Making Space Speak," in *Nothing to Do with Dionysos?* ed. John Winkler and Froma Zeitlin, p. 355–360.

24. A. W. H. Adkins, *Merit and Responsibility*, pp. 48–54.

25. Jones, *Aristotle and Greek Tragedy*, p. 35.

26. Frank L. Lucas, quoted in Jones, *Aristotle and Greek Tragedy*, p. 35.

27. Yosal Rogat, quoted in Hannah Arendt, *Eichmann in Jerusalem*, p. 277.

28. G. Hermann, Preface to his *Euripidis Opera* (1831), quoted and discussed by Nussbaum, *Fragility of Goodness*, p. 399. In this same context she notes that Arrowsmith now agrees with her interpretation of *nomos* as "convention," p. 400. The Loeb Classical Library translation of *Hecuba* by Arthur Way translates *nomos* simply as "Law," which is actually less misleading (800).

29. See Winnington-Ingram, *Sophocles*, p. 302.

30. Jean-Paul Sartre, *Existentialism and Human Emotions*, p. 23.

31. Ludwig Binswanger, *Being in the World*, from the introduction by Jacob Needleman, pp. 91–92.

32. Sartre, *Existentialism and Human Emotions*, pp. 72, 68.

33. Sartre, *Being and Nothingness*, pp. 52–53. This is the existential-psychological version of Sartre's more general argument in *Being and Nothingness* that consciousness is absolute, making consciousness of oneself a precondition of consciousness of things but not vice versa. Similarly, consciousness of pleasure is constitutive of pleasure, says Sartre. From here it is but a small step to claim that consciousness of the unconscious is constitutive of the unconsciousness. It is not the last small step but the first big one—that consciousness of oneself is a precondition of consciousness of things but not vice versa—that is so problematic.

34. Binswanger, *Existentialism and Human Emotions*, quoted by Needleman in his introduction, p. 93.

35. Sartre, *Existentialism and Human Emotions*, pp. 16, 32.

36. Charles Taylor, "The Concept of a Person," pp. 112–113.

37. Max Horkheimer and Theodor Adorno, *Dialectic of Enlightenment.*

38. In *The Self in Social Theory*, pp. 35–44, I deal with Lacan's fascination and play with language in some detail, arguing that they sometimes serve as a defense (especially by those critics who focus on his language) against his stunning conclusions.

39. Jacques Lacan, "Some Reflections on the Ego," pp. 11–12.

40. Lacan, *Le séminaire*, 1:22, my translation.

41. Lacan, *Ecrits*, p. 300.

42. Louis Sass, "The Self and Its Vicissitudes," pp. 600–601.

43. Stuart Schneiderman, *Jacques Lacan: The Death of an Intellectual Hero*. There is an ironic double meaning to Schneiderman's subtitle that need not be addressed here.

44. Vernant, in Vernant and Vidal-Naquet, *Myth and Tragedy in Ancient Greece*, p. 139.

45. Jane Gallop, *Daughter's Seduction*, pp. 49–50, 95–96. Thanks to Denise Valentino for clarifying *jouissance*.

46. Jones, *Aristotle and Greek Tragedy*, p. 110.

47. Lacan, "Mirror Stage as Formative of the Function of the I."

48. Jones, *Aristotle and Greek Tragedy*, p. 108.

49. Ibid., p. 110.

50. Michel Foucault, "Polemics, Politics and Problemizations," p. 388. In *Situation and Human Existence*, Sonia Kruks argues that Foucault does not so much soften his stand as reverse it, so that this formulation regarding thought "reverts instead to the classical conception of the autonomous subject" (p. 188).

51. Alexander Nehamas, "The Rescue of Humanism," p. 33.

52. Emmanuel Levinas, *Difficult Freedom*, p. 10.

53. Jacques Derrida, " 'Eating Well,' " *Who Comes after the Subject?* ed. Eduardo Cadava, Peter Connor, and Jean-Luc Nancy, pp. 114–115. How to come to terms with the horror of Auschwitz is a theme of this essay, and the organizing principle of Lyotard's *Differend*. There is, I believe, a deeply ethical passion behind the postmodern critique of the subject. Its origins are virtually identical to the ethical passion of the Frankfurt school of critical theory, which also sought to explain why Western reason posed no barrier to Auschwitz: because the deeply instrumental orientation of Western reason involved it from the very beginning in the project of domination, including the destruction of those who could be identified as mere nature. For Lyotard (but not Derrida, I think), however, the issue fundamentally concerns the destruction of language. "In exterminating the Jews, Nazism eliminated a phrase regimen" (*Differend*, p. 106). True enough, but Nazism did much more, which is also worth remembering.

54. Derrida, " 'Eating Well,' " *Who Comes after the Subject?* ed. Cadava, Connor, and Nancy, p. 112. The work of both Heidegger and Levinas, says Derrida, "remain profound humanisms to the extent that they do not sacrifice sacrifice" (p. 113). Derrida would, it appears, sacrifice sacrifice—that is, render the subject not merely hostage to the other, but a virtual non-entity except in relationship to the other.

55. Lyotard, *Differend*, p. 107.

56. Michel Foucault, "What Is an Author?" p. 138.

Chapter 6 Pity and the Foundations of Civilization

1. Albert O. Hirschman, *Passions and the Interests*, p. 41.

2. *The Federalist* (1787–1788), numbers 72, 51.

3. David Johnston, *Rhetoric of* Leviathan.

4. Immanuel Kant, "Grundlegung zur Metaphysik der Sitten," 4:25–26 (Akademie edition, 4:399–400; BA 12–14), Kant's emphasis. My translation of the passage that begins "is benefi-

cence from duty" is based upon, but alters, that of Lewis White Beck in Kant, *Foundations of the Metaphysics of Morals*, p. 16. A popular translation by Carl J. Friedrich in the Modern Library *Philosophy of Kant* edition renders *pathologische* not as "pathological" but as "psychological" (p. 147), helping the reader to gloss over the stringency of Kant's opposition to compassion.

5. David Hume, quoted in Hirschman, *Passions and the Interests*, p. 66.

6. Bishop Butler, quoted in Hirschman, *Passions and the Interests*, p. 35.

7. A .W. H. Adkins, "Arete, Techne, Democracy and Sophists"; Adkins, *Merit and Responsibility*; Adkins, *Moral Values and Political Behavior*.

8. H. D. F. Kitto, *Greek Tragedy*, p. 123. Not always the most reliable guide to Greek tragedy, Kitto hits the mark on this point. My argument about pity is, however, my own; it does not depend upon Kitto's comments on *Ajax*.

9. Bennett Simon, *Mind and Madness in Ancient Greece*, p. 136.

10. Jean-Jacques Rousseau, "Discourse on the Origin and Foundations of Inequality among Men," p. 131. More on this comparison with Rousseau follows in the conclusion to this chapter.

11. Jean-Pierre Vernant, in Jean-Pierre Vernant and Pierre Vidal-Naquet, *Myth and Tragedy in Ancient Greece*, p. 26.

12. J. Peter Euben, *Tragedy of Political Theory*, p. 90. In spite of all the disagreement over the resolution of the *Eumenides*, few would deny that the *Oresteia* concerns the transformation of the lex talionis under the influence of such civilized values as mercy and pity.

13. Simon Goldhill, "Great Dionysia and Civic Ideology," *Nothing to Do with Dionysos?* ed. John Winkler and Froma Zeitlin, p. 114.

14. R. P. Winnington-Ingram, *Sophocles*, p. 328.

15. Edmund Wilson, "Philoctetes: The Wound and the Bow."

16. The reader will recall that in the Homeric tradition Neoptolemus kills Priam at Troy. Sophocles obliquely refers to Neoptolemus' future at lines 1440–1445. In this passage Heracles tells Neoptolemus to act with piety (*eusebeia*) when he sacks Troy. This might lead one to posit a tight link between pity and piety among the Greeks, as tight as in the Christian era (as pointed out previously, the English term *pity* has its origins in the Latin *pietas*, "piety"). In fact, my thesis is that pity is something quite different, a distinctly human virtue—what humans can offer each other that the gods cannot. Piety concerns people's relationship to the gods and to each other, as this relationship is mediated by a respectful attitude toward the gods. Pity is a strictly human relationship, unmediated by the gods. See my comments on Christian pity, below.

17. James Scully and C. John Herington, introduction to *Prometheus Bound*, trans. Scully and Herington, pp. 13–14. Their translation captures this schizoid quality especially well.

18. Werner Jaeger, *Paideia*, 1:n.p.

19. Stephen Salkever, "Tragedy and the Education of the *Demos*," *Greek Tragedy and Political Theory*, ed. J. Peter Euben, p. 295.

20. W. B. Stanford, *Greek Tragedy and the Emotions*, p. 24.

21. Pietro Pucci, *Violence of Pity in Euripides' Medea*, p. 127.

22. Richard Sewall, *Vision of Tragedy*, p. 5.

23. Translation from Martha Nussbaum, *Love's Knowledge*, p. 375; it captures the spirit of *suggnome* well.

24. Both quotations from James Grotstein, *Splitting and Projective Identification*, p. 202.
25. William Arrowsmith, introduction to his translation of *Alcestis*, by Euripides, p. 6.
26. Hans J. Morgenthau, "Love and Power," in his *Restoration of American Politics*, p. 13.
27. Diskin Clay, introduction to his translation, with Stephen Berg, of *Oedipus the King*, by Sophocles, p. 16.
28. Nussbaum, *Fragility of Goodness*, pp. 45–46.
29. See Alford, *Melanie Klein*, pp. 33–37.
30. From the conjunction of the desire for self-preservation and pitié, says Rousseau, one can derive reason and natural law "without the necessity of introducing [the principle] of sociability" ("Discourse on the Origins and Foundations of Inequality among Men," pp. 95–96). For an extended discussion of this aspect of Rousseau's thought see my *Self in Social Theory*, chap. 8, on Rousseau.
31. Hirschman, *Passions and the Interests*, pp. 56–67.
32. James Boswell, *Boswell's Life of Johnson*, quoted in Hirschman, *Passions and the Interests*, p. 58.
33. Hirschman, *Passions and the Interests*, pp. 130–133.
34. *Psychoanalytic Terms and Concepts*, ed. Burness E. Moore and Bernard Fine, entry entitled "Perversion."
35. Robert N. Bellah, et al., *Habits of the Heart*.

Chapter 7 Conclusion

1. Martha Nussbaum, *Fragility of Goodness*, pp. 389–398.
2. Martin Heidegger, "*Aletheia*: Heraclitus, Fragment B 16," *Early Greek Thinking*, 102–124.
3. See Peter Gay, *Freud*, p. 292, and Phyllis Grosskurth, *Melanie Klein*, pp. 262–275.
4. Heinz Kohut, *Restoration of the Self*, pp. 30–32; Kohut, *How Does Analysis Cure?* pp. 99–103. See also Alford, *Self in Social Theory*, pp. 27–31, on Kohut's concept of transmuting internalization.
5. Evelyn Waugh, *Brideshead Revisited*, pp. 259, 337.
6. Jacques Lacan, quoted by Bice Benvenuto and Roger Kennedy in *Works of Jacques Lacan*, p. 207.
7. Alaisdair MacIntyre, *Whose Justice?* p. 347. See also MacIntyre, *After Virtue*, pp. 123–136, on the coherence of the poets' worldview.
8. Charles Segal, *Tragedy and Civilization*, p. 42.
9. J. Peter Euben, "Political Corruption in Euripides' *Orestes*," *Greek Tragedy and Political Theory*, ed. J. Peter Euben, p. 235.
10. Hanna Segal, "Psycho-Analytical Approach to Aesthetics," p. 400.
11. Arthur Ganz, *Realms of the Self*, p. 214.
12. Charles Segal, *Tragedy and Civilization*, p. 44.
13. H. D. F. Kitto, *Greek Tragedy*, p. 252.
14. Sigmund Freud, *Civilization and Its Discontents*, p. 77.

Appendix

1. See David Claus, *Toward the Soul*, p. 13. Though I disagree with some of Claus's conclusions about the Homeric psyche, his is a marvelous and subtle book.

2. Bennett Simon, *Mind and Madness in Ancient Greece,* pp. 62–64; *Tragic Drama and the Family,* pp. 13–27.

3. Paul Fussell, *Wartime,* p. 281.

4. Joel Kovel, "Mind and State in Ancient Greece," in his *Radical Spirit,* pp. 208–225.

Works Cited

Note: Classical sources cited in the form that is usual in classical studies are not repeated here.

Adkins, A. W. H. "Arete, Techne, Democracy and Sophists: *Protagoras* 316b–328d." *Journal of Hellenic Studies* 93 (1973): 9–12.

———. *Merit and Responsibility*. Oxford: Clarendon Press, 1960.

———. *Moral Values and Political Behavior in Ancient Greece*. New York: W. W. Norton, 1972.

Adorno, Theodor. *Prisms*, trans. S. Weber and S. Weber. Cambridge: MIT Press, 1981.

Alford, C. Fred. *Melanie Klein and Critical Social Theory*. New Haven: Yale University Press, 1989.

———. *Narcissism: Socrates, the Frankfurt School, and Psychoanalytic Theory*. New Haven: Yale University Press, 1988.

———. "Psychoanalysis and Social Theory: Sacrificing Psychoanalysis to Utopia?" *Psychoanalysis and Contemporary Thought* 13, no. 4 (1990): 1–25.

———. *The Self in Social Theory: A Psychoanalytic Account of Its Construction in Plato, Hobbes, Locke, Rawls, and Rousseau*. New Haven: Yale University Press, 1991.

Arendt, Hannah. *Eichmann in Jerusalem: A Report on the Banality of Evil*. Rev. ed. New York: Viking Press, 1965.

———. *The Human Condition*. Chicago: University of Chicago Press, 1958.

Arrowsmith, William, trans. and ed. *Alcestis*, by Euripides. Oxford: Oxford University Press, 1974.

Artemidorus. *The Interpretation of Dreams*. Translated by R. J. White. Park Ridge, N.J.: Noyes Press, 1975.

Barbu, Zevedei. *Problems of Historical Psychology*. 1960. Reprint. Westport, Conn.: Greenwood, 1976.

Baudrillard, Jean. *L'échange symbolique et la mort*. Paris: Gallimard, 1976.

Bellah, Robert N., Richard Madsen, William Sullivan, Ann Swidler, and Steven Tipton. *Habits of the Heart: Individualism and Commitment in American Life*. Berkeley: University of California Press, 1985.

Benvenuto, Bice, and Roger Kennedy. *The Works of Jacques Lacan*. New York: St. Martin's, 1986.

Binswanger, Ludwig. *Being in the World: Selected Papers of Ludwig Binswanger*. Edited and with an introduction by Jacob Needleman. London: Souvenir, 1975.

Bion, Wilfred. *Attention and Interpretation*. New York: Basic Books, 1970.

Boss, Medard. *Psychoanalysis and Daseinanalysis*. Translated by Ludwig Lefebre. New York: Basic Books, 1963.

Bourdieu, Pierre, and Jean-Claude Passeron. "Sociology and Philosophy in France since 1945: Death and Resurrection of a Philosophy without a Subject." *Social Research* 34, no. 1 (Spring, 1967): 162–212.

Bowles, Paul. *The Sheltering Sky*. New York: Vintage, 1949.

Bowra, C. M. *Sophoclean Tragedy*. Oxford: Oxford University Press, 1944.

Braun, Richard Emil, trans. *Antigone,* by Sophocles. New York: Oxford University Press, 1973.

Bremer, J. M. *Hamartia: Tragic Error in the* Poetics *of Aristotle and in Greek Tragedy*. Amsterdam: Adolf Hakkert, 1969.

Brown, Norman O. *Life against Death*. New York: Vintage, 1959.

Burkert, Walter. *Greek Religion*. Translated by John Raffan. Cambridge: Harvard University Press, 1985.

Butler, Bishop. *Analogy of Religion,* in *Works,* vol. 1. Oxford: Clarendon Press, 1896.

Cadava, Eduardo, Peter Connor, and Jean-Luc Nancy, eds. *Who Comes after the Subject?* New York: Routledge, 1991.

Chasseguet-Smirgel, Janine. *The Ego Ideal*. Translated by Paul Barrows. New York: W. W. Norton, 1984.

Claus, David. *Toward the Soul: An Inquiry into the Meaning of Psuche before Plato*. New Haven: Yale University Press, 1981.

Clay, Diskin, and Stephen Berg, trans. *Oedipus the King,* by Sophocles. New York: Oxford University Press, 1978.

Conacher, D. J. *Aeschylus'* Oresteia: *A Literary Commentary*. Toronto: University of Toronto Press, 1987.

Cousineau, Robert Henri. *Humanism and Ethics: An Introduction to Heidegger's "Letter on Humanism."* Louvain: Nauwelaerts, 1972.

Detienne, Marcel, and Jean-Pierre Vernant, with essays by Durand, Georgoudi, Hartog, and Svenbro. *The Cuisine of Sacrifice among the Greeks*. Translated by Paula Wissing. Chicago: University of Chicago Press, 1989.

Devereux, George. *Dreams in Greek Tragedy: An Ethno-Psycho-Analytical Study*. Berkeley: University of California Press, 1976.

Dodds, E. R. *The Greeks and the Irrational*. Berkeley: University of California Press, 1951.

Douglas, Mary. *Purity and Danger: An Analysis of Concepts of Pollution and Taboo*. Harmondsworth, England: Penguin, 1966.

Elshtain, Jean Bethke, "Antigone's Daughters Reconsidered: Continuing Reflections on Women, Politics, and Power," in *Life-World and Politics: Between Modernity and Postmodernity. Essays in Honor of Fred R. Dallmayr,* edited by Stephen White, pp. 222–235. Notre Dame, Ind.: University of Notre Dame Press, 1989.

———. *Public Man, Private Woman: Women in Social and Political Thought*. Princeton, N.J.: Princeton University Press, 1981.

Elshtain, Jean Bethke, ed. *The Family in Political Thought*. Amherst: University of Massachusetts Press, 1982.

Erikson, Erik. "On the Generational Cycle: An Address." *International Journal of Psycho-Analysis* 61 (1980): 213–223.

Euben, J. Peter. *The Tragedy of Political Theory*. Princeton, N.J.: Princeton University Press, 1990.

Euben, J. Peter, ed. *Greek Tragedy and Political Theory*. Berkeley: University of California Press, 1986.

Ferry, Luc, and Alain Renaut. *Heidegger and Modernity*. Translated by Franklin Philip. Chicago: University of Chicago Press, 1990.

Finley, M. I. *The World of Odysseus*. Rev. ed. Harmondsworth, England: Penguin, 1978.

Foucault, Michel. *The Care of the Self: The History of Sexuality,* vol. 3. Translated by Robert Hurley. New York: Vintage, 1986.

———. "Polemics, Politics and Problemizations: An Interview," in *The Foucault Reader,* edited by Paul Rabinow, pp.381–389. New York: Pantheon, 1984.

———. "Truth and Power," in *Power/Knowledge,* edited by Colin Gordon, pp.109–133. New York: Pantheon, 1980.

———. "What Is an Author?" in *Language, Counter-Memory and Practice,* edited by Don Bouchard, pp. 113–138. Ithaca, N.Y.: Cornell University Press, 1977.

Freud, Sigmund. *Civilization and Its Discontents*. Translated by James Strachey. New York: W. W. Norton, 1961.

———. *The Standard Edition of the Complete Psychological Works of Sigmund Freud*. Edited by James Strachey. 24 volumes. London: Hogarth Press, 1953–1974.

Fussell, Paul. *Wartime: Understanding and Behavior in the Second World War*. New York: Oxford University Press, 1989.

Gallop, Jane. *The Daughter's Seduction: Feminism and Psychoanalysis*. Ithaca, N.Y.: Cornell University Press, 1982.

Ganz, Arthur. *Realms of the Self: Variations on a Theme in Modern Drama*. New York: New York University Press, 1980.

Garland, Robert. *The Greek Way of Death*. Ithaca, N.Y.: Cornell University Press, 1985.

Gay, Peter. *Freud: A Life for Our Time*. New York: W. W. Norton, 1988.

Gilligan, Carol. *In a Different Voice*. Cambridge: Harvard University Press, 1982.

Girard, René. *Violence and the Sacred*. Translated by Patrick Gregory. Baltimore: Johns Hopkins University Press, 1977.

Glotz, Gustave. *The Greek City and Its Institutions*. New York: Knopf.

Goldhill, Simon. *Reading Greek Tragedy*. Cambridge: Cambridge University Press, 1986.

Gomme, A. W. *The Population of Athens in the Fifth and Fourth Centuries B.C.* Chicago: Argonaut, 1967.

Gouldner, Alvin. *Enter Plato*. New York: Basic, 1965.

Greene, William Chase. *Moira: Fate, Good, and Evil in Greek Thought.* New York: Harper and Row, 1944.

Grene, David, and Richmond Lattimore, eds. *The Complete Greek Tragedies.* 9 volumes. Chicago: University of Chicago Press, 1953–1959.

Grene, Marjorie. "Heidegger" in *The Encyclopedia of Philosophy,* edited by Paul Edwards. Volume 3. New York: Macmillan Publishing and The Free Press, 1967.

Grosskurth, Phyllis. *Melanie Klein: Her World and Her Work.* Cambridge: Harvard University Press, 1987.

Grotstein, James. *Splitting and Projective Identification.* Northvale, N.J.: Jason Aronson, 1985.

Guntrip, Harry. *Psychoanalytic Theory, Therapy, and the Self.* New York: Basic Books, 1971.

Habermas, Jürgen. *Theorie des kommunikativen Handelns.* 2 vols. Frankfurt am Main: Suhrkamp, 1973.

Havelock, Eric. *Preface to Plato.* Cambridge: Harvard University Press, 1963.

Heidegger, Martin. *Brief Über den Humanismus.* Frankfurt am Main: Klosterman, 1947.

———. *Discourse on Thinking [Gelassenheit].* Translated by John Anderson and E. Hans Freund. New York: Harper and Row, 1966.

———. *Early Greek Thinking: The Dawn of Western Philosophy.* Translated by David Krell and Frank Capuzzi. New York: Harper and Row, 1984.

———. *Holzwege.* Frankfurt am Main: Klosterman, 1950.

———. "What Is Metaphysics?" Translated by R. F. C. Hull and Alan Crick. In *Existence and Being,* 353–393. Chicago: Regnery, 1949.

Hirschman, Albert O. *The Passions and the Interests: Political Arguments for Capitalism before Its Triumph.* Princeton, N.J.: Princeton University Press, 1977.

Horkheimer, Max, and Theodor Adorno. *Dialectic of Enlightenment.* Translated by John Cumming. New York; Herder and Herder, 1972.

Hume, David. *A Treatise of Human Nature.* Books I and II, 2 vols. Edited by L. A. Selby Bigge. Oxford: Oxford University Press, 1888.

Jaeger, Werner. *Paideia: The Ideals of Greek Culture.* Translated by Gilbert Highet. 2d ed. Volume 1. New York: Oxford University Press, 1945.

Johnston, David. *The Rhetoric of Leviathan: Thomas Hobbes and the Politics of Cultural Transformation.* Princeton, N.J.: Princeton University Press, 1986.

Jones, A. H. M. *Athenian Democracy.* Oxford: Basil Blackwell, 1957.

Jones, John. *On Aristotle and Greek Tragedy.* New York: Oxford University Press, 1962.

Kant, Immanuel. *Foundations of the Metaphysics of Morals.* Translated by Lewis White Beck. Indianapolis: Bobbs-Merrill, Liberal Arts Press, 1959.

———. "Grundlegung zur Metaphysik der Sitten," in *Immanuel Kant: Werke in Sechs Bänden,* edited by Wilhelm Weischedel, 4:11–102. Wiesbaden: Insel-Verlag, 1956.

Kellner, Doug. *Jean Baudrillard: From Marxism to Post-Modernism and Beyond*. Stanford: Stanford University Press, 1989.

Kitto, H. D. F. *Greek Tragedy*. 3d. ed. London: Methuen, 1961.

Klein, Melanie. *The Writings of Melanie Klein*. 4 vols. Edited by R. E. Money-Kyrle. New York: Free Press, 1964–1975.

Knox, Bernard. *Oedipus at Thebes*. New Haven: Yale University Press, 1957.

Kohut, Heinz. *How Does Analysis Cure?* Edited by Arnold Goldberg. Chicago: University of Chicago Press, 1984.

———. "Remarks about the Formation of the Self," in *The Search for the Self: Selected Writings of Heinz Kohut, 1950–1978*, edited by Paul Ornstein, 2:737–770. New York: International Universities Press, 1974.

———. *The Restoration of the Self*. New York: International Universities Press, 1977.

———. *Self Psychology and the Humanities*, edited by Charles Strozier. New York: W. W. Norton, 1985.

Kovel, Joel. *The Radical Spirit: Essays on Psychoanalysis and Society*. London: Free Association Books, 1988.

Kruks, Sonia. *Situation and Human Existence: Freedom, Subjectivity and Society*. London: Unwin Hyman, 1990.

Lacan, Jacques. "The Mirror Stage as Formative of the Function of the I," in *Ecrits*, translated by Alan Sheridan, pp. 1–7. New York: W. W. Norton, 1977.

———. *Le séminaire de Jacques Lacan*. Volume 1. Edited by Jacques-Alain Miller. Paris: Editions du Seuil, 1975.

———. "Some Reflections on the Ego." *International Journal of Psycho-Analysis* 34 (1953): 11–17.

Lasch, Christopher. *The Culture of Narcissism*. New York: Warner, 1979.

———. *The True and Only Heaven: Progress and Its Critics*. New York: W. W. Norton, 1991.

Lattimore, Richmond. Introduction to *Alcestis*, by Euripides. Translated by Richmond Lattimore, in *Complete Greek Tragedies: Euripides I*, edited by David Grene and Richmond Lattimore. Chicago: University of Chicago Press, 1955.

———. Introduction to *Helen*, by Euripides. Translated by Richmond Lattimore, in *The Complete Greek Tragedies: Euripides II*, edited by David Grene and Richmond Lattimore. Chicago: University of Chicago Press, 1956.

Lebeck, Anne. *Oresteia: A Study in Language and Structure*. Cambridge: Harvard University Press, 1971.

Levinas, Emmanuel. *Difficult Freedom: Essays on Judaism*. Translated by Séan Hand. Baltimore: Johns Hopkins University Press, 1990.

Lifton, Robert Jay. *The Broken Connection: On Death and the Continuity of Life*. New York: Basic Books, 1983.

———. *The Nazi Doctors: Medical Killing and the Psychology of Genocide*. New York: Basic Books, 1986.

Lloyd-Jones, Hugh, trans. *Agamemnon; The Libation Bearers; The Eumenides,* by Aeschylus. Englewood Cliffs, N.J.: Prentice-Hall, 1970.

Löwith, Karl. *Max Weber and Karl Marx.* Edited by Tom Bottomore and William Outhwaite. London: George Allen and Unwin, 1982.

Lucas, Frank. L. *Tragedy.* Rev. ed., New York: Macmillan, 1957.

Lyotard, Jean-François. *The Differend: Phrases in Dispute.* Translated by Georges Van Den Abbeele. Minneapolis: Univeristy of Minnesota Press, 1988.

MacIntyre, Alasdair. *After Virtue.* Notre Dame, Ind.: University of Notre Dame Press, 1981.

———. *Whose Justice? Which Rationality?* Notre Dame, Ind.: University of Notre Dame Press, 1988.

Marcuse, Herbert. *The Aesthetic Dimension.* Boston: Beacon, 1978.

———. *Eros and Civilization.* Boston: Beacon, 1966.

Meltzer, Donald. *The Kleinian Development.* Perthshire, Scotland: Clunie Press, 1978.

Millett, Kate. *Sexual Politics.* New York: Avon, 1971.

Moore, Burness E., and Bernard D. Fine, eds. *Psychoanalytic Terms and Concepts.* New Haven: Yale University Press, 1990.

Morford, Mark P. O., and Robert Lenardon. *Classical Mythology.* 3d ed. New York: Longman, 1985.

Morgenthau, Hans J. *The Restoration of American Politics.* Chicago: University of Chicago Press, 1962.

Muller, John P. "Ego and Subject in Lacan." *Psychoanalytic Review* 69, no. 2 (1982): 234–240.

Nehamas, Alexander. "The Rescue of Humanism," *The New Republic* 203, no. 20 (November 12, 1990): 27–34.

Nietzsche, Friedrich. *The Birth of Tragedy,* in *Basic Writings of Nietzsche,* translated by Walter Kaufmann, pp. 3–144. New York: Modern Library, 1968.

Nussbaum, Martha. *The Fragility of Goodness: Luck and Ethics in Greek Tragedy and Philosophy.* Cambridge: Cambridge University Press, 1986.

———. *Love's Knowledge: Essays on Philosophy and Literature.* New York: Oxford University Press, 1990.

Ogden, Thomas. *Projective Identification and Psychotherapeutic Technique.* New York: Jason Aronson, 1982.

Pound, Ezra, and Rudd Fleming, trans. *Elektra,* by Sophocles. New York: New Directions, 1990.

Pucci, Pietro. *The Violence of Pity in Euripides' Medea.* Ithaca: Cornell University Press, 1980.

Rilke, Rainer Maria. *Duineser Elegien.* Leipzig: Insel-Verlag, 1923.

Rousseau, Jean-Jacques. "Discourse on the Origin and Foundations of Inequality among Men [Second Discourse]," in *The First and Second Discourses,* translated by R. Masters and J. Masters, pp. 77–228. New York: St. Martin's, 1964.

Sartre, Jean-Paul. *Being and Nothingness*. Translated by Hazel Barnes. New York: Philosophical Library, 1956.

——— . *Existentialism and Human Emotions*. New York: Philosophical Library, 1985.

Sass, Louis. "The Self and Its Vicissitudes: An 'Archaeological' Study of the Psycho-analytic Avant-Garde." *Social Research* 55 (Winter, 1988): 551–608.

Scarry, Elaine. *The Body in Pain: The Making and Unmaking of the World*. New York: Oxford University Press, 1985.

Schneiderman, Stuart. *Jacques Lacan: The Death of an Intellectual Hero*. Cambridge: Harvard University Press, 1983.

Scully, James, and C. John Herington, trans. *Prometheus Bound,* by Aeschylus. New York: Oxford University Press, 1975.

Segal, Charles. *Interpreting Greek Tragedy: Myth, Poetry, Text*. Ithaca, N.Y.: Cornell University Press, 1986.

——— . *Tragedy and Civilization: An Interpretation of Sophocles*. Cambridge: Harvard University Press, 1981.

Segal, Hanna. "A Psycho-Analytical Approach to Aesthetics," in *New Directions in Psycho-Analysis,* edited by Melanie Klein, Paula Heimann, and R. E. Money-Kyrle, pp.384–405. London: Maresfield Library, 1955.

Sewall, Richard. *The Vision of Tragedy*. New Haven: Yale University Press, 1959.

Simon, Bennett. *Mind and Madness in Ancient Greece*. Ithaca, N.Y.: Cornell University Press, 1978.

——— . *Tragic Drama and the Family: Psychoanalytic Studies from Aeschylus to Beckett*. New Haven: Yale University Press, 1988.

Slater, Philip. *The Glory of Hera: Greek Mythology and the Greek Family*. Boston: Beacon Press, 1968.

Snell, Bruno. *The Discovery of Mind: The Greek Origins of European Thought*. Translated by T. G. Rosenmeyer. Cambridge: Harvard University Press, 1953.

Stanford, W. B. *Greek Tragedy and the Emotions*. London: Routledge and Kegan Paul, 1983.

Steiner, George. *Antigones*. Oxford: Clarendon Press, 1986.

Tallis, Raymond. *Not Saussure: A Critique of Post-Saussurean Literary Theory*. London: Macmillan, 1988.

Taylor, Charles. "The Concept of a Person," in *Human Agency and Language, Philosophical Papers,* 1:97–114. Cambridge: Cambridge University Press, 1985.

Thomas, Dylan. *The Collected Poems of Dylan Thomas*. New York: New Directions, 1957.

Turner, Victor. *The Ritual Process*. Chicago: Aldine, 1969.

Vernant, Jean-Pierre, and Pierre Vidal-Naquet. *Myth and Tragedy in Ancient Greece*. Translated by Janet Lloyd. New York: Zone, 1988.

Waugh, Evelyn. *Brideshead Revisited: The Sacred and Profane Memories of Captain Charles Ryder*. Boston: Little, Brown, 1945.

Weber, Max. *The Protestant Ethic and the Spirit of Capitalism*. Translated by Talcott Parsons. New York: Scribners, 1958.

White, Stephen K. *Political Theory and Postmodernism*. Cambridge: Cambridge University Press, 1991.

Whitman, Cedric. *Euripides and the Full Circle of Myth*. Cambridge: Harvard University Press, 1974.

Williams, C. K., and Gregory Dickerson, trans. *Women of Trachis*, by Sophocles. New York: Oxford University Press, 1978.

Wilson, Edmund. "Philoctetes: The Wound and the Bow," in *The Wound and the Bow: Seven Studies in Literature*, pp. 223–242. New York: Oxford University Press, 1965.

Winch, Peter. "Understanding a Primitive Society." *American Philosophical Quarterly* 1 (1964): 307–324.

Winkler, John, and Froma Zeitlin, eds. *Nothing to Do with Dionysos? Athenian Drama in Social Context*. Princeton, N.J.: Princeton University Press, 1990.

Winnicott, D. W. *Holding and Interpretation*. New York: Grove, 1986.

———. *The Maturational Processes and the Facilitating Environment*. New York: International Universities Press, 1965.

Winnington-Ingram, R. P. *Euripides and Dionysus: An Interpretation of the* Bacchae. Cambridge: Cambridge University Press, 1948.

———. *Sophocles: An Interpretation*. Cambridge: Cambridge University Press, 1980.

———. *Studies in Aeschylus*. Cambridge: Cambridge University Press, 1983.

Wolfenstein, Eugene Victor. "Eating Psychoanalytic Marxism: *Anti-Oedipus* and Human Emancipation." Paper presented at the Annual Meeting of the American Political Science Association, San Francisco, August 1990.

Index

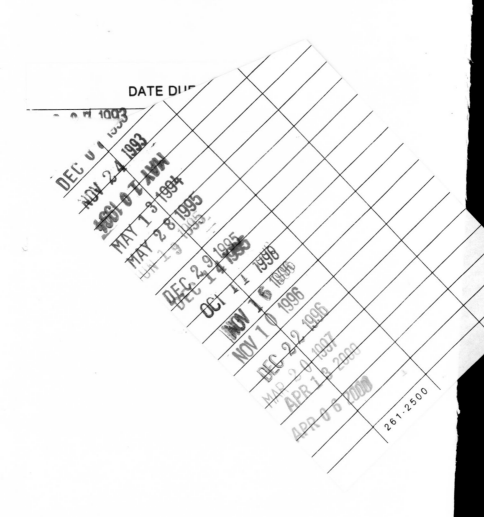